'Oren Gozlan is a profoundly original and incisive psychoanalytic thinker whose work demonstrates an unparalleled ability to engage with the most complex and urgent questions of gender and sexuality. Drawing on a close reading of psychoanalytic theory, this brilliant book challenges traditional views, offering fresh conceptual tools for understanding gender in psychoanalysis, as well as a daring rethinking of gender not as identity but as a psychoanalytic event of becoming.'

Prof. Dana Amir, *Ph.D.,* *Head, The Interdisciplinary Doctoral Track in Psychoanalysis, School of Therapy, University of Haifa, Clinical Psychologist, Supervising and Training Analyst, The Israel Psychoanalytic Society*

Gender with Sexuality

This book explores the changing attitudes and clinical responses to gender and transition in psychoanalysis and psychotherapy.

It examines gender as a dynamic and elusive psychic situation—lived through affect, phantasy, and symbolic pressures. Gozlan argues that gender shapes experience not only in patients' lives but also in theory—where it unsettles coherence, challenges neutrality, and brings forward what is lost or unsymbolized. Engaging figures such as Sullivan, McDougall, Stoller, and Quinodoz, he reimagines the analyst as implicated in the transmission of gendered meanings, where the mind becomes a site of ethical and aesthetic reworking. This extends to the psychic life of psychoanalytic institutions, where gender's fate and its impact on the analyst's own transformation are examined. The book also interrogates the conditions under which the analyst's thinking shifts—or resists shifting—and invites readers to rethink how gender circulates through psychoanalysis, theory, and institutional life.

With a deep and nuanced understanding of gender in the clinic and beyond, this book is essential reading for psychoanalysts, psychotherapists, and other mental health professionals seeking to update their thinking and practice around gender and transitioning.

Oren Gozlan is a psychoanalyst in Toronto and a member of the Committee for Gender and Sexuality of the International Psychoanalytical Association (IPA). His book, *Transsexuality and the Art of Transitioning* (Routledge), won the American Academy and Board of Psychoanalysis's annual book prize (2015).

Gender with Sexuality

Situations of Psychoanalytic Learning

Oren Gozlan

R Routledge
Taylor & Francis Group

LONDON AND NEW YORK

Designed cover image: ©Alamy

First published 2026
by Routledge
4 Park Square, Milton Park, Abingdon, Oxon OX14 4RN

and by Routledge
605 Third Avenue, New York, NY 10158

Routledge is an imprint of the Taylor & Francis Group, an informa business

British Library Cataloguing-in-Publication Data
A catalogue record for this book is available from the British Library

ISBN: 978-1-032-57735-7 (hbk)
ISBN: 978-1-032-57736-4 (pbk)
ISBN: 978-1-003-44075-8 (ebk)

DOI: 10.4324/9781003440758

Typeset in Optima
by Apex Co Vantage, LLC

For Marcelle Obadiah-Lawee and Solange Gozlan

Contents

Acknowledgments

Writing is never solitary, even when it demands solitude. This book is the trace of encounters—intellectual, emotional, and transferential—that have shaped its questions as much as its hesitations. To acknowledge these voices is not merely to list names but to recognize that thought is always borrowed, interrupted, and carried forward by others. Ideas take root in conversations, in the silent pressure of a question, in the patient listening that allows something unthought to emerge. The development of this book has been enriched by invitations and participation in conferences and productive engagement with colleagues in the Sexual and Gender Diversity Studies Committee of the International Psychoanalytical Association (IPA).

Some debts are obvious, others less so. Some have been written into the fabric of this book; others persist in its margins, as absences, as hesitations, as the echoes of conversations that have shaped the way I have learned to think. It is with these debts in mind that I offer my thanks. I particularly want to thank psychoanalyst and poet Dr. Dana Amir and committee chair Dr. Leticia Glocer-Fiorini. My engagement with their work has been both intellectually expansive and profoundly moving, shaping not only the direction of my thinking but also the emotional texture of my writing.

My deep appreciation and thanks to Routledge editor Susannah Fearson, who first heard my idea for this book during our meeting in New York and believed in its potential. I am also grateful to Jane Woodhead for her careful editing. I would also like to thank my dear friends Paola Bohorquez and Angela Facundo for their careful reading and thoughtful edits of several chapters, and my dear friend Marilyn Learner for her continuous engagement with both clinical and theoretical ideas throughout this journey.

This book carries the fingerprints of Distinguished Prof. Deborah Britzman in ways that go far beyond citation. Her thinking—restless, rigorous, and always capacious—has shaped not only my work but also how I have learned to think, to listen, and to sit with the emotional demands of ideas. It is through Prof. Britzman that I first came to understand education, psychoanalysis, and even friendship itself as affective, emotional, and transferential situations—spaces where we are undone and remade in ways we cannot always predict.

But more than that, Prof. Britzman's presence in my life has been a gift. Her generosity, wit, and intellectual companionship have made the difficult work of writing feel less lonely, even at its most disorienting. This book, in many ways, is the product of countless conversations, moments of shared curiosity, and the kind of thinking-together that lingers long after words have been spoken. For all of this—her work, her friendship, and the many ways she has shaped both—my gratitude is boundless.

And finally, to my wife and best friend, Agnieszka Gozlan, whose presence embodies a form of care beyond words, shaping not only this book but the very life in which it was written. For that, and for all the ways the world becomes more intelligible, livable, and full of love, my gratitude knows no bounds.

Parts of this book originally appeared in edited volumes of others and as articles in journals. I thank the following for permission to reprint previous work:

A shorter version of Chapter 11 will be published in Gherovici & M. Stainkholer (Eds.), *Routledge International Handbook of Psychoanalysis and Gender* (forthcoming).

Portions of the case of "D." (Chapter 12) also appear in my book *Gender: A Contemporary Introduction* (forthcoming). In that volume, the case was used to consider how gender takes shape as a subjunctive and aesthetic situation, enacted through repetition, refusal, and the strain of recognition. In this book, I return to the same material with a different emphasis. How the social enters the clinic and how listening might remain open to the enigmatic. All identifying details remain altered to preserve confidentiality.

I acknowledge Taylor & Francis for permission to reproduce a revised and much-abridged version of Chapter 13, "Crafting of a Self," which was originally published in *The Psychoanalytic Quarterly* as "Novel Revolts as Crafting of a Self. The original version is available at http://www.tandfonline.com.

A shorter version of Chapter 14 was published under the title "In-Difference: Feminism and Transgender in the Field of Fantasy," in P. Gherovici & M. Stainkholer (Eds.), *Psychoanalysis, Gender and Sexualities: From Feminism to Trans* (pp. 212–221), Routledge.

"And the future enters into us, in order to be transformed in us, long before it happens."

—Rainer Maria Rilke, *Letters to a Young Poet*

Introduction

Gender with Sexuality: Situations of Psychoanalytic Learning explores gender as an emotional and aesthetic situation rather than as a fixed identity. Drawing on psychoanalytic theory, clinical practice, and literary sensibility, the book reimagines gender as a psychic encounter—shaped by affect, phantasy, and symbolic forces. It challenges traditional views of gender, proposing it as a libidinal experience that binds and unbinds, securing meaning even as it threatens to unravel it. By examining gender through the lens of psychoanalysis, the book explores how gender functions not only in individual lives but also within the institutional structures of psychoanalysis, where it disrupts theory, transference, and learning. Using Winnicott's concept of dependence and relationality, it suggests that gender's complexities are mirrored in the psychoanalytic process itself, which is always bound by emotional conflicts and resistances. The book interrogates the tensions between learning and unlearning, highlighting how psychoanalytic education often bypasses emotional complexities and fails to engage with the psychological dimensions of gender and learning. Through this exploration, the book presents a new way of thinking about both psychoanalytic practice and pedagogy, emphasizing the vulnerability inherent in both understanding gender and engaging with knowledge itself.

A few years ago, I was asked to teach an extension course in one of the psychoanalytic institutes on the topic of transsexuality and gender transitioning. The request came following a book I had written a year before, in which I had taken an aesthetic approach to the question of gender, by which I mean considering experiences of gender as something which exceeds identitarian claims—a way of opening representations of gender to their underside, to what was not meant to be represented.[1] I considered gender as an artistic project, as the creation of a self, and I imagined transsexuality from a kaleidoscopic viewpoint: as a question of representation, as a particular translation, as an insistence and an address to the other, and as an enigma that belongs to the question of gender. With this notion of aesthetics in mind, I picked the title "There is no such thing as a transsexual" in reference to Winnicott's well-known formulation *there is no such thing as a baby without a mother*. This idea was articulated by Winnicott out of a belief that babies cannot

DOI: 10.4324/9781003440758-1

become human by themselves. According to Winnicott, subjective life can only come into being in relation to the body of an other in order to constitute something like a self.

Winnicott's statement, far from a dismissal or erasure of the baby, is concerned with the question of humanity and with the capacity to maintain our humanity through a link to what is imagined as foreign, unintelligible, or unknown. It also expresses a situation of dependency that makes it impossible to conceive of individuality in isolation, because the human being is always beholden to an other. *Such*, I suggested, *is the situation of gender*. Gender is most often spoken of as a category of identity, a position one takes or is placed within. It is variously understood as performance, assignment, discourse, or self-expression. But what if gender is not only that? What if gender is not simply a social location or descriptive term but something far less containable—something that belongs to the terrain of psychic life? To ask this is not to evacuate its social meanings but to inquire into how gender functions as a linchpin of unconscious life—as that which binds and unbinds, which secures meaning even as it threatens to unravel it. I proposed that gender is not a "thing" in and of itself, not a coherent object of thought, but a libidinal experience—infused with pleasure and pain, shaped by proximity to other psychic intensities: age, illness, beauty. It names not an identity but an encounter. It emerges from what is archaic and unnameable in us, from what resists symbolization yet exerts an undeniable force on thought and perception.

The title I chose was not meant to provoke, but it did. Before the course even began, it had become something else; circulating as rumor, as accusation, as a kind of cipher for all that could not be said. Emails arrived. Warnings were whispered. Posts multiplied. I was told I had denied the reality of trans lives, that I was dangerous, that I needed to be stopped. It didn't matter what I said—my clarifications only deepened the mistrust. What I had imagined as an invitation to think was taken as a refusal, a negation. And maybe that's the deeper problem: when thought itself becomes suspect, when the act of asking is mistaken for an act of harm. What does it mean, I kept wondering, when a title—just a title—can summon such intensity? What does it expose about our shared vulnerabilities, our hopes for recognition, and our dread of misrecognition?

The situation I have just described is an emotional one. It arose out of the anxiety of not knowing but also from wanting to know. My insistence throughout this book follows Britzman's (2015) view of pedagogy as an emotional situation, one that engages both interior and exterior worlds and, as we will see, unfolds as a transferential scene. This is because learning is inevitably bound up with conflicts, those that make up our relationship to social bonds and our relationship to cultural impressions and transmissions. It involves scenes of mentality which are libidinal in nature—meaning it has to do with affects, phantasies, and resistance to change. We can venture to say that learning is also traumatic. This traumatic aspect of learning is tied to the human condition of dependency on the other—adult figures, institutions— which creates tension with our self-perception as self-sufficient beings. This vulnerability creates a conflict in the experience of education and learning; a phantasmagorical measure of how others should act.

Attention to transference, I suggest, must also be part of psychoanalytic institutional teaching. Looking back at the reactions to my proposed course, the preconceptions orienting such responses suggest an understandable fear that the course's orientation was hostile to transsexuality. It was as if the course title alone crashed all students' expectations, and in response, the course itself needed to be destroyed. I would argue that this logic—so characteristic of our era's "cancelling culture"—reveals dominant tendencies in our collective experience and understanding of gender. In reading this scene as an analyst, I am curious about how gender structures we have not created shape our current perceptions of the world.

The first thing the reader needs to know about gender—and what the classroom scene already makes evident—is that it is a wild exaggeration. That is why it provokes such affect. Gender dramatizes psychic life—its impossibilities, its repetitions, its needs for recognition. The idea of gender as an emotional situation is not new. We could say that it really came to light at the turn of the 20th century, with Freud's psychoanalytic notion of unconscious processes (1905). While the concept "gender identity" did not exist in Freud's time, his elaboration of the notions of masculinity and femininity as psychical entities, rather than biological givens, already addressed what we now term "gender" as psychic constructions, hard to define, laden with conflict and anxiety around loss, separation, and dependency. All of these experiences migrate onto different places and constitute "theatre of the mind" (McDougall, 1989), where gender colors how power and desire play out through various relationships.

But with unconscious processes come profound defenses. And yet, psychoanalytic institutes fail, by and large, to engage deeply with the emotional and psychological dimensions of teaching and learning. One example that comes to mind concerns a class on perversion that was offered in my fourth year of analytic training. The lecturer asked us to watch *The Piano Teacher*, a film which depicts a complex and unsettling sadomasochistic relationship between a teacher and her student. After watching the film at home, one of the students expressed anger at the lecturer for not warning the class about the disturbing content of the film. She then refused to participate in the class and left the room crying. One by one, the students left the room to comfort her, until only three students were left in the class. The surprising aspect, however, is the fact that the experience was never referred to by the lecturer of the class. The experience itself—charged, evocative, brimming with the very themes of perversion, power, and transgression that the film depicted—was bypassed entirely. Why, I wonder, can we not be curious about what is happening in a class when we encounter difficult emotional situations as part of our psychoanalytic training?

The problem I am trying to elaborate is not simply this classroom event. This event is an exemplar for the ways in which the structure of the institute is both personal and dissociated at the same time. It is personal to the extent that you may be taught by your analyst, but there is also a progress committee who wants to know who your analyst is. There is a certain sadistic quality to institutional education, in which, if we go by Kernberg (2016), there are 30 ways it destroys candidates' creativity. The structure of the psychoanalytic institute itself, he suggests, mitigates against frank discussions on the question of how we learn and what is difficult for us to tolerate.

Ironically, the experience I describe took place in a relationally oriented institute. And yet, relationality appears verboten. The avoidance of discussion, in my view, speaks both to the institute's concern over controversy and a tendency to individualize experience and conceptualize education as a personal difficulty that is devoid from the larger problem of education, one that is tightly linked with the structure of the institution itself. The question of pedagogical orientation and the capacity to bear "difficult knowledge" *is* education. Similarly, in teaching, the analyst also meets the history of their own learning, which returns, Britzman (1998) observes, "to haunt education in the form of its contested objects: as conflicts, as disruptions, as mistakes, and as controversies" (p. 19). "Educators rarely acknowledge these repressed psychic events," she adds, "yet they nevertheless exist and demand attention" (Britzman, 1998, p. 19).

The psychoanalytic institute creates the illness of the student. One of the ways it does this is through its fear of controversy, which prevents it from treating students as individual subjects. In my example, the teacher was eventually blamed by the institute for having shown the film at all. The absence of discussion about education has an infantilizing effect on candidates who have no say about their education, and what is taken away is a degree of freedom. It concerns the question of how we think about difficult emotional situations in education over time and what role students have in that discussion in a way that psychoanalytic education becomes a conversation rather than a passive experience. In this way, education makes us sick.

This moment in the classroom that I have described is an exemplar for a larger point. It reveals a profound lesson: the inherent difficulties of engaging with the psychic life of learning, where masochism and sadism operate as structuring forces. Learning is not only a site of knowledge acquisition but also an arena of unconscious struggles—between desire and resistance, mastery and submission, love and aggression. These tensions shape the emotional and relational contours of education itself. In entering into difficult or incomprehensible experiences, we are susceptible to transference, projection, and splitting: "that is not me," "I could never be or do that," or "that happened to me and the teacher is evil for showing this." These are ways of disclaiming the experience that one is studying. Psychoanalysis, however, is of another order of learning. This order is of learning by implication: in approaching phenomena we do not understand, such as masochism, sadism, transgender or nonbinary identities, we must wonder about ourselves. We cannot step outside the experiences we encounter in learning because in psychoanalysis there is no such outside. This is a very different way of thinking about understanding, learning, and meaning in a psychoanalytic education.

Education, therefore, is an emotional situation. It requires its own theory to help us conceptualize what we understand, after the inevitable experience of a failure. Another dimension of its failure belongs to communication. Trying to speak gender is like working with a palimpsest—each new layer obscures and carries traces of what came before. What we attempt to express or "declare" about gender never coincides with something we call "gender." In learning, we enter into incoherence, and this is a dilemma for both teachers and analysts, as well as writers and readers. There will always be a degree of inchoateness in our attempt to understand the other—the dilemma of human interaction is shared across the board. An ethics for teaching and learning hinges, therefore, on an understanding of care—tolerating ambivalence, engaging with psychic pain, and recognizing resistances—particularly in this age of misunderstanding (to put it in its most banal terms) that we are facing worldwide. This is the case particularly in broader questions that touch on the realm of gender: abortion, lesbian and gay rights, and, significantly, the trans child. These conflicts break open in and outside of the psychoanalytic institutes. A psychoanalytic mode of thinking is of particular interest for formulating what can be said about our pedagogical situation in the arena of both learning and gender and how we may think about the play between the internal and external conflicts, and their effect on our theories of practice.

The very idea of a theory of learning is already paradoxical. Psychoanalytic institutes, for all their concern with thought and formation, offer little sustained reflection on how learning happens—or fails to happen—in their own spaces. And yet it matters. To think about learning is to confront its fragility, its resistances, its unconscious refusals. The same is true for thinking about gender. Here too, concepts do not simply accumulate or resolve; they waver, undo themselves, require us to live with instability. Perhaps this is the deeper convergence: that to remain in relation to gender's movement, one must learn—and unlearn—in ways no theory can fully prepare. Institutional education, however, often resists this reckoning, treating uncertainty and controversy not as generative conditions for thought but as disruptions to mastery. We might therefore consider how learning about gender is not only an intellectual endeavor but also an affective and relational one, implicating the learner in the very scene of study. To approach gender within a psychoanalytic framework is to confront how education itself is structured by unconscious investments—by fantasies of coherence, by defenses against psychic pain, and by the resistances that arise when knowledge unsettles subjectivity. It is in this way that both learning and gender remain ongoing processes, bound not to certainty but to the vulnerabilities and contingencies that shape the conditions of thought itself.

A situation we are in

The question of how minds change—how one teaches or learns in the charged terrain of gender and sexuality—bears directly on psychoanalytic work with trans, nonbinary, and gender-nonconforming patients. But this is no simple matter of acquiring new knowledge or adopting new guidelines. It asks something harder: what does it mean to meet an other who asks us to listen differently—to words, to phantasies, to forms of life that unsettle our inherited categories? In the space of psychoanalytic education, this question returns with particular force: how do we recognize where we remain entangled in normative ideologies, even as we seek to think beyond them? And how do such entanglements shape what our patients can say, or feel, or become?

The unease analysts so often feel in the face of new gendered experiences is not incidental. It tells us something—not just about gender but about the limits of our own capacity to learn. These encounters do not ask simply for new terminology or updated frameworks. They disturb the very wish for mastery, the belief that concepts can shield us from contradiction. What they expose are transferential knots: theory breaks down, listening turns defensive, and the analyst's phantasies take hold. Gender is not an object of study but a scene we enter, half-knowing and already implicated.

It unfolds through phantasy,[2] through social insistence, through desire and disavowal. To speak of gender at all is to be caught in its tensions: between what can be said and what insists beyond symbolization. And so the problem of learning returns, not as acquisition but as an undoing; a kind of unlearning that leaves us altered, unfinished, perhaps more able to hear.

Psychoanalysis has long been preoccupied with thresholds—those between the conscious and unconscious, the known and unknowable, the self and the other. But today, it finds itself at another threshold: it is confronted with new ways of living gender and remaking the self. Many psychoanalytic practitioners recoil at these transformations, drawing old lines with renewed urgency. In psychoanalytic discourse and institutions, we see a mounting anxiety in response to the changes unfolding in gender's cultural and subjective life—a return to rigid categories and an insistence on stability where there is none. This discomfort with gender fluidity reveals a reluctance to sit with what queerness and transness expose: that identity is always in process, never fully possessed. When trans experience is treated as either sacrifice or pathology, psychoanalysis inadvertently exposes the very anxieties it seeks to master—the fear that the self might no longer be anchored in the familiar coordinates of psychoanalytic thought, and that the rearticulation of gender destabilizes the very terms psychoanalysis uses to understand subjectivity.

Sergio Benvenuto's article "Genderification" (2024, p. 124) and David Bell's "First Do No Harm" (2020) exemplify a defensive reaction—not only as intellectual positions but as affective maneuvers against the unsettling force of gender's becoming. For Benvenuto, transness is a "mystical devotion": "It is a path of pain and renunciation in exchange for happiness" (p. 4). The term *mysticism* here describes a representation of reality as preordained. This is how Benvenuto relates to masculinity and femininity for the cisgender person. For biological males or females like himself, gender appears predetermined, fixed, oceanic in its superstition. Bell similarly frames transgender identity as a perilous misstep, a suffering that analytic thought must resist rather than engage. His metaphors—contagion, castration/amputation—position transitioning youth as tragic, partial objects. Both critiques share an assumption: trans life is inherently tragic, a symptom of misguided desire rather than a mode of self-fashioning; a foreclosure rather than an opening.

Roberto D'Angelo's recent paper "Do we want to know" in the *International Journal of Psychoanalysis* reanimates an equally enduring fantasy in psychoanalysis: a wish for an "origin story," the belief that the analyst's task is to discover and treat the "underlying cause" of gender variance in youth. Beneath D'Angelo's analytic posture of neutrality and concern lies a tired suspicion toward trans identification—"a suspicion framed as clinical precaution but tethered to an almost melancholic wish for psychoanalysis to reclaim its paternal function as guardian of the psyche against cultural distortion" (Gozlan, 2025, p. 849). Similar positions emerge among some French colleagues who, drawing on a facile and reductive reading of Butler, Derrida, and Bion, interpret transgender experience as an omnipotent refusal of reality—an alleged failure to recognize and accept limits as imposed by the reality principle. Transition, in this view, signals a breakdown of what Keats (1817) called "negative capability"—the capacity to tolerate uncertainty—and a fantasy of deconstructing what society has constructed. What unsettles me in this framing is the way gender transition becomes the emblem of failed negative capability—as if uncertainty were not an analytic condition but a punishment. The term is wielded not to open thought but to foreclose it, as though to transition is a flight from thought and constraint, rather than a psychic reckoning with their intractability. In this frame, "negative capability" is less a concept for holding ambiguity than a moralizing diagnosis—its failure attributed to those who trouble normative boundaries.

Such critiques often do not proceed through argument alone; they arrive charged with affect, shaped by the destabilizing pull of gender. Deconstruction, after all, is not a dismantling of reality; it reads the fractures already present, the seams where meaning has long threatened to give way. It brings us closer to the contradictions that structure even our most intimate categories: sex, gender, identity. And perhaps transition itself, so often cast as refusal or flight, might be thought otherwise: not as escape from psychic work but as its intensification. A renewed struggle with the body, with the symbolic order, with forms of recognition that were never assured. To read transition merely as denial of limits is to misread what psychoanalysis should know: that mourning, transference, and the labor of making a life are never simple acts of negation. Perhaps it is not transness that veers toward mysticism but the fantasy that sex could offer final truth; that the body might speak a destiny rather than a text still unfinished, still in the process of being written.

Psychoanalysis teaches us that the body does not speak—it is spoken for, shaped by fantasy, desire, and cultural inscription. If biology is already imagined the moment it is perceived, why cling to gender as fixed rather than as unfolding—an aesthetic process felt more than seen, sensed more than assigned? What is most difficult to accept is the uncertainty: we cannot say with finality what biology is, what gender is, or where either begins. From such indeterminacy, political struggle emerges, and absolutism takes hold. The deeper tension is not between sex and gender but between what is declared immutable and what is experienced as shifting. Sex, after all, expands beyond gender—yet only if we allow it to escape the grip of normativity. Loosened from biological authority, it spills over, shaped by desire and phantasy. Gender, in this light, is not a containment of sex but one of its many possible expressions—a creative negotiation between soma and psyche.

If gender is a creative negotiation between soma and psyche, does that make it essential to psychoanalytic thinking? In my view, the concept of gender cannot be given up, just as concepts like transference, Object *petit a*,[3] or phantasy cannot be relinquished either. For me, gender remains a central linchpin in the capacity to imagine psychical life. When we hear statements in the clinic such as: "I hate my body," "I want to be beautiful"—we are hearing derivatives of gender. We are hearing experiences of gender that are tied to desire and belong to the self. As long as pleasure vacillates across the categories of gender, it is very difficult to separate gender from sexuality. And yet, femininity and masculinity are social experiences that play out in the field of gender as the capacity to be recognized on our own terms. What if gender transition were not a break from reality but a reparative act, an imaginative remaking of psychic space? What, then, would it mean to think of gender as something not to be perceived but something to be felt? Partly, this would allow for the concept to be susceptible to something more. Perceived as a constellation, gender can be conceptualized in ways that we cannot imagine, or in ways that we wish to imagine. And yet, this affective pull is also subject to concreteness, where femininity and masculinity are treated as something known. But can we go beyond such terms?

Within the changing landscape of gender, there is a growing recognition of the right of transgender, nonbinary, gay, and lesbian individuals to decide how they want to live and how they want to be cared for by the "mental health" establishment. This pressures us to think. Medical establishments, psychoanalytic institutions, and academic institutions are being pushed to rethink and reorganize their approach to gender in ways that will be relevant to trans and nonbinary individuals seen in clinics, medical institutions, and educational institutions. While tracing the manifestations of gender will not lead us to an origin, gender itself structures and contains the conditions of existence, making the self's truths accessible through interpretation and open to continual elaboration. If, following Freud, the unconscious ensures that subjectivity is always marked by parallel realities that can never fully align, what would it mean for psychoanalysis to take this dilemma as its starting point in thinking about gender? It would, in my view, mean approaching gender not as a fixed identity to be clarified but as a site of psychic contradiction.

The first time I began to seriously think about the question of teaching classes on gender was when I was asked to teach an introductory course on psychodynamic psychotherapy to first-year candidates in a psychoanalytic psychotherapy program. As I prepared for this teaching, I asked myself, "What makes a good novice analyst?" Freud certainly does not leave us with the impression that the analyst relies on the clinic alone for their thinking. For Freud, it is the attempt to open up to what one doesn't know. Freud started with a fascination with ancient cultures, Greek mythology, literature, and philosophy, making a tradition in psychoanalysis of going beyond the couch to study psychic life through the world of literature, music, art, and culture. I would say that this is how the analyst feeds their mind on problems of symbolization. In turning to art, the analyst moves beyond the constraints of social cohesion, conducting themself in a way that resists mere functionality. Crucially, the analyst's engagement with cultural representation is not about "getting to know" in any definitive sense. Culture—whether gender, race, or politics—is not something wholly knowable, nor something the clinic can simply disavow. Rather, the analyst listens to the material scenes that enter the clinic as borderline concepts, oscillating between actuality and the echoes of psychical reality.

Psychoanalysis, however, is not complicit with culture. It considers two kinds of understanding of the "residues" of social experiences that patients bring to the clinic: the external world and the internal world. Yet, at the same time, psychoanalysis is not outside the scenes of culture from which it has emerged and hence is always at risk of collapse of reality and fantasy. To make a third space, however, the analyst must work against their own subjectivity and be prepared to lose their theories so they can reach the patient and at the same time understand how their work affects their own selves. But change, Bion suggests, is always catastrophic, because it involves the breakdown of an existing structure. It is experienced as loss.

Pedagogy is not a neutral exchange of knowledge but a transferential experience—suffused with unconscious investments, repetitions, and desires. What is taught circulates with what cannot be taught: the anxiety of knowing, the pressure to be recognized, the echo of prior scenes. In this sense, learning is never only intellectual. It is affective, embodied, shaped as much by what is sought as by what must be defended against. Samuel Weber addresses the paradox of psychoanalytic thought in *The Legend of Freud* (Expanded ed., 2000), asking in the Preface:

> Can psychoanalytic thinking itself escape the effects of what it endeavors to think? Can the disruptive distortions of unconscious processes be simply recognized, theoretically, as an object, or must they not leave their imprint on the process of theoretical objectification itself? Must

not psychoanalytical thinking itself partake of the dislocations it seeks to describe?

(pp. xiii–xiv)

In essence, Weber is asking us to think about the ways in which our transference to a concept shapes theory and, in turn, how our libidinal attachment to a theory shapes and maintains the concepts it seeks to describe. Psychoanalysis, he suggests, cannot remain unaffected by the very phenomena it seeks to understand and describe.

It is with this dilemma—how the disruptive distortions of the unconscious leave their imprint on theory itself—that I approach the ways in which psychoanalytic thought engages contemporary questions of gender. In particular, I consider how normative discourse is produced and repeated within psychoanalytic education. In writing this book, I am attempting to think through the breakdowns of meaning that emerge in both the transmission and reception of ideas, focusing on the ways we come to understand something called "gender" and its relation to sexuality. It is not that gender begins somewhere but that we find ourselves already inside it—inside its grammar, its refusals, and its emotional demands. Gender, in this frame, is an emotional situation where the psyche wrestles with what has been handed down, what has been refused, and what remains to be figured. I will explore the various stages upon which our conflicts, fantasies, enjoyments, dispersals, and suffering are played out. These are not scenes of development in any linear sense but fields of psychic movement, where gender becomes one way—perhaps the most intimate way—of staging what the psyche cannot fully know but must nonetheless inhabit. In this sense, gender becomes a kind of playground for the procedures of psychic and social life—a gateway to uncertainty and a space for negative capability. One has no control over what one is given, but one can decorate it, stretch it, love it, hate it—all without fully knowing it or anticipating its effects.

Gender is not simply a personal identity or social category but a building block of human subjectivity because it poses a fundamental problem of recognition—a blur between the psychic and the social that resists neat separation. I will approach this blur through four contentions: translatability, dimensions of change and resistance, matters of concern, and the world of others. These, I argue, are not fixed categories but heuristic devices—lenses through which to interpret how things not thought of as gender nevertheless land as gender. If gender is libidinally charged, so too is body image, although each may follow distinct psychic paths. While the body appears as a public image, psychoanalytically it also inaugurates a psychic space—one shaped by fantasy: the aging body, the young body, the sick body, the fantasized body. Gender and sexuality meet here in a strange confluence, structured not only by the question "what am I?" but also "how do I think I am seen?"—an image that resists finality. As André Green (2000) observes, the image, like history, is difficult for the psyche.

In the clinic, gender and sexuality often emerge obliquely—not through grand declarations but in tonalities, intensities, metaphors, and oppositions. Everything a patient says may carry gender's trace. Yet in theoretical discourse, gender is often treated as if it were a coherent structure rather than a psychic movement—a defensive concretization of what is, in fact, uncertain, transitional, and conflicted. When the Oedipal structure is understood not as a fixed blueprint but as a shifting field of identifications, prohibitions, and desires, gender appears less as an object than as a mobile scene of positioning, force, and deformation—a conflictual staging of subjectivity. To think of gender as an emotional situation—*a contact zone between exteriority and interiority*— is to imagine a complex world where recognition always arrives too late, and where sexuality and gender cannot be cleanly separated. In this manuscript, I will emphasize their mutual instability: not to dissolve them into abstraction but to explore how they are endured, elaborated, and suffered. One way to approach this instability is through art and literature—where we "think in cases," and where theory loses its grip. Here, gender becomes a force field—a site of presence and absence, marked by failed translations, psychic interferences, and the breakdowns of meaning. It is named, enforced, performed, and yet it continually slips—across language, across bodies, across scenes of desire.

The failure to capture gender is not incidental; it is its very condition. Like *Das Ding*—that archaic, unrepresentable "thing" in the Freudian-Lacanian tradition that resists symbolization—gender presses on thought from the outside: unnameable, affective, and impossible to fully integrate. It cannot be integrated, only circled around, projected into, or anxiously symbolized. This book will trace how institutions—including psychoanalysis itself—are caught in the gravitational pull of this thing that cannot be fully thought but must still be managed. The institutional imaginary forms around gender not simply to make sense of it but to contain its excess: to discipline what resists legibility, to narrate what haunts, to reframe what threatens with too much fluidity. And yet, the very presence of gender in analytic work, in classroom conflict, and in clinical hesitation signals that Das Ding has not disappeared—it returns, unclaimed, as the impossible object of theory, the repressed tradition, the force that shakes the institution's confidence in its own conceptual inheritance.

The scenes gathered in this manuscript may frustrate the reader's desire for coherence or political clarity. But such frustration, I argue, is not a failure of explanation. It is an encounter with gender's uncanniness and with the transference to institutional forms of knowledge—an encounter with their resistances, disavowals, and occasional openings. To think gender psychoanalytically is to risk thinking beside the institution, not against it, but through the holes in its fabric, in order to reimagine what kind of symbolic life remains possible. Speaking of gender as *Das Ding!* is a kind of a partial lifting of the constraints imposed by rigid definitions and categories. Here, we are no longer asking, "What is gender?" but rather, "What does it mean for something—an experience, an object, a relation—to be gender?" To speak of gender as an enigmatic object—one that resists symbolization—is not to deny the force of its hegemonic ideals, nor the ways its forms can be lived, at times, as stable. It is to remain with its paradox: that what seems most solid is also most haunted by instability. In speaking gender, we mark its edges and undo them at once—an articulation that is also a negation.

Clinical cases, John Forrester suggests, do not simply exemplify theory; they are scenes where meaning falters and is taken up belatedly. Their impact resists closure, continually revised in the deferred temporality of writing (Gozlan, 2025). To write a case is to stay within this field of partial understanding, where what speaks also withholds. Gender sharpens the tension, opening onto broader questions in psychoanalysis: time, sexuality, identification, and even the status of metapsychology as a paradigm (Simpson, 2022). Freud (1937a) himself likened metapsychology to conjuring a witch: "We can only say: So muss denn doch die Hexe dran! [So we must call the witch to our aid!]—the witch Metapsychology. Without metapsychological speculation and theorizing—phantasying, one might say—we shall not get another step forward" (p. 225). The point is its speculative, even mystical, character—less concerned with truth than with possibility. Freud's metapsychological papers—*Instincts and Their Vicissitudes*, *Repression*, *The Unconscious*, the supplement to the theory of dreams, and *Mourning and Melancholia*—do not offer a theory of gender per se.

but they do offer a scaffolding for how we might begin to think of gender as a psychic structure, not a fixed identity. These essays mark Freud's effort to theorize the dynamics of the mind from within—to track how meaning is produced through conflict, compromise, and loss. And while none of them "explain" gender, each offers a conceptual aperture. We can speak of gender in relation to repression, to melancholia, to unconscious formations that refuse integration. A metapsychological approach to gender, then, does not seek to uncover some originary moment but instead traces how gendered experiences acquire meaning and psychic weight. Freud's (1917) "Mourning and Melancholia," for example, offers a compelling analogy: just as the processes of mourning and melancholia map out libidinal attachments and losses, so too can gender be understood as a melancholic structure—an enduring, dynamic interplay of identifications with masculinity, femininity, and their many interwoven forms. But more fundamentally, the question arises: Why does attachment itself occur? What compels the mind to invest meaning in the raw materiality of the body?

Looking back at the history of the reception and exploring case studies, we are able to see something of how psychoanalytic ideas became sedimented. This excavation is also a form of resistance. Likewise, resistance is also the basis for engagement in analytic thinking because psychoanalysis is, after all, a theory of conflict: our investment in ideas, including those in psychoanalysis, is libidinal. Studying how psychoanalytic ideas have been transmitted, received, and thought about by analysts over the years, the respective chapters aim to present different sides of a perennial problem in psychoanalysis; namely, the status of time in thinking. In particular, the idea of deferred action—a temporality that returns but not in the same way that it was experienced—will be explored. This strange *nachträglich*[4] temporality is why, in my view, we will go back to Robert Stoller's case of Agnes, and why we will use memoirs to see *how* we can enter into the paradox of psychoanalysis, where time is not linear.

If we go back to the psychoanalytic concept of *nachträglichkeit*, we see that it encompasses a sense of history that is very close to the notion of the drive in the sense that there is an affective experience before something can be known. The ego's ability to defer is therefore difficult to tolerate. There is an animation, an instinctual urge, before something can be understood, and this urge, to understand our own acts and our own reception of ideas, puts the psyche to work. By examining situations of change and resistance through the lens of *nachträglichkeit*, I am also tracing the slow undoing and reforming of my own thinking. I return to the "crime scenes" of the classroom, the institute, and the clinic, not to verify what happened but to ask again what failed to take place—what was longed for, misrecognized, deferred. These are not simply read as past situations but as scenes that refuse closure—psychic remains that trouble the line between what happened and what could not happen. They hold the weight of unrealized gestures, of speech that missed its moment, of encounters that dissolved under the pressure of too much knowing or too little imagination. This return does not put an end to the frustrations of institutional learning, yet it changes their register. Frustration becomes less an endpoint than a kind of resonance—something to be worked through, for the possibility of a more interesting question. Something that could not be said, now turned into a style of listening.

Why this book now

In the history of psychoanalysis, it is well known that the idea of femininity and masculinity, which today we think about as gender, is foundational to the conception of intersubjectivity. Gender has always been a site of contestation because it is intertwined with sexuality, the centerpiece of psychoanalysis. We see this in cultural debates, in the family, in the problem of sexuality, and in questions of love and hate. To speak of gender through sexuality is to encounter the association between sex and biology, which presses the conversation back toward normative closure. Freud himself never used the concept of gender. Early on, however, there was a deep preoccupation in psychoanalysis with a question of female sexuality and mothering. It is only within the last few decades, however, with the advancement of women's rights, gay and lesbian rights, divorce laws, and the partial disassembling of patriarchy, that the constellation we call gender has started to be spoken about beyond the publicity of Hollywood and fashion advertisements. These cultural tropes have been what traditionally animated the ways in which gender is received;

they are a sort of "implantation" (Laplanche, 1992), and hence, gender is a site of seduction.

Today, we see another kind of activism tied to sexual liberation and the opening of a broader range of ways to conceptualize the self: gay, lesbian, trans, bisexual, two-spirited, nonbinary, etc. What we encounter with nonbinary individuals is that gender can no longer be an identity or an attribute. Instead, it is a situation—an articulation of an emotional state that is expressed in a different kind of way. Bion would say that our vocabulary is inherently insufficient for the experience. If we start there, the question of gender for the psychoanalytic field is tied to the capacity to think together about a topic that we all have strong ideas about and that are, in addition, difficult to communicate. We see this difficulty in both the clinic and in the analytic classroom, and our tools to try to conceptualize this dilemma will, much like gender, be made through the veil of phantasy: not only the phantasy structuring psychic life but also the phantasy that theory can name it—a recursive entanglement that becomes visible in transference and countertransference.

What the emotional situation of gender and sexuality suggests is that to study their effects we must begin with the uncertainties, surprises, and affrays that characterize intersubjective life. The classroom experience I mentioned earlier, of attempting to teach courses on gender and sexuality, is a prime example of how gender is a site of contention but also of intrigue and desire: there are loyalties, ideologies, and certitude. The collapse of gender into identity leads to the "confusion of tongues" that Ferenczi describes as the trauma that occurs when the child's "language of tenderness" meets the adult's language of passion and sexuality (Soreanu, 2018, p. 44). This confusion is not only the situation of the child. Its aftereffects reverberate in all experiences of authority and submission. The classroom quickly turns to a site of contestation but also to a place of possibilities, where the calcification of both anxiety and knowability are agitated by the enigmatic nature of communication, its inherent compromise, and the impossibility of translation. The problem of intersubjectivity lies at the heart of gender's psychical experience, because the pursuit of humane learning, Britzman (2024) suggests, does not introduce fragility so much as reveal the fragilities that have always structured intersubjective life (p. 47).

At the same time, ideals take shape under what Ferenczi describes as the "paternal and maternal hypnosis"—the interplay of fear and love, a dynamic that Soreanu (2018) notes appeals to "a lifelong element of infantile obedience in all of us" (p. 45). In this sense, learning is another word for transference, where the eerie delay between experience and meaning (Britzman, 2024) supplies a breathing space for new interpretations. Rather than assert a specific way of transcending our limits in understanding gender, I turn to psychoanalytic situations of learning to elaborate a constitutive problem with understanding itself. It involves the contradiction of having to give up knowledge in order to understand something about the other. If, in the realm of gender, psychoanalytic teaching seems to have stalled, the question this book engages with is: where did our understanding turn against itself and fall apart? Each chapter will address the question of the reception of knowledge in a different way and examine its falling apart. At the same time that I present a falling apart, I will argue for this very collapse as the grounds for learning itself.

The question of the reception and transmission of psychoanalytic theory is evidently bound up with the problem of intersubjectivity because ideas about gender are also places of unconscious psychical and libidinal investments. From this emotional realm, the question of reception touches upon the inherent compromise of communication, the impossibility of translation, and how it is subject to erotic traces of dependency that constitutes transference. This volume examines the conditions that have both enabled and challenged previous psychoanalytic understandings of gender. It does so by bringing together theories of learning and unconscious temporality, highlighting the dilemma of unpreparedness: in learning, experience comes before understanding. It is then within the gap between receiving and learning that also allows for new translation.

There are different ways of studying transformation in the conceptualization of gender and resistance to change within our field. Psychoanalysis is a very intimate practice, and if we want to study the ways in which analysts change their mind to also explore the question of what constitutes openness, we must, in my view, study not only the resisting movement or the shift in concepts but also the person experiencing that shift. One way is through looking at case studies where analysts have changed their mind on the question of gender. This process draws on Forrester's method of "thinking in cases" (2017); the ways he describes reading case studies as entering an experience that is other to me by "climbing into the writer's head," an imaginative reach that, nonetheless, cannot go beyond an entrance point to the reader's phantasy. The writing of a case, he suggests, is already an aftereffect of the transference and, in this way, reading cases is an intersubjective experience.

Cases, Forrester suggests, are exemplars. Not because they can be generalized but because they present a threshold: cases give us access to a social, political, emotional, and pedagogical situation. Drawing on Forrester, I engage with reading cases by attempting to enter the writer's mind from the *nachträglich* temporality of my own transferential reading. From the perspective of "thinking in cases" (Forrester, 2017), reading clinical vignettes is akin to reading narratives. What the reader encounters in a case is a text implicated by the aftereffect of the transference, which brings a series of disguises. In this sense, the book will approach narratives and cases as dream texts, that is, as "compositions" subject to the logic of displacement and condensation and to the temporal movements of anticipation and retroaction.

About the structure of the book

The book is framed by four parts that nonetheless are intertwined: **Part 1: Translatability**, attends to the gap between what we inherit and how we interpret it—between the public language of gender and its clinical intima-cies, where meaning is always slightly misaligned and never fully our own. **Chapter 1** begins with a question: how do ideas of gender and sexuality travel—between people, across time, within institutions? Here, reception is treated not as passive intake but as a scene of susceptibility, where thought leaves its residue, like a fingerprint. Drawing on Freud's concept of *nachträgli-chkeit* (deferred action), the chapter explores the temporal and affective dis-tance between what is transmitted and what is understood. Reception, in this view, is less a moment than a process—haunted by phantasy, by seduction, by the failure of language to contain what it seeks to name. In this space, trans-ference becomes not only a clinical phenomenon but a structure of learning, where knowledge is entangled with desire, inheritance, and resistance.

Chapter 2 turns to the troubled legacy of Harry Stack Sullivan, as read through Naoko Wake's *Private Practices*. What emerges is not simply a biog-raphy but a study in transference—across analytic scenes, political histories, and disciplinary borders. Sullivan's navigation of homosexuality, psychiatry, and American liberalism becomes a way to think about how the personal and the institutional are never separate. The chapter suggests that the dilemmas of recognition, self-disclosure, and normative pressure that marked Sullivan's life also structure how psychoanalytic ideas are mediated today. Here, trans-ference exceeds the clinic, shaping the very conditions of public thought, institutional memory, and what can be said.

Chapter 3 examines how theories of gender, even in their most critical forms, can become complicit in the structures they seek to resist. The focus shifts to the institution as a scene of seduction—where knowledge is passed not only through instruction but through unconscious arrangements of desire, rivalry, and identification. Psychoanalytic education becomes a group pro-cess, saturated with the very norms it might otherwise question. The chapter stays with the question of how institutional pedagogy stages gender through affect, repetition, and misrecognition, revealing that what is learned is never only content but also position, belonging, and defense.

Part 2: Dimensions of Change and Resistance traces how the mind changes through transference—not through will or cognition but through the scenes where one's theories of self and other are lived, revised, or defended against. Chapter 4 turns to Joyce McDougall's apologetic paper "Gender Identity and Creativity" (2001), which presents the paradox of how theory cannot lead but only tag along with the emotional situation of the clinic. I use this case as an example of how theory is always out of step and consider the conditions for its revision. Chapter 5 turns to Robert Stoller's case of "Agnes," in his 1964 paper and his re-consideration of the case. It explores how transference shapes the interpretation and presentation of evidence, while also considering the role of agency and desire in defining gender. Chapter 6 will focus on a reading of Danielle Quinodoz's paper "Termination of a Fe/Male Transsexual Patient's Analysis." It will look at the question of transference as key to understanding current psychoanalytic responses to the dilemma of gender transitioning.

Part 3: Matters of Concern signals those affective intensities that refuse to stay in place—the things we worry over, argue about, and come to feel as gendered, even when gender is not the stated issue. Chapter 7 plays with the scene of gender through Eve Sedgewick's memoir of her therapy. As with the chapter on Stoller and the case of Agnes, one of the questions the chapter looks at is that of agency, represented through dialogue. Here, Eve Sedgewick's concept of the capacity for "middle range of agency" will be considered as a condition for thinking. Chapter 8 tackles the question, "How do we know something like gender?" I revisit Eve Sedgwick's concept of the "middle range of agency"—the space between passivity and reactivity—this time in relation to scientific inquiry. This is framed through Isabelle Stengers' idea of science as something that remains open to what it needs in order to develop. Using Stengers' distinction between "matters of concern" and "matters of fact," the chapter explores how not knowing the history of how we've come to know something can block the possibility of changing that knowledge. What, for example, does psychoanalysis need to create a science that does not pathologize?

Chapter 9 considers a particular mode of giving in to a situation that is inexplicable. It then considers how this condition allows for something new. Through Dana Amir's abstract notion of "forgiveness" as a human and radical form of ethics, I consider a third space, beyond the binary of ruthlessness and helplessness, with which to listen to gender. Chapter 10 considers the capacity of the analyst to not be deadened or seduced to come to any kind of a conclusion about a phenomenon through Saito's depiction of the Otaku culture—a community of individuals who have a deep libidinal attachment to anime characters—as a way to think about gender differently and posit reality and fiction in creative, nonbinary ways.

Part 4: The World of Others invokes the interpsychic—the ethical and aesthetic problem of becoming in relation to those we cannot fully know, yet who leave their imprint on us. Chapter 11 turns to the classroom as a scene of care and conflict, where gender emerges through educational encounters shaped by libidinal histories. Classroom "characters" are read not as types but as expressions of psychic life and group dynamics. Like the clinic, the classroom becomes a space for imagining relationality, where certainty may harden into defense or soften into responsiveness. Through reflections on adolescent ruthlessness (Gozlan, 2022b), group psychology, and the confusion of tongues, the chapter asks how tenderness might become a form of listening.

Chapter 12 revisits the notion of the *social unconscious* to ask how dominant ideologies shape our technical listening, especially when it comes to gender. Which world are we attuned to—the material, the emotional, the ideological, or the unconscious? Chapter 13 explores four memoirs of transition to show how gender intersects with broader experiences of change—across illness, aging, sexuality, and relationality—each offering new ways of imagining what transition can mean. Chapter 14 introduces the idea of a psychic space of *in-difference*, complicating the phrase "the personal is political" by showing how, for the transgender subject, politics and embodiment are mutually implicated. The chapter proposes a space of intermediacy between feminist and trans discourses, rather than opposition.

The book concludes with a coda by revisiting Canguilhem's conception of the *norm* not as a fixed standard but as an aesthetic, affective process of individuating life, and pairs it with Richard Prum's evolutionary argument that beauty—not fitness or adaptation—is a primary motor of change. It follows how beauty, desire, and gender's shifting forms unsettle identity itself—inviting a movement from certainty toward an aesthetic and affective experience of embodiment, where attraction emerges as something unmastered and in flux. Aesthetic orientation, I suggest, reopens the Oedipal conflict—not as a structure to be resolved through symbolic law but as an encounter with unresolvable difference that invites creativity, ambiguity, and relational invention.

Notes

1 An example of that can be found in a short novel by Stefan Zweig—*Letter from an Unknown Woman*, where the narrator is fixated on a man's hands. Not even the whole hand, perhaps—only a gesture, a curl of the fingers mid-sentence, a careless reach. The body disassembles itself under the pressure of desire. Gender appears here as part objects: a hand, a voice, a detail too small to be named—these become the scaffolding of meaning. One does not find gender; one stumbles into its debris, animates it, gets caught.
2 The reader will notice that I alternate between *phantasy* and *fantasy*. I use *phantasy* to signal unconscious formations in the Kleinian sense, while *fantasy* refers to more conscious, imaginative elaborations.
3 Lacan's notion of paradoxical object that does not satisfy desire but instead elicits and sustains it. It is not an object one can possess; rather, it marks the structural lack that organizes subjectivity and desire. Seminar XVI: *From an Other to the Other* (1968–69).
4 The way in which a meaning of an event can only be understood as an aftereffect. It is a structure for understanding how people learn: something that is happening now that is calling into action things that haven't been resolved.

Part I

Translatability

This section examines the space between what is given and what is made of it: the languages handed down in the name of gender and the unpredictable ways they are taken up. Here, translatability does not promise clarity but names a tension between inheritance and reworking, reception and resistance. From the receptive vulnerability that makes thinking possible, to the transference that binds private and public life, to the seductions that animate pedagogy, these chapters ask: What does knowledge turn into when received in the unconscious, where it is never intact? Knowledge does not pass unchanged. It takes shape in relation—inflected by receptivity, transference, and pedagogy. What arrives in the other is altered: translated, resisted, or desired. Such distortions may be the very form in which truth becomes thinkable.

DOI: 10.4324/9781003440758-2

1 Inheritance and transmission

Freud's capacity for a tender and uncertain mode of investigating the mind begins with his desire to step back into his own past, where he discovers his fantasies, wishes, and infantile theories of sexuality. He then shows us how these fantasies and the internal representation of the world on which they are based are tightly linked to our infantile perceptions of our parents, which are then projected forward to shape our future:

> The child's first and most significant love-object is the mother, and this relationship forms the prototype for all later love relationships. The internal representations of these early experiences are carried forward and influence future relationships and behaviors.
>
> (Freud, 1917, p. 366)

In Freud's phylogenetic view, what we inherit from the mother is an internal world that is always in contact with the external world. Psychic experience, for Freud, is situated in an uncanny space, where the past and present continuously interact. Winnicott extends this idea through his notion of the "creative space of culture" (1971, p. 100), a term he uses to describe the history of transmission that culminates in each individual in a highly particular way.

I would like to extend this notion of transmission further, imagining education as one of its primary scenes—particularly in how theories of gender function as sites of seduction, transference, and reception. Just as psychic life is shaped by traces of the past, so too is learning structured by the histories of thought that precede us. There is a transference to education itself, a force of history that shapes our becoming, because new learning hinges on the reception of what came before. One way to conceptualize this scene of transmission is through the metaphor of fingerprints: something enigmatic that leaves its trace on us—impressions formed not only by explicit teachings but also by distant cultural meanings, symbolic collapses, and unrecognized desires.

Laplanche (1995) names this process *seduction*—not in the vernacular sense of lure or intent but as a structural relation. Sexuality, for him, is not innate to the body but arises in the wake of a message the infant cannot fully

DOI: 10.4324/9781003440758-3

decode. In the act of caregiving, the mother—or whoever takes up that position—does more than feed or soothe. She transmits something else, something excessive: traces of her own unconscious, her own erotic life. These messages arrive encrypted, enigmatic, addressed to a subject not yet formed. It is in responding to this foreignness, this *message without code*, that sexuality begins to stir. The infant, in turn, is susceptible to the unconscious of the adult in this asymmetrical relationship of care—what Laplanche (1987, Trans. 2016) calls the "anthropological situation":

> A body of thought about the essential foundations of the human being. One of these foundations, perhaps the most important one, is the fact of the little human's entry into the world of adults. . . . It is a "universal" for human beings . . . the fundamental anthropological situation.
>
> (pp. 19–20)

As a body of thought, meaning is necessarily delayed because the infant is unprepared for the saturated sexuality of the adult world. The messages received from the other are compromised, requiring ongoing translation (Scarfone, 2015). This is also where ethics enter the picture—because the encounter between the adult and the infant is a volatile mixture. And this volatility is what we call sexuality. The anthropological situation itself is seductive: it is a condition of helplessness, yet what makes it significant is its enigmatic nature. The gaps between what we are given and how we receive it require us to think through the instability of meaning. Interpretation is inherently haunted by the presence of desire—both our own and that of the "other"—something unconscious, beyond immediate understanding, but also in futurity. We cannot predict how we will be affected by the "messages" we receive or what meanings will emerge from them. This is the space where new narratives take hold, where something previously unthought—such as a new gender formation or identity—demands consideration.

To think of gender formation as a process of transmission, then, is to return to the most basic condition of being born—our prolonged gestation, our radical immaturity, our fundamental dependence on language. To be born is to be formed, impressed upon, to be vulnerable to the world before we can even name it. This openness to impression and susceptibility to dependency is not incidental to gender but constitutive of it. Gender, in this sense, is always maternal—not in the biological sense but in the way it entwines with what Winnicott called the "maternal environment" (1971), the psychic holding space where affective madness, aggression, depression, and helplessness can be lived through. This maternal environment need not be a mother, nor even a woman; it is whoever assumes the task of holding, of containing, of witnessing the infant's psychic experience. But gender is not only born here—it is continuously reborn in the unfolding enigma of human life. The anthropological situation (1987, 2016) describes not only the development of gender but also the human condition itself. It speaks to our fundamental unpreparedness for life's unpredictability—our perpetual entanglement with enigmatic messages, histories, and desires that exceed our capacity to know.

This asymmetry—between adult and infant, between analyst and analysand, between teacher and student—repeats itself across the transferential landscapes of psychoanalysis and education. Learning is not exchange. Like the analytic encounter, it stirs the transference; it seduces. To be taken in by education is to be drawn into its desires—its histories, its positions, its wounds. Theories do not stand apart from this. They attract their own forms of loyalty, their own idealizations; they become screens for collective identifications. And what passes between teacher and student—like what passes in the clinic—is never what was intended. No transmission is clean. What is received is altered, refracted, shaped by forces neither side can fully know. Perhaps this is the deepest lesson psychoanalysis offers to its own education: that every act of learning folds back into the scene of desire.

The transferential experience of being affected by education—how it is transmitted and received—complicates our ability to recognize our own emotional susceptibility to historical positions. This presents a dilemma for our capacity to see that our theories are not omnipotent or absolute but rather sites of seduction. As long as we are in this position of reception, we cannot fully grasp either the nature of what has been received or the unconscious dimensions of transmission itself. In psychoanalysis, the seduction of theory within institutional education relates to group psychology, asymmetry, and the vulnerability of dependency In education.

Laplanche (1987) situates miscommunication not as an accident of transmission but as its structural condition. Education, in this sense, cannot secure the purity of what it imparts: what is taught is already altered in the act of reception, shading into what is taken up, leaving traces that linger in afterlives we cannot anticipate. Nowhere does this turbulence press more sharply than in questions of gender. Theories meant to unsettle may find themselves caught in familiar circuits—repeating the very forms they hoped to disturb: normativity, institutional desire, collective fantasy. Yet, this is not failure, nor cause and effect. It is the work of reception—thought shaped and reshaped as it moves through the transferential life of the institution. The transmission of ideas in psychoanalytic education is rarely examined as a process in its own right. What tends to be overlooked is not simply what is learned but how—how education is mediated through institutional life, through identifications, group anxieties, loyalties, refusals. The question of transference is central here: it unsettles any fantasy of direct communication. In the analytic institute, as in the clinic, theory does not travel unmarked. Theories of gender, especially, gather psychic investments as they move—becoming sites of conflict, resistance, and unconscious rewriting. Between what is offered and what is taken up, something happens that no curriculum can script. It is in this gap—in what cannot be foreseen—that the work of interpretation begins again.

Psychoanalysis has never been neutral on the question of gender, although its terms have shifted across time. From Freud's *Three Essays on the Theory of Sexuality* (1905) onward, the question of what we now call gender has been inseparable from the problem of sexuality itself. It must have been a shock, in 1905, to encounter Freud's assertion that sexuality is not confined to genitality, that perversion is not an aberration but a fundamental structure of desire. He wrote: "Human beings are sexual beings right from the start," and "Sexual excitation is not restricted to genitalia, as pleasure is achieved through erotic attachment to any area of the body" (Freud, 1905, p. 182). Desire, he insisted, does not conform to the categories we impose upon it; it exceeds them, proliferates beyond them, undoes them. In this, Freud opened a door that psychoanalysis has never quite been able to close.

In his *Three Essays*, Freud is grappling with multiple interwoven ideas: seduction theory and trauma, the Oedipal structure, the origins of sexuality, and autoeroticism, all of which are linked to the broader question of the origins of the mind. His thinking is initially guided by the concept of libido, first understood as a biological force and later as a psychical one. For Freud, sexuality is the primary site from which we defend against the drives. In the *Three Essays*, he conceptualizes sexuality as a property of the body, but with the abandonment of seduction theory, he begins to shift his focus toward phantasy. By the third essay, which centers on adolescence and latency, Freud's notion of sexuality and its destiny becomes somehow more rigidified. His privileging of genital primacy and the division between fore-pleasures and end-pleasures folds sexuality back into a more traditional script—one in which heterosexuality arrives as the telos of psychic development. Oedipalization seals this alignment: through its repetitions, the heterosexual couple becomes an unquestioned figure in the architecture of everyday fantasy, but this is not a neutral inheritance. The history of psychoanalytic thought is itself a scene of transmission—gender shaped, constrained, and reiterated through the pathways by which ideas are carried, received, and sedimented over time.

It is impossible to account for this conservative turn in the third essay, and we can only hypothesize retrospectively on whether Freud's theory was affected in part by concern over the way in which psychoanalysis would be received in the social environment of his time, given his drawing upon contemporary sexologists—Krafft-Ebing, Magnus Hirschfeld, and Albert Moll—all of whom were oriented toward a non-pathological view of homosexuality and the question of freedom. *Nachträglichkeit* invites us to ask how this history continues to shape the ways we now narrate gender—and whether Freud's third essay might have held to the openness of the first two, had the fear of pansexualism not shadowed its later revisions. His ongoing struggle with *Three Essays* can be traced in the revisions and footnotes (see Leader, *Freud's Footnotes*)—marks of an argument not only with the social climate but also with the resistances gathering within psychoanalysis itself. Freud's narrative is saturated with its historical moment. And in its wake, we must also attend to the aftershocks of postwar history—how cultural upheavals left their impress on the theoretical life of the field. What historians of postwar psychoanalytic theory observe (Wake, 2011; Roudinesco, 2016; Kahn, 2022) is a turn to biology, where the site of the actual body is normalized and romanticized. Psychoanalysis began as an unfolding of ideas in the aftermath of the Holocaust, whose effects were devastating and ground-shifting on both a personal and theoretical level for Freud. It was in the United States that psychiatry and psychoanalysis were very much in tune with the illegality of homosexuality. The use of standardized measures and the alliance with conventional medicine led to a rigidification of psychoanalytic practice, Laurence Kahn (2022) suggests, and constrained its creative aspects.

Reading Freud's *Three Essays* in the 21st century, it seems that the greatest freedom in those essays lies in his discussion of infantile sexuality, perhaps because of our own infantile amnesia. From a *nachträglichkeit* perspective, infantile sexuality functions as a kind of Rorschach test—open to myriad translations and expressions. The case is different with adolescence, however, because puberty continues to be associated with volatility, idealization, and passion. Adolescence is a particularly vulnerable period for any gender, especially due to the capacity for pregnancy. The question of care and the adolescent's need for adult protection is especially dominant in current debates on gender transitioning. The adolescent's capacity for agency, decision-making, and independent thought is often doubted. One of the challenges we face is that adolescence is conceptualized simultaneously as a biological and developmental phenomenon and as a historically constructed concept subject to transmission and translation.

The very term *adolescence* is a late arrival. It did not emerge in its current form until the postwar decades of the 1940s and 1950s. Before then, other figures crowded this space: *youth, wayward youth, delinquent*—each freighted with moral anxiety. The idea of adolescence as a distinct developmental stage is not a natural fact but a historical invention, one still unsettled. As Britzman (2020) observes, analysts have long struggled to conceptualize adolescence; it is not something simply encountered but something conjured—by theory, by culture, by transference. Yet, psychoanalytic thought often forgets this instability. Bound to developmental frameworks, it risks treating adolescence as a given, just as recent debates about transgender adolescents often do (Gozlan, 2022b). Winnicott's (1971) idea of adolescence as a *transitional space*, a *borderline concept*, suggests otherwise: adolescence is never one thing. It is a lived state, a phantasy of those no longer young, an institutional figure, a "paper adolescent" in need of rescue—or control. Perhaps the real question is not how to define adolescence but how to bear its uncertainties. For the adult—and for the analyst—the work is not to master adolescence but to create a frame spacious enough to think with its contradictions: of development, of normativity, of sexuality. A frame that does not foreclose what remains in motion.

What these dilemmas bring into view is the instability of concepts. Gender too is a modern concept tied to social and governmental and medical structures: passport, identity card, medical discourse, not a natural occurrence. It reached its nadir in pop culture, with the idea of reaching your inner potential, being a better person or a "true self." There is a contest of meaning to masculinity and femininity within Freud's corpus and in culture. And what we receive from cultural transmission is therefore an *intermediacy*. At the same time, the persistence of ideologies of gender in psychoanalytic education point to a resistance to change. What we witness, Fiorini (2019) and Gullestad (2024) suggest, is a tendency to fall back on normative theorization and paradigms of binary logic. Femininity and masculinity in the Freudian corpus are unstable constructs—at times a maternal trace, a physical element, a pressure point, and at other times the destiny of anatomy. This is also the quality of the experience of gender, which evokes uncannily mixed feelings of recognition and foreignness. There is something in gender that resists cohesion. This is gender's uncanniness.

Glocer Fiorini (2019) identifies central ideals that persist in the face of Freud's paradigmatic shifts, which provide a broader sense of conceptualizing heterogeneous paths to gender: current bifurcated ideals of the "masculine/feminine pair" (p. 1263), the conception of "a universal notion that can only envision a normative, dual outcome of the construction of sexuated subjectivation" (p. 1263). Such ideals run counter to Freud's notion of the unconscious, which decenters the idea of a unitary subject and presents us with a conception of subjectivity as a "network of psychological multiplicities" (p. 1263). These ideals are grounded on heteronormative notions of gender that are deeply rooted in culture. What they obfuscate is the question of desire, which is beyond the cultural, the social, and the political, and toward the psychoanalytic notion of phantasy and creativity. The persistence of ideals presents an active disavowal of the transformations that are occurring in culture, which are evident in the clinic. What is defended against is the loss of certainty, of control, of cultural touchstones, and loss of footing.

What is at stake in the question of the fate of the concept of gender in psychoanalytic education, however, is not the nature of Freud's work. Rather, it is our relation to his work, from the backward glance of today. And here we may wonder what sustains the continued disavowal of Freud's uncanny text. What maintains the difficulty of approaching psychoanalytic meta-psychology paradigmatically (Simpson, 2022), that is, as a paradox, rather than universal truths? The defense against uncanniness is, of course, a multifaceted problem that hinges on dilemmas of recognition (something familiar becomes unhomely and strange) and existential anxiety over unintelligibility and annihilation (Freud, 1919; Weber, 2024).

Freud's placement of uncanniness—a concept that is unworldly, familiar and unfamiliar—at the core of psychoanalytic science that is supposed to be in the world, addresses a conflict in psychic reality: we are susceptible to the historical movements that are us but that we don't know and that nonetheless we feel. The uncanny is a bridge between reality and phantasy. It is a banister concept to the ways psychical reality leans towards projective identification under the guise of perception. From this vantage point, gender will be conceptualized as a cover-up for this internal difference and the proliferation of this difference. Freud identifies the ultimate source of anxiety associated with the uncanny as the projected loss of a bodily organ: the "development of the fear of castration" (Freud, 1933, p. 147), associated with helplessness. The experience of the uncanny brings to the fore the idea that events are both inner and outer, self and not-self, present and past. Its disavowal functions as a defense against the anxiety of not knowing.

The resistance to change in psychoanalytic education, particularly in relation to concepts like gender, is not only a matter of theoretical inertia but also of transference. If learning itself is shaped by unconscious attachments, anxieties, and desires, then shifts in knowledge—especially those that challenge foundational beliefs—become sites of conflict and repetition. That "difficult knowledge" is a relationality, an encounter with our own history of education, which suggests there is an infantile structure to learning. Put more clearly, learning will bring back infantile desires to secure love from the other, or in turn, an omnipotent wish to be the parent (Britzman, 1998, p. 34). To consider this dynamic in the context of institutional education, we might consider candidates' desire to be all-knowing as she/he imagines the training analyst to be. The candidate and the institute are involved in a psychological situation of dependency, asymmetry, vulnerability, and difference. Aulagnier (2001) imagines the child's entrance to the adult world as one of saturation. The mother's unconscious desire saturates, infiltrates, and intrudes. The child, she argues, meets the "word bearer"/mother's "violence of interpretation." The way in which susceptibility for ideality enacts what Alice Balint called "identificatory thinking" (in Pitt & Britzman, 2003, p. 34)—a means of adhesive identification "not yet replaced with understating" (Pitt & Britzman, 2003, p. 34)—suggests that infantile structures of infancy return to rattle our learning in violent and intrusive ways. And yet, there is no direct correspondence in unconscious communication. The child encounters maternal violence with creativity: the capacity to lie and have secrets is the space where "the I must come about" (p. 71). "Words," Britzman writes, "demand something of us and may feel persecutory. In times of safety, words may be permitted their aggression and destruction" (p. 35). Such are the conditions for sublimation.

The backdrop of our learning is created from attachments to others and a desire for love. Our learning too will therefore be susceptible to repetition, anxiety, loss, and hence to transference neurosis, transference love, and transference resistance. This involves the transference that bears on reception to new ideas: "it is not only that new ideas affect the ideas one already holds. Rather, the affect involved with ideas we already hold transfers into the reception of new ideas and to the figure of the teacher" (Britzman, 2015, p. 43). Freud (1914) describes the transference as a "playground" where the patient's compulsion to repeat is allowed to expand in almost complete freedom (p. 150). Transference, he suggests, is where startling, unexpected knowledge emerges. Freud's insistence that analysts learn from the tumult of transference presents us with a dilemma. Can candidates and psychoanalysts press against the soft spots of their learning to begin to recognize what Britzman (1998) describes as "the force of resistance to the destiny of one's mental acts that sinks the buoyancy of symbolization" (p. 35)?

If our capacity to learn something new hinges on our ability to accept that we are seduced or deceived by what we think we know, we are also confronted by another dilemma: how do we know we are deceived? This is a transferential dilemma, because there is no outside to transference. In the psychoanalytic institute, both candidates and analysts are caught within it, and education stalls. At stake is the recognition that belief is a libidinal situation: the experience of belief binds through commitment, through professionalism. Even when confronted with truth, refusal persists.

Libidinal attachments will register change as a conflict between "loyalty to the known and anxieties over loss of love" (Britzman, 2015, p. 43). The "seduction to ambition" (Britzman, p. 39), the determination to apprehend knowledge, comes with omnipotence that must be shattered in the process of coming to know. But the dynamic of transference—its conflicts and places of collapse—are also the grounds for change. Change, Anna Freud suggest, comes with a conflict and is itself a conflict. Interference, she states, is the nature of education and the dilemmas psychoanalytic institutes face in being able to create a space for learning, and is the capacity to "find a way between the Scilla of non-interference and the Charybdis of frustration" (Freud, p. 149, in Britzman, p. 34). Learning will hinge on the ability to withstand conflict—to admit psychoanalysis' divided nature, its tipsy-turvy affected, wounded course, and contain destruction of meaning.

If the tight spot we must get at with gender is the recognition of where meaning breaks down, then the question we also face is whether psychoanalytic institutes can begin to affect their own imaginary. Here we are faced with a dilemma: how do we open the archive to its own otherness? Given the challenges psychoanalysis faces in conceptualizing gender, we might ask: how do we make room for what psychoanalysis does not yet know? If we return to Freud (1958), education begins not with mastery but with an openness to what one doesn't yet know. Psychoanalysis offers an aesthetic vision of the human: we are structurally susceptible to and shaped by that which we do not know. This requires engagement with spaces outside psychoanalysis.

There is a long tradition in psychoanalysis of going beyond the psychoanalytic couch to study the problems and situations of psychical life in the worlds of literature, art, and culture. Freud was drawn to ancient cultures, Greek mythology, literature, and philosophy. In the realm of gender, a turn to art, film, and literature allows the analyst to imagine gender's creativity, instability, and its dynamic of relationality. The aesthetic lens of art and literature places our preconceived ideas that might stabilize meaning at bay. Encountering different situations of gender through literature, memoirs, and art allows us access to a wider world of experience—that is both outside our own and at the same time ours—and to a dreamy notion of gender: the

ambiguities of partial, contradictory, ambivalent, and unconscious identifications. It also involves, however, the task of narrating gender's reception within
the psychoanalytic field, its conceptual transformations, uses, breakdowns,
and contradictions. In this way, the concept of gender is bound to time. Just
as psychoanalytic theory itself is shaped by historical shifts and unconscious
receptions, gender too can only be understood in *nachträglichkeit* time—
through its ongoing reinterpretations and echoes within culture and the analytic field.

2 Unbridgeable gap

Reading cases is also an encounter with the echoes of history—what Deborah Britzman (2024) describes as the transferential process of working through time. To study the conditions for change is to remain with absence—with what does not link, with the distances between past and present, knowing and not knowing. For Britzman, education unfolds in this uncertain space, where meaning arises not only from what can be taught but also from what resists being known. My work with cases does not seek resolution. It follows the tremors in analytic life: moments when meaning breaks down, when attention drifts, and when hesitation interrupts the exchange. Such tremors mark how psychic life resists smooth narration. The temporal gap between what registers and what returns belatedly raises a central question: how does change move between inner life and the public world? My concern here is the discord between the clinical encounter and its institutional afterlife—in publications, classrooms, and supervision—where private uncertainties become public certainties.

Harry Stack Sullivan (1882–1949) moves in this archive as a spectral figure—one whose contradictions illuminate the uneasy traffic between public ideals and private struggle. A neo-Freudian psychiatrist without formal psychoanalytic training, Sullivan developed what became known as *interpersonal theory*: a vision of mental life in which illness, sexuality, and suffering are saturated by the social. Against the biological determinism of his time, Sullivan insisted that societal attitudes toward homosexuality and mental illness penetrate psychic life, shaping the very texture of experience. But the cost of this insight was not small. His own life bore the marks of its impossibility: a project of liberation shadowed by personal concealment, a critical stance undone by the institutions through which he sought to sustain it.

Two studies trace the tensions he encountered: Naoko Wake's account of his two-decade investigation into homosexuality and Mark Blechner's 2005 paper, "The Gay Harry Stack Sullivan" (*Contemporary Psychoanalysis*, 41(1): 1–20). In Blechner's account, Sullivan becomes a figure of historical ambivalence: a closeted man whose prescient thinking strained against the constraints of his public life, an uneasy precursor to the language of gay rights that had not yet arrived. He lingers on an unconventional act of

DOI: 10.4324/9781003440758-4

altruistic devotion—Sullivan, in an effort to secure legal protection for his much younger partner, James Iscoe, adopted him as his son, a maneuver that granted them the privileges of a heterosexual couple. Wake, by contrast, turns our gaze to Sullivan's radical clinical work in the early 1920s at the Sheppard and Enoch Pratt Hospital near Baltimore, where he carved out a space for gay men to speak openly about their experiences—an audacious move for its time.

Wake traces Sullivan's movement through shifting circles—anthropologists, sociologists, psychoanalysts—among them Edward Sapir, John Dollard, Margaret Mead, Ruth Benedict. His inquiry into sexuality was never just an academic pursuit. It carried a vision: a hope for a more livable world for those psychiatry had pathologized and society had cast aside (Wake, p. 2). Yet Sullivan remained ensnared in the very structures he sought to undo. The work of liberation did not extend to his own life. His position was fraught: an iconoclast wary of collaboration, a closeted man whose writings at times reinforced the very homophobic logics he might have opposed, a theorist whose later turn toward eugenics revealed the contradictions he could not escape. His legacy is not one of simple progress. It leaves us with a more unsettling question: how does one think—let alone teach—beyond the conditions that shape one's own blind spots? What can it mean to change minds when one's own remains caught in the tangle of public ideals and private impossibilities?

Wake's study tells us little of Sullivan's own sexuality, leaving his subjectivity an open question. Indeed, attempting to grasp Sullivan the man proves elusive—his figure wavers between the lines of psychological textbooks, presenting the outline of someone who strove for a more humane clinic but whose inner life remains occluded. Yet in Wake's study, the reader catches glimpses of him—not just in the finished work but in the act of its making, where we see the cracks, the obstacles, the unresolved internal tensions that shaped his approach.

The life history interview

Wake describes a moment when men of both the bourgeoisie and the working class entered Sullivan's clinic at the Sheppard and Enoch Pratt Hospital, where he was director of clinical research in psychiatry, and later at St. Elizabeth's Hospital in Washington, D.C., where he worked under Allanson White. It was there that he crafted an interview method not merely to collect psychiatric data but to invite his patients to reflect on their own experiences, to bring into focus the ways in which the architecture of their social world shaped their emotional lives.

For Sullivan, the willingness to pose questions about sexuality without moralism, without the dulling force of judgment, were the conditions for humanity. His most enduring contribution, the "life history interview," was born from his conviction that mental illness had sociological origins. His early advocacy for deinstitutionalization grew out of his clinical work and his insistence on centering patient subjectivity. Unlike the detached, regimented structure of conventional medical diagnostic interviews, Sullivan's method allowed patients to become active participants in shaping their own narratives. In a gesture that broke with medical authority, he even permitted patients to turn the tables, to interview him. He sought not merely information but intimacy—speaking of affection in a warm, open vocabulary, creating a space where desire could be named without shame.

Through this collaborative approach—not simply, "Tell me about your life," but "What do you think of it?"—Sullivan endeavored to unearth the erotic undercurrents of experience. His life history interview was designed to listen for the textures of subjectivity: first kisses, moments of awakening, the places where desire stirred. Here was an attempt to move away from science as taxonomy and toward something more experiential, more phenomenological. In speaking of what people did together and, crucially, what it felt like, he pointed toward a new kind of psychoanalytic listening. Pre-war shifts in thinking found an uneasy foothold in clinics such as Sheppard and Enoch Pratt, where some psychiatrists began to approach homosexuality as variation rather than pathology—another thread in the fabric of human experience. Sullivan's work, at once radical and unresolved, remains a testament to both the promise and the difficulty of changing minds. His legacy resists easy closure: a record of insight shadowed by contradiction. It continues to unsettle the ways we think about the entanglements of private life and public discourse, desire and discipline, self and structure.

Wake's analysis highlights how Sullivan's work emerged during a moment of intellectual openness, when a more ambiguous notion of sexuality was gaining traction across anthropology, sociology, and psychoanalysis (e.g., Mead, Benedict, Sullivan). Yet, this intellectual openness did not extend beyond the clinic into broader social acceptance of sexual minorities. She shows how Sullivan's work took place during a period before World War II when progressive views on homosexuality were flourishing among liberal intellectuals both in and beyond the United States. This was a moment in psychoanalysis when artists, lay analysts, and marginalized individuals—including drug addicts and gay people—sought to give voice to the unconscious through music and art, embracing a freedom that would later be curtailed.

After the war, this openness gave way to a rigid ideological imperative—patriotism, paternalism, and an aversion to ambiguity. The expressive freedoms of the pre-war period were replaced by conformity, leaving little room for the nuances of sexuality and desire. The intimate and erotic nature of Sullivan's interviews, particularly with homosexual men, became culturally forbidden and unthinkable, particularly in institutions like the military.

Nor did this prior openness allow scientists and professionals who were themselves sexual minorities to come out publicly. The drive to gain acceptance in the postwar era demanded a strict separation between private life and public stance. Wake shows that while Sullivan cultivated an atmosphere of frankness within his clinic, this remained deliberately hidden from public view. The Sheppard and Enoch Pratt Hospital, as Wake describes it, was less an asylum than a kind of retreat. Here, doctors were encouraged to spend extended time with patients—who were mostly articulate, socially connected, but deeply troubled men, alongside some women. Sullivan urged his colleagues to listen closely: to the intricate weave of these patients' familial entanglements, social contradictions, and economic pressures. Behind closed doors, his clinic operated as a space of remarkable openness, yet Sullivan's public persona told a different story. Although he embraced a progressive approach to homosexuality in private clinical work, the constraints of professional discourse required him to publish within the prevailing medical framework, reproducing the very pathologizing terms he sought to resist. He cast effeminate behavior in homosexual men as evidence of psychic failure—a refusal or inability to achieve a coherent sexual self. In doing so, his public writings aligned him with the very pathologizing discourse he sought, elsewhere, to resist. The contradiction was not merely theoretical; it exposed the fragility of his own position—caught between private recognition and the demands of public legibility.

Here, we start to see indications of an extremely defended man. Wake suggests that Sullivan's defenses revolved around rigid ideologies of masculinity, a preoccupation that became ever more pronounced in his later work. He introduced a dichotomy of the "good" and "bad" homosexual, the latter equated with effeminacy—a quality he associated with lack and pathology, and one he viewed as the root of social hatred toward "real" (masculine) homosexuals. Wake portrays Sullivan as a man whose chauvinism and narrow focus on treating men shaped both his practice and his prejudices. He was known to be particularly "frustrated and disagreeable" with female patients, dismissing women as unstable and unreliable narrators. In this too, a disjunction emerges: while Sullivan's private views on homosexuality and gender were more tolerant, his public stance reinforced the very structures of pathologization he resisted in the clinic.

Sullivan, as Wake illustrates, also sought to elevate psychiatry's professional standing by applying the personal interview method in the context of wartime efforts. In trying to shield homosexual men from military conscription, Sullivan reinforced their marginalization. His strategy bound them to those labeled psychologically unfit for service, adding "homosexual proclivities" (p. 166) to a roster of so-called deviations marked by weakness, effeminacy, and unreliability. The pathologizing did not stop there. In public writings, Sullivan elaborated these associations, drawing sharper lines between forms of same-sex desire and folding moral judgment into clinical language. He framed homosexuality as a developmental phase—one to be outgrown if psychic health were to be achieved. More troubling still was his typology: a division between the "mature" homosexual—masculine, independent, *urethral*—and the "immature"—effeminate, dependent, *oral*. For Sullivan, effeminate men appeared not only as failed mimics of femininity but as subjects trapped in longing—for father figures, for unachieved resolution, for coherence that eluded them. Their supposed immaturity became, in his narrative, a refusal of integration—a sign of psychic incoherence that disqualified not just their desires but their capacity to author a life. What began as a gesture of protection thus gave way to a more enduring form of injury: one in which the desire to help was bound to the pathologizing gaze it could not escape.

The question of subjectivity

What emerges from *Private Practices* is the idea that Sullivan's most enduring legacy—what remains most visible in the public sphere—is his *life history interview*. This method staged an unsettling shift: subjectivity was no longer outside the frame of scientific inquiry but drawn into it; exposed, yet never fully captured. His interest in patients' personal narratives of Eros—whether masturbation, cruising, experiences of fellatio, or even molestation—was not about pathologization but about destigmatization. Sullivan encouraged patients to speak about themselves, their relationships, and their erotic lives with the belief that experience was central to the formation of selfhood. At Pratt, Wake shows, Sullivan's approach to sexuality was broad and fluid. Rather than rigidly distinguishing between heterosexuality and homosexuality, his interviews focused on the lived realities of desire, recording sexual activities, interests, and experiences without imposing moral judgment. The repression of these desires, he believed, was at the core of many psychiatric illnesses. More than just a diagnostic tool, the *life history interview* introduced a new model of self-care: one in which treatment was not merely symptom-driven but structured around the act of storytelling itself—where patients were invited to narrate their pain.

Wake's account highlights Sullivan's effort to engage with culture, particularly in the narratives people bring to the clinical encounter—not as fixed or fully knowable but as shaped by historical and social forces. The *life history interview* reveals not just an individual's psychological state but their position within a broader social world. Sullivan understood that the structures of psychiatry were affected by power relations—the rigid hierarchies of doctor and patient, authority and submission. Sullivan broke with the analytic fiction of neutrality, stepping into the scene of the therapeutic encounter. He invited questions, spoke openly of marriage, of sexuality, allowed himself to be seen—but only in ways he could still control. To center subjectivity was not a simple act. What surfaced could not be held steady; the act of bringing it forward unsettled the frame that sought to contain it. The life history interview made this visible. It was meant to give space to the speaking subject. Yet in its wartime deployment, something shifted. The interview was turned outward—toward sorting, toward classification, toward the service of an institution's anxieties. Listening gave way to judgment. The homosexual men Sullivan had once wished to protect were now caught in this reversal—named through the very categories the method had once sought to exceed. What had begun as an opening returned as a closing but not cleanly: its contradictions remained folded into the gesture itself.

But this was not simply a professional compromise. As Wake shows, Sullivan's clinical work and personal life were bound in ways he could not undo. His own experience as a closeted man sharpened his empathy but may also have fueled his reliance on rigid classifications. In public, he pathologized effeminacy as arrested development; in the clinic, he traced desire's ambiguities with more freedom. The tension was not resolved; it was enacted. The very project of centering subjectivity exposed how fragile that center could be. The army made this dynamic brutal. Here, repression did not erase homoeroticism; it organized it. The institution performed denial through its very rituals—hierarchy, masculinity, and the discipline of what could not be named or metabolized. Sullivan, determined to preserve a certain masculine self, moved within this structure. His distinctions—between "mature" and "immature," between forms of same-sex desire—became ways of managing an anxiety that no classification could settle. If his aim had been to make space for open speech, the result was a doubling of silences: for the institution, and perhaps, for himself.

Wake's depiction of Sullivan suggests that his conservative psychoanalytic commitments—especially his association of maturity with the ability to produce a coherent self-narrative—led him to idealize a specific notion of the "modern self," one that excluded effeminacy, lower-class homosexuality, and women's accounts of their own experiences. What emerges from Wake's study is a portrait of a man whose internal conflicts shaped his professional theories in ways that reinforced social hierarchies. Sullivan's belief that a cohesive life story was a precondition for psychic health reveals his investment in a conservative vision of gender and sexuality, where masculinity was aligned with intellect and self-mastery, and femininity with instability and lack. This anxiety over femininity echoes the logic of homophobia itself: in a society where homosexuality was stigmatized, the idea of a "manly homosexual" became an impossibility, and any association with femininity a threat to one's legitimacy as a man.

Theories, too, are private practices. They bear the traces of what their authors can and cannot bear to know. They are shaped by the theorist's unconscious desires, anxieties, and identifications. Sullivan's formulations of gender and sexuality drew from sedimented cultural fantasies—homosexuality as arrested development, femininity as immaturity, intellect as a marker of psychic stability. Such theories did not emerge in neutral space; they worked defensively, allowing Sullivan and his peers to hold certain identifications—and certain anxieties—at bay. In Wake's telling, this is not only a history of Sullivan but a study in the fragility of knowledge itself: how ideals harden into defenses, how professional authority may serve less to clarify than to shield. The difficulty at the heart of *Private Practices* is not simply epistemological but psychic: how to bear one's own subjectivity in the very act of inquiry. Sullivan's effort opened something—but never cleanly. The pull toward sexual exploration remained knotted to the work of exclusion. The space he built was never free of what it sought to refuse. There is no legacy here that can be neatly claimed. Wake leaves us not with resolution but with a scene still in motion—where recognition folds back into disavowal, and where the wish to know becomes caught in what cannot be said. And psychoanalysis? No differently situated. The histories it draws on, the fantasies it stages, remain within the room—unfinished, unsettled, implicated in the very struggles they would seek to name.

A perfect storm

Sullivan sought to open new ways of thinking subjectivity, but foreclosure marked his path. Wake's study makes this refusal visible: a closeted gay man sustaining homophobic structures, caught in a contradiction that shaped what he could offer and what he could not bear to know. He pursued an account of intersubjectivity—of how experience takes shape between minds, of how emotional life is narrated and lived. The structures within which he worked were saturated with hierarchy and exclusion. Sullivan's professional ambitions were closely tied to preserving certain ideals—his masculinity, his scientific authority, and his ability to maneuver within institutional power structures. At Sheppard-Pratt and again in the army selection process, his work bore the imprint of the very contradictions he could not resolve. Care and control, knowledge and exclusion, folded into one another—unsettling the space he tried to claim as neutral.

Wake's depiction suggests that Sullivan was not merely a progressive thinker constrained by his time but an active participant in reinforcing the very structures he sought to challenge. His equation of maturity with a coherent life narrative, for example, was not just a diagnostic tool but an exclusionary mechanism—one that labeled effeminate men, working-class homosexuals, and women as "immature" and unfit for the institutional spaces he controlled. Beyond the ideological contradictions, Wake also highlights the interpersonal and institutional dynamics that contributed to Sullivan's limitations. What began as collegial exchange, with Erich Fromm, Karen Horney, Margaret Mead, and Lawrence Frank, became strained by Sullivan's need to assert authority. What passed for collaboration gave way. Distance grew, not announced but felt—in the sidelong glance, in the meeting that did not happen. The silence held too much; words would not hold it. Drawing on Clifton Read's memoir, Wake traces a man increasingly preoccupied with defending a fragile authority—one hardened through masculinized postures and disavowals. Effeminacy became an object of scorn; proximity to the feminine, a threat. Sullivan shaped his relations defensively—professional, personal—building positions that mirrored what could not be faced. What he sought to banish returned, unbidden.

The clinical forms he devised—interpersonal technique, life history interview—could not escape this movement. Openings turned; what had made room for the speaking subject began to close, to classify, to bind. The harm was not incidental. It threaded beneath what appeared as care. Wake's study does not sort contribution from failure. It returns us to the question: what happens when the effort to reform cannot outpace the structures—and the fantasies—that resist it? And how to approach conviction here? The archive does not yield Sullivan's mind. Only the text—charged, partial, transferential. Not a stable figure but a scene: where political, psychic, institutional currents cross and snag. Sullivan's conservatism—gesture, symptom, defense? The categories blur. What disturbs is that conviction—conscious, progressive— offered no shield. The same was true of the field around him. Diagnosis, too, was unsettled—psychoanalysis, biology, behaviorism vying for ground that would not hold. The asylum was no neutral space; the analytic circle no haven. Stigma moved through them all, threading madness to homosexuality in ways no theory could untangle.

In Wake's book on Sullivan, we encounter the fragility of psychoanalytic education and the idealistic belief that the openness of the clinic can create conditions for social debate. Wake portrays a clinician at a crossroads— caught between the early conceptualization of a non-pathological homo- sexuality and the effort to transform his field, while facing tremendous resistance. The conditions of his profession—both psychiatry and psychoa- nalysis—worked against transformation. Sullivan's nuanced approach to same-sex affection was met with heavy criticism, and his attempts to imple- ment an interpersonal approach were hindered by the rigidity of institutional structures. He grew more withdrawn—not only from others but also from the ambitions that had once carried him. Wake offers no reassuring portrait: here is a man who had once imagined the clinic as a space of ethical possibility, yet found that very hope turning against itself. His failure to reconcile pri- vate beliefs with public discourse—even among liberal clinicians, including himself—meant that he never fully embraced or advocated for a progressive view of homosexuality.

The shift Sullivan had imagined failed to take hold. At Pratt, suspicion began to gather—not all at once, but in currents difficult to track, impossible to dispel. His departure from the hospital left no simple narrative. It was a residue of forces already in motion—forces he could sense but not name and could no longer resist. Wake's study tarries here, attuned to the undercurrents that shape institutional life: anxieties that attach to ideas, libidinal invest- ments that shadow alliances, and loyalties that fray under pressure. What can be thought—and what must be refused—is never a matter of individual will alone. At the heart of her account lies an older question, unresolved: how do minds change, and how do the structures around them change in turn? And the paradox sharpens. The more open a possibility becomes, the more resist- ance it evokes. But what is openness? Not the performance of inclusion, nor the shield of progressive stance. Wake shows us something more unsettling: that openness remains fragile, exposed, undone by the very dynamics it seeks to welcome.

What is at stake is not theoretical position but the analyst's own implication in shifting discourses, paradigms, and identifications. Change that remains external—declared but unexamined—repeats the very closures it claims to undo. When analysts turn away from this entanglement, something vital is foreclosed. Wake's account prompts us to consider what remains foreclosed in both clinical work and psychoanalytic education when the analyst's subjectivity is abandoned. And these evasions do not remain outside thought; they shape its very conditions. To approach Sullivan's position is to enter an entanglement. He did not stand outside the forces that shaped him—education, institutional discourse, the medical imaginary—but moved within them, marked by their claims and refusals. His predicament cannot be prised apart from this scene: his struggle to rethink gender, his refusal of public identification as a gay man, his complicity in the medical classification of homosexuality as pathology—all bound to the history that both constrained and enabled his thought.

Psychoanalysis, after all, is not immune. It lives in the charged space between internalization and the pressures of the external world. For Sullivan, the relation to gender, to culture, to authority was never only personal. It was transferential—shot through with the desires and defenses of his professional world and of his own. Identity, in Wake's account, remains fragile, knotted to the shifting play between psychic life and social field. Sullivan's legacy does not settle. What it stages—and what it troubles—is not otherness as object but as a relation: one that implicates the analyst, disturbs the frame, and undoes the possibility of clean knowing.

Failure of translation

Wake's project gestures toward a central paradox: to understand the analyst at work is to encounter a series of contradictions. The split between Sullivan's clinical practice and his public life was not simply a tactical separation—an effort to shield his work from a conservative world—but rather the very structure through which he lived. Sullivan's position, as Wake shows, was never stable. He moved within a space marked by contradiction—between the privacy of his desires and the institutional demand to disavow them. The negotiation was constant but not resolving: personal and institutional forces pressed against each other, leaving neither coherence nor escape. The freedom of the analytic encounter—of transference, play, and unconscious elaboration—does not pass unbroken into the world beyond the clinic. What is opened within the frame resists transcription into institutional life. As Britzman observes, self-knowledge does not, in itself, guarantee transformation of the world (2021, p. 24). The world outside the clinic remains opaque to the transformations that occur within it; there is no smooth passage from psychic to social change. Sullivan's failure to establish a non-homophobic psychoanalytic practice, his complicity in the very structures he sought to resist, and his fear of exposure cannot be disentangled from his desire to elevate his profession. His dream of a clinical liberalism extending into the public realm ultimately shattered against the conservatism of his time. His view of homosexuality as mere variation did not take hold, failing to gain transference beyond those already inhabiting the confluence of sexuality and freedom.

But another problem persists, one that Wake's work leaves us to consider: the problem of secrecy and interiority. The private space of the clinic is not only a space of elaboration but also a space of concealment, of unmetabolized remnants—fantasies, identifications, defenses—that resist articulation. The unthought known insists in the folds of discourse—caught in the self-theorizing movements of the analyst, of the culture, of the space between them. Here, we might recall Aulagnier's (2001) notion of secret thoughts: those traces of an internal dialogue that puncture the phantasy of the other's omnipotence, allowing for the discovery of one's own mind. What emerges, then, is not only the failure to effect change but also the impossibility that underlies it: that the analytic encounter and the public world do not meet on the same terms.

The privacy of the clinic, with its fluidity and openness to meaning, stands in stark contrast to the rigid normativity of the institute, the Kantian demand that ideas be declared, systematized, and made coherent. The tension does not resolve. It presses against thought—against. It presses against thought—against its limits, against what exceeds them. Meaning fragments.

What is given risks being undone, and learning, if it comes at all, must move through what cannot fully be represented. As soon as we consider teaching and learning within psychoanalysis, we are subject to a "failure," for learning from psychoanalysis and learning about psychoanalysis can be at odds. To engage with an idea is not the same as to change one's mind. The institute's demand for knowledge, for legibility, can be at variance with the more uncertain, more unsettling movements of psychic transformation. And it is in this gap—between knowing and unknowing, between thought and its resistance—that the problem of psychoanalytic education remains suspended.

3 Institutional life

Sullivan's failure to shift psychoanalytic discourse on homosexuality reveals the limits of clinical liberalism—a failure that lingers in the very architecture of psychoanalytic education. The questions his case raises—about subjectivity, institutional change, and the uneasy history of psychoanalysis in relation to homosexuality—remain largely buried in the analytic archive. Wake's study, then, can be read as a cautionary tale: of what happens when one attempts to unsettle the normativity of sexual conformity, and in doing so, becomes subject to the pain of difference. Psychoanalysis emerges here as both fragile and fraught—its capacity for openness haunted by the very institutional enclosures meant to sustain it.

The instability of identity, the porous relation between mental and social space, the emotional weight of theoretical inheritance—these shape not only the analyst's subjectivity but also the very conditions of learning itself. As Žižek (2001) notes, to truly grasp what people want, one must first listen to what they believe—what is defended, repeated, taken as given. The institution forgets slowly. The past is not distant: homosexuality as developmental failure, as the trace of an unresolved Oedipal scene. Today, the discomfort has shifted but not passed. It gathers now around gender—around the trans child, the question of agency, the uncertainty of becoming. The scene has changed; the tension remains.

To think within gender is to enter a field where certainty fails. Yet psychoanalytic theories still cling to gender as something to be named, located; as if consciousness could be pinned to form. But belief is never absent here (Kristeva, 2009); it saturates the scene, shapes what can be thought and what is refused. Within the institution, intersubjectivity is not neutral. It moves through us—in relations with supervisors, candidates, teachers—marking both the scope of our imagination and its constraints. Group psychology, professional loyalties, unworked residues—all combine to produce a volatile atmosphere. In such a field, defenses gather quickly: certitude, compliance, the comforts of repetition. And the cost? It is not abstract. Change wounds. The question is not whether education can avoid wounding but whether it can remain porous enough to be wounded—and to think from within that wound.

DOI: 10.4324/9781003440758-5

This returns us to the problem of transmission and reception: our theories of gender, like our education as a whole, are "parented" (Britzman, 2009, p. 132)—our subjectivity shaped by the necessity of interpreting the unknowability of the other's unconscious. Laplanche reminds us that theory must not only be applied; it must also be interrogated—turned back upon itself. At that point, resistance asserts itself. If to be changed by theory is to be affected, why does psychoanalytic education so often refuse this wound? Britzman names this the curriculum's defense: emptied of its own debates, shielded from its own contradictions. The cost is not only the loss of controversy but also the loss of vitality—the movement through which psychoanalysis might rethink what it teaches and what it cannot yet bear to teach.

Britzman (2009) extends Laplanche's insistence by addressing the seductive nature of education—how, left unexamined, it reproduces its own infantile theories. What follows is that any theory will be an attempt to bind the enigmatic message of the other. But this then means that our attempts to make, learn, or apply theory carry an erotic quality—what Lacan (1977), bringing us back to the question of education, describes as "a passion for ignorance" (p. 121, in Britzman, 2009, p. 133). The problem, then, is not only that the analytic curriculum is made safe from controversy but that, in doing so, it reinforces the very structures of knowledge that prevent thinking. Nowhere is this more striking than in the handling of sexual identity and the choice of the object, where the weight of history insists itself through the lingering authority of the Oedipal complex.

This moment reanimates a fundamental dilemma: why does psychoanalytic training so rarely include a direct engagement with Sophocles' *Oedipus Rex*? Had we begun with the myth rather than its doctrinal appropriation, we might have been better equipped to conceptualize sexuality not as an origin story but as a shifting and unstable mythology—one of love, of knowing, and of the unknowable. To think mythologically is to engage the imagination, to acknowledge the historicity of our concepts (Green, in Levine, 2023, p. 75), and to recognize where theory itself has become an object of fixation. Britzman (2021, p. xv) delineates five ways in which psychoanalysis approaches change—ways that set it apart from other fields, including pedagogy. First, psychoanalysis is uniquely attuned to the inner life: to transference and phantasy, to the question of what prevents change rather than what facilitates it. Second, its "estranged temporality," modeled after the dream, fosters a relation to creativity that resists linear understanding. Third, change depends on a willingness to embrace unpreparedness—the analyst's ability to listen to the not-yet-known, to observe how their subjectivity is affected by the other (countertransference), by the other's history, and by the otherness of history itself. Fourth, psychoanalysis remains attentive to what is missed or left behind, to the incidental and the accidental—dreams, parapraxes, jokes, fantasies, obstacles, even the mind's wandering. These, Britzman suggests, form the fictions of intersubjective life (Britzman, 2021).

Finally, there is the essential task of continuing to debate meaning. Change, Britzman argues,

> depends on interpreting the shifting sands of language and affect and, in doing so, on finding new value in meanings tucked away—meanings that allude to events so distant that they are never thought of as affecting the currency of our attitudes, concepts, and desires.
>
> (p. xv)

If change depends on the ability to tolerate uncertainty, then we must ask: what does the curriculum disavow in its insistence on safety? Why does it strive to "empty itself of debate" (Britzman, 2009, p. 132), to make itself safe from controversy? And more pointedly: how does the very structure of our theories betray a reluctance to change our minds?

Given that psychic life is "mainly an intersubjective impression" (p. xv), its conditions for change of mind will be resisted. This is a difficulty Britzman observes, for a theory aimed at containing the anxiety and frustration over the uncertainties and intermediacy framed by the dimensions of material reality, phantasy, and history: there will be a "resistance to resistance" (Britzman, 2009, p. 136). There is a resistance to resistance in moralistic aspects of particular analytic approaches to gender, approaches that are found in the design of institutional education of psychoanalysis. What would it be, for example, to consider the *Oedipus Rex* myth's flexibility and capacity for pliability; qualities which led Freud to insist that sexuality is there from the beginning of life?

Reading *Oedipus* as a metaphor, play, concept, dynamic, and a mode of inquiry shifts it from a developmental fact to a *libidinal* fact. In a way, the Oedipal structure is an "inside out" experience told from the vantage point of the child, not the parents. It is the parents (the king and queen) who have the Oedipal problem—the child—that interferes in their capacity to be a couple. That sexuality is also the experience of the infant also means that love and hate are there at the beginning of life, and the most dramatic story of love and hate is a story of a tragedy. But it is ultimately the writer and the poet, Sophocles, who is the hero of the play.

The hero, Freud suggests, is the one who can wrest themselves from the group psychology, and Freud praises the imagination of the writer (Sophocles): "He relates to the group his hero's deeds which he has invented. At bottom this hero is no one but himself" (*Group Psychology*, 1921 pp. 136–37). Freud's assertion gets at the heart of the value of narrating one's experience, which of course writers do. What would it take for psychoanalytic education to wrestle itself out of group psychology so it can begin to reclaim its narratives and handle theories as over-determined, as places of seduction, as paradoxes and as failures of translation? Approaching psychoanalysis paradigmatically also means that the very structures we are attempting to theorize create the structures we are theorizing. It is the construct of the Oedipal complex, for example (the discourse on the problem of authority and the problem of not knowing), that structures the Oedipal. The implication is that there is no one cause that causes every cause.

Group psychology

In the clashes within psychoanalytic institutes over gender, history often functions not as a settled archive but as a potential space—a site of conflict, desire, and possibility. History here does not offer a fixed archive of theory but rather a terrain still marked by what it has failed to hold. Where understanding was absent, something belated takes shape—but this is not a smooth becoming. It is uneven, caught in the return of the very traumas it seeks to address, never quite able to settle what it brings back into view. Institutes defensively cling to orthodox histories to ward off the destabilization that new conceptions of gender provoke, but in doing so, they reveal that loss—of certainty, coherence, authority—has an afterlife. It remains as anxiety, as resistance that finds new forms, as affects that do not fade. History here is not a foundation but a site of return—haunted by what it could not hold and by what returns in its name. Change may begin there but not without the weight of what has already been refused.

The analyst, Laplanche (1992) suggests, is an effect of a field that has the capacity of closing in on itself, partly through its professionalization and creating what Bion (1965) talks about as curiosity, arrogance, and stupidity: the desire to know "at all costs." At the same time, analysis "is not a profession" (Laplanche, 1992, p. 5); it cannot propose an aim, provide instructions, strive at adaptation, or have a preconceived knowledge of meaning. The cost of the incapacity to tolerate uncertainty is a dismissal of the other's reality or omnipotent knowledge: the belief that truth gives us control. Groups, Bion suggest, make us susceptible to conformity, groupthink, and can easily become what Kuhn describes as a "community of agree-ers," a term that encapsulates Kuhn's (1962, p. 59) critique of how scientific communities often operate more through consensus and allegiance to a paradigm than through open rational debate.

Looking back at my own experience of training in two separate psychoanalytic institutes, one contemporary and one traditional, I am intrigued by the effect of group psychology, how institutes are subject to the authority of the social and the authority of the institute, and by the idea that, at times, there is no difference between those two things. This was reflected in a curriculum that tended to repeat the previous generation's education; an education that is subject to sexism, homophobia, transphobia, racism. Contemporary resistance to new conceptualizations of gender include the dissociative way in which the subjects of transsexuality and transitioning are commonly presented as phenomena that concern only a few. One enters a phantasy of the analysts and students as unaffected bystanders who are unfamiliar with the struggles of embodiment, recognition, and the tension between sexuality and identity. Another example relates to the ways in which gender is deemed "knowable": a memorable scene is one where a transman psychoanalyst was persistently addressed as female in all written communications. The same transman was deemed by a member of the institute to be an inappropriate choice as a speaker for a panel on gender because in the eyes of one of the panelists, he was "a closeted trans." These situations describe an ambivalence with gender: the institute both wants and does not want the trans. It is thought of as a good transsexual who "comes out" and a bad one that does not. But even coming out is not sufficient, because there is a refusal to recognize that the other can change.

Another place of ideality is paradoxically operative in recent pedagogical commitment to tolerance, which often takes the forms of repetition: the trans person is depicted as a victim of the normative other, limiting the complexity of identification to a scene of "us and them." The central question in this pedagogical maneuver becomes the ways in which the body is addressed by normalcy. This question can also be framed along the lines of Butler (1990) and Britzman's address to pedagogy: can psychoanalysis admit the unthinkability of normalcy and how it is constituted again and again? (Britzman, 1998, p. 85). The other side of this dilemma involves an education subject to hypothetical universals (Gozlan, 2014, 2018, 2022b, 2022c)—"the child," "the adolescent," "the trans," without a body.

Even when bodies appear, however, they show up as exceptions or are used as "poster." Young-Bruehl makes this case when she points to how, for example:

> Over the decades of psychoanalysis' history, psychoanalytic investigation of female homosexuality has been relatively neglected. But, at the same time that female homosexuality was being judged relatively unimportant, a creature known as "the female homosexual" was quite remarkably pathologized; the specter of a very disturbed, father-identified, mother-fixated, narcissistic Child Amazon came to haunt the feverish case studies of analysts who were hard put even to imagine what their subjects did in bed.
>
> (2000, p. 97)

By asking "what is THE homosexual woman?" Young-Bruehl opens a broader dilemma about the ways gender and sexuality are at times collapsed with the question of origin. If psychoanalysis offers a science of the particular, Young-Bruehl asks, how can such a science yield a theoretical universal?

Young-Bruehl enters the historicity of ideas, not only their history and what the concepts are, but the form that gives rise to the story—that is, the conceptual apparatus that provides that backward look in the first instance. By giving us a panoramic view of the turns in gender theory in Freud and beyond, Young-Bruehl's article on the homosexual woman focuses on the uses of theory and moves theory closer to the theorist's phantasy of what it is they are defending. Theory, she suggests, is a subjective object.

The educational situations I described animate a desire for a stable object that is known, one that can be either discarded or helped, attacked, or rescued. There is an intensity that belongs to the topic of education because it is a site to which we bring our own desires, our hatred of dependency and development, and our tacit fantasies of what it takes to change minds. The issue for education, as Forrester and Cameron's study suggests, is that while an attempt to engage in new theories and change saturated ideas in ways we could not have done before is compelling, we are also faced with the problem of having to be affected by the idea, without knowing "where they land" (Britzman, p. 102). The problem of change, Bion argues, is affected by the agony of not knowing and the fear of uncertainty. What the adult learner fears is coming into contact with the history of their own experiences of dependency and helplessness. The effect of this uncanniness is that theoretical change is experienced as a loss—and thus, as cataclysmic.

What is it to enter the imaginary of gender with the pre-conceptions we have considered? Do these preconceptions constitute what we understand about gender? And then, once the bodies can counter those ideas, what happens then? The other aspect of learning is that education is always group psychology. There is a central problem of the ego in group psychology, because our susceptibility to others makes us subject to influence, dependency, fantasies, defenses, and speech. These are the major elements that are mental health. In theorizing how people learn, we must also think about how people learn in a group. The pressures of influence are atmospheric.

The normative current

Recent conceptualization of femininity, masculinity, sexual difference, and the Oedipal situation have been put into question by the advent of transsexuality and nonbinary subjectivities. The visibility of transgender and nonbinary subjectivities in media, education, advertising, and military affairs had followed suit in psychoanalytic institutes, who are now seeing a growing numbers of trans or nonbinary-identified candidates at the same time that analysts are now encountering trans and nonbinary patients in their clinics. The new landscape of gender has also brought slow theoretical reconceptualization of gender beyond identarian and anatomical differences (Harris, 2005; Gozlan, 2008; Gherovici, 2010; Glocer Fiorini, 2017; Saketopoulou & Pelegrini, 2023). We can see a growing body of psychoanalytic literature attempting to work against normative discourse by exposing its brittle structure through the question of what it is that must be taken for granted to walk through the world without being bothered, and what are the tacit encouragement, within and without psychoanalysis, that help maintain this structure.

Despite these piecemeal changes, the structures that sustain the relation of power within the institute have not changed: the lack of separation between teaching and treatment (as candidates are also taught by their analysts); the hierarchical structure of training analysis; the requirement for analysis with a didactic focus—and hence nonanalytic aim—as well as the narrow focus of training that is largely not interdisciplinary in nature—all contribute to the maintenance of a closed solipsistic structure. This is a conflict, Safouan (2000) suggests, and it is always threatening to blow up. In her introduction to Moustafa Safouan's text on *Lacan and the Question of the Psychoanalytic Clinic*, Jaqueline Rose (2000) posits this conundrum as a piece of resistance and an act of regression when she asks: in what ways might an institution constitute a piece of acting out against its own main discovery? The blurred lines between didactic education and the analytic scene presents a pedagogical dilemma, because, as Kernberg observes:

> the same people train, teach, and supervise, a cautious attitude tends to prevail, focusing on who is the training analyst of any particular candidate, as if any criticism of the candidate might reflect on the training analyst, or any negative evaluation of the candidate be considered an attack on his training analyst.
>
> (p. 802)

Rose points to an affective investment in a disavowal of a conflict—one that is then repeated. This has to do with the pedagogical problem of ideality, where institutions become caught in the libidinal structure of pedagogy as a relation marked by "fealty, its perversions and its discontents" (1993, p. 202). On the one hand, there is a narcissistic investment on the part of the analyst in their analysand's success. On the other, the position of the analyst confounded with the authority professionally accruing to the figure of the teacher creates an inevitable pull, both conscious and unconscious, on the part of the candidate to identify and incorporate their training analyst's views and style of practice. Psychoanalytic education today, Kernberg argues, "is all too often conducted in an atmosphere of indoctrination rather than of open scientific exploration. Candidates as well as graduates and even faculty are prone to study and quote their teachers, often ignoring alternative psychoanalytic approaches" (p. 801).

While psychoanalysis continues to flourish in dissipated forms, there remains a question of why has its education not transformed since its arrival in North America? Emma Leiber (2023), drawing from Freud's image of the *navel of the dream*—that point at which a dream "is joined onto the unknown"—proposes that the navel marks the limit of institutional legibility, a reminder of the unassimilable tie to the maternal and the pre-symbolic. She repurposes the navel as a figure of institutional ambivalence: both a remnant of dependence and a wound of separation. Just as the dream's navel resists full interpretation, the psychoanalytic institute cannot fully account for its own origins or affiliations without reactivating what it has disavowed—its dependence on maternal traces, its nonlinear affiliations, its unconscious investments.

The institute, in this light, is less a space of coherent transmission than a body structured around a cut it cannot name. The fantasy of pedagogical lineage strains under this tension; what is passed on is never only knowledge but also the traces of what must be kept out. The training analyst does not stand simply as a symbolic father but rather as a figure caught in impossible affiliations—haunted, still, by the maternal remainders the institute cannot fully repudiate, even as it tries. To invoke the navel is to return to this question—not only of who belongs but of what forms of belonging remain unthought, unacknowledged. Gender here unsettles the terms of institutional inheritance: not identity, not adaptation, but a psychic persistence that refuses the ease of transmission.

For the analyst, this fact perhaps is not surprising. Why wouldn't a theory of conflict be anything other than conflicted and conflicting? Safouan points to this paradox when asking: "What happens when a radical theory, whose radicalness resides at least partly in its unique critique of power as identification, becomes mired in charismatic authority?" (p. 8). The reasons for the shifts in psychoanalysis are multiple, as we have seen in Wakes' analysis of Sullivan's situation. Partly, the discourse has shifted by a push for measurement, a desire for categorization and medicalization as a way of handling situations such as PTSD and war deserters. These converging factors culminate in something called testing, which in turn culminates into something called intelligence or self-esteem. What is also brought to light through the history of concepts is the formation of the 'psy' (psychiatry, psychology, psychoanalysis) professions as a creation of an apparatus that, in turn, creates the qualities it accounts for. The 'psy' apparatus utilized concepts from science (measurements) to justify methods as scientific. *Once psychoanalysis is instituted, it becomes subject to the law.*

In her introduction to Safouan's critique of psychoanalytic training, Rose begins by asking whether psychoanalytic institutes "may not tolerate their own psychoanalysis" (Rose, p. 42, in Britzman, 2006, p. 164). The paradox lies in the tension between the psychoanalytic idea that the "unconscious . . . repeatedly empties all utterances of their authority" (Rose, p. 42) and the institute's pedagogical failure to engage in questioning its own modes of ideality. Britzman insists:

> If the unconscious is its own reason and cannot know its own grounds, just as representation cannot know its own activity of metabolization, then an education that centers this paradox must also be prepared to engage displacement and connotation in terms of its psychical consequences, its defenses, and its resistance to insight.

Sullivan sought to transform both a field of thought and a field of practice, yet the very conditions of that field were already working against the possibility of transformation. Rose takes up this question of fragility, arguing that institutions, learning, and psychoanalysis cannot be thought apart from transference and repetition. Rose's introduction to Safouan's analysis of psychoanalytic institutes, alongside Wake's study of Sullivan, draw us into the fissures of institutional life—not merely the practice of psychoanalysis itself but the analysis of its own institutional practices. This, for Rose, is where the problem deepens: why is it that institutes cannot, as it were, bear their own self-analysis? The reasons are manifold. Rose suggests that part of the difficulty lies in the hierarchical structures of governance, which foreclose the very conditions for self-renewal and transformation. Safouan, working within a Lacanian framework, articulates this dilemma at its core:

> The analytic act is something else. In principio, in the beginning was the act. It is born, not of a form of power to be actualized, but of nothing, ex nihilo. It is an act which found itself on nothing whatsoever; it is its own foundation. It rests on, comes with, and brings no guarantee.
>
> (cited in Rose, 2000, p. 44)

Safouan imagines the analytic act as a kind of genesis—a threshold, a becoming—something that appears to be springing from nothing and that no theory is adequate to explain how it comes about, except to describe its mechanics. The analytic act carries this enigma since identifications, defenses, and projections cannot be justified or stopped. Our transference is both a psychic function and a method of knowing, and because it remains unconscious, it inevitably resists full translation and transparent communication. This vulnerable beginning carries an affective charge—not the certainty of knowing but the fragile movement between understanding and being understood, where something of relation is always at risk. As Rancière suggests in *The Ignorant Schoolmaster* (1991), this link is grounded in the presupposition of intellectual equality—the idea that one learns not by being filled with knowledge but by assembling one's own thoughts in response to another (Rancière, p. 23, cited in Britzman, p. 69).

The notion of an act as springing from "no-thing" paradoxically provides us with a banister with which to approach psychical questions, because, from the place of unknowability, we observe their unfolding—their movement, dispersals, activities, and characters—without falling into explanations to cover it over. There is an ethical proposal in this articulation of analysis as vulnerable beginning because the only way into uncertainty is to claim nothing. Here we hear Bion's echo urging us to approach analysis without memory or desire. The paradox we face in both education and psychoanalysis lies in the difficulty of imagining learning outside what has happened to us—and this brings us to the problem of recognition, tied to the complexities of libidinal investment. How do we recognize the other's experience that is outside of what we know? Britzman describes this paradox aptly when she suggests that "we would have to notice meaninglessness: times when thoughts fall apart, when experience loses its foothold in the world of others, and when social denial obliterates a second chance" (2022, p. 69).

The difficulty of learning is that we cannot approach education except through the traces of our earliest theories—infantile, affect-laden, unfinished. Both analysis and education remain scenes of emotional life, and in that sense they remain equally enigmatic. To speak of unknowability here is not to introduce a paradox but to acknowledge that the very idea of education may not be something we can hold apart from this not-knowing. This uncertainty, however, may open a space that allows us to ask: if we do not know what education is, might this freedom allow psychoanalysis to engage with "nothing"?

The capacity to enter another's experience and endure its estrangement begins with the vulnerability of not knowing. Yet, both the schoolmaster and the analyst are inevitably shaped by their own childhoods—their grades, their teachers, their parents, the rigid knowledge structures, hierarchical power, moralism, and the equation of learning with punishment and obedience. The autocracy of education is almost airtight, while "what has happened" remains a history that is involuntary, beginning from "nothing," in the sense that it is unconscious. The analytic act is rooted in the capacity to meet unconscious experience. It begins in the anxiety and vulnerability tied to dependency, asymmetry, and helplessness—conditions carried through transference. Hence, communication will always be partial, for what transfers in both education and analysis are messages that remain enigmatic for the very messenger. These messages are both new and old, familiar and strange, and this uncanniness, this failure in translation, is also a challenge to the presumption of equality in the dynamics of learning and analysis—not in the sense of sameness between teacher and student, or analyst and patient, but in terms of their irreducible differences.

Both education and psychoanalysis are intersubjective scenes steeped in dependency on psychic life. This generates the conditions of vulnerability that the fantasy of authoritative knowledge—manifested in the "subject supposed to know"—tends to foreclose. For Rancière, the ability to be curious without resorting to stultifying explications is what allows an intellect to reveal itself (Rancière, in Britzman, p. 69). The dilemma for psychoanalysis and its institutes lies in the fragility of learning: analysis depends on the enigmatic nature of communication, yet education is still difficult to imagine outside the frame of our own experience. This fragility, as Safouan suggests, lies at the center of why institutes are not able to analyze their own acts, and it is in part, he suggests, the institutes' hubris, their autocracy (its hierarchical structure that perpetuates power through identification), and idealization that already foreclosed the capacity to ask questions. And while we learn through Lacan that psychoanalytic teaching "does not just reflect upon itself but turns back upon itself so as to subvert itself, and truly teaches only insofar as it subverts itself" (Felman, p. 90, in Rose, p. 7), the pragmatism of psychoanalytic training and the IPA has failed—"through their very success with which it continues to reproduce itself" (Rose, p. 9)—to relate to its own history without explication. That is, to teach and learn beyond what it knows.

Freedom

As we consider what prevents institutions from transforming by inventing "new modes of instituting" (Safouan, 2004, p. 9), we are also grappling with the tension between desire and identification. This is not only because sexuality has the power to subvert any origin story of identity and its "delusional stability" (Rose, p. 10) but also because such origin stories are "not so easy to shift" (Rose, p. 9). The challenge of historicizing psychoanalytic discourse—that is, understanding how our concepts are shaped by history—allows our discourse to creep into superego structures or even to constitute them. The traditional formulation of Oedipus is where analysis absolves itself of the world's inequities and where the field silences its own ideological history.

Yet, there can be no direct transmission of psychoanalytic theory or technique, because the profession itself forecloses the very capacity to tolerate the necessary helplessness that education demands—namely, the problem of metabolizing what we do not know. This inevitable gap, as Britzman suggests, "renders education interminable" (p. 165), because knowledge always carries with it a "wish for what can be learned" (Britzman, 2006, p. 165). In this sense, pedagogical fact, much like the "analytic fact" (Caper, 1999), is an attempt at "communicating what cannot be shown" (Reeder, 2004, p. 131, in Britzman, 2006, p. 165). This intermediary space between what is transmitted and what is received becomes a site of both frustration and freedom. For while the capacity for interpretation is constrained by institutional "violence," a term Aulagnier uses to describe the powerful effect of maternal discourse, it is also an opportunity for the interpretation of violence itself. Institutional conditions—dependency on the other's evaluation, the need to please, and the pressure to conform—may stifle the imagination. Yet, there will always be an opening through the struggle for conflicting narratives. In the very effort to understand, we create new meaning.

The question of reception of ideas and the capacity for new translations returns me to the Oedipal story, which has been a central paradigm for the psychoanalytic understanding of gender formation. Its traditional theorization is by and large a cisgender structure that represents the thinking in Freud's time. We cannot do away with the paradigmatic notion of the Oedipal, not because it can in any way account for the variability of gender, but because—when read less as a fixed structure and more as the psychic scene in which authority comes into being—it reveals a capacious and enduring significance, the capacity for the subject to come into its own. Ironically, the gay and trans movements, in part, help us open this concept to other configurations. From today's perspective, it is very much a story of transitioning, a narrative for the installation of sexuality—not as a family romance but as a story of transformation: Oedipus spends a lot of time thinking that he has a family. He remains insistent in searching for his parents, no matter what other people have said about his family. By Bion's account, he is a stupid and arrogant adolescent who seeks the truth at "all costs." When he finally realizes that he has been carried away by his fate and that by attempting to avoid it he met it head on, he realizes that he has been blind. And so, he blinds himself.

Read as a story of education, *Oedipus Rex* is an allegory for the paradox of coming to know: the human condition of being oriented by something we do not know but think we do. It is also a metaphor for disillusionment and reillusion: when we realize that our parents are not who we think they are, that means we too are no longer who we think we are. The capacity to let go of the parental imago of childhood, which return in the form of institutes, supervisors, and analysts, means facing the dilemma that we never coincide with who we think we are. From today's vantage point, we could use it as a moral quandary, as a problem of self-knowledge, as a problem of origin and a problem of learning: Oedipus's wish to be king comes from what is already a reaction formation to something that happens much earlier—he was not going to be king but was rather destined to be killed. The refusal of difference, the incapacity to open one's narrative to its difference, is where education becomes another term for a refusal of the unknown.

The Oedipal story is, at its heart, a lesson in belatedness—discovering too late the terms of one's inheritance. Institutionalized psychoanalysis risks repeating this structure in its pedagogy. In transmitting theory, the institute often idealizes what cannot be absorbed, presenting knowledge as if it were fixed and detached from the histories and affects that shaped it. Yet transmission is never seamless. Hesitation, refusal, or the moment when thought breaks down all reveal the aesthetic and affective dimensions of learning. These moments unsettle theory and return it to what it always is: a scene of encounter with the potential to change us.

Part II

Dimensions of change and resistance

Now that I've outlined the structural dilemmas of psychoanalytic institutes, a second question arises: what is it like to live there? When I think about changing minds in relation to gender, three analysts come to mind: McDougall, Stoller, and Quinodoz. Each is an exemplar of how clinical experience unsettles theory—shaped by cases, readings, encounters, and desires we cannot fully trace. As Forrester (2017) notes, "the process of their writing obeys the same laws of transference and countertransference as the analytic situation itself" (p. 65). Reading them, I am drawn into the tension between sameness and difference, because interpretation is never outside the transference. These cases are exemplars not only of theoretical revision but also of theatres of desire, where gender and sexuality stage the problem of changing minds.

DOI: 10.4324/9781003440758-6

4   Scene of transference

Following Bion, we might say resistance is a response to the catastrophe that change demands. Learning can feel catastrophic: we change, and yet something resists. There is hatred, too, in development—the strange violence of having to move from one psychic position to another, the loss that becoming demands. It is not the change of mind that holds me but the conditions that make change possible—the disruptions that unsettle theory, the moments when thinking loses its footing. What comes into view is not mastery but exposure: every theory marked by the very sexuality it struggles to contain.

There is a moment in clinical writing where you can see a crossroad where the analyst can go one way and stay loyal to a viewpoint or become open-minded. One example of such a *carrefour* can be found in Joyce McDougall's paper "Gender Identity and Creativity" (2001), which serves as a reconsideration of the broad generalizations she previously made in "Homosexuality in Women." Aware of the limitations of her earlier perspective, McDougall openly reflects on the critiques it provoked, acknowledging how they led her to rethink certain clinical and theoretical impasses in her understanding of sexual orientation. In this later work, she moves away from a universalizing theory of female homosexuality—one she had previously aligned with perversion—toward a more nuanced and self-critical position. "Gender Identity and Creativity" is an admission of her blind spots. In this reparative paper, she presents her work with Mia, a woman in her forties who is experiencing intolerable pain over the breakup of a 15-year relationship with her female partner, Cristina, a French actress. Mia's work and creativity, she writes, has suffered since the breakup, and she tells her analyst that her life "is no longer worth living" after Cristina had reportedly turned to another woman and wanted Mia to join in establishing a *ménage à trois*. McDougall provides a retrospective account of how her encounter with Mia, whom she had seen eight years prior to writing her "Gender Identity and Creativity" paper, has shifted her views on the universality of her claims.

In the preface to her paper, McDougall offers an apology for her inexperience but also reflects on how she was affected by cultural shifts and

DOI: 10.4324/9781003440758-7

atmospheric pressures that contributed to a crisis in education. She finds herself having to reconsider everything she thought she knew:

> Whether we are considering homosexual or heterosexual object orientation, there is no evidence that a psychic representation of core gender identity is inborn. Core gender and sexual role identity are shaped in large part by the experiences of early childhood and the parental discourse on sexuality and sexual role. Many years ago, the author wrote a paper entitled "Homosexuality in Women," which was based on a small number of analysands, and the author mistakenly drew conclusions that she believed could apply to female homosexuality in general. With time, and through the shifting scene of her own self-analysis and her work with lesbian analysands, the generalizations she had once offered no longer held. What emerged instead was a sense of how situated those earlier claims had been—tied to the specific experiences of the analysands she had quoted, and no longer able to stand in for more.

She later adds:

> The criticisms stirred up by that outdated paper have given the author much food for thought and have helped her reflect on certain clinical and theoretical impasses in her early attempts to understand the complexities of sexual orientation. In this paper, the author presents a female patient in order to explore to what extent family circumstances and the unconscious wishes of the patient's parents may have contributed to her adult sexual orientation, as well as the role these played in her creative activities.
>
> (2001, p. 5)

There are many things that McDougall is known for. *Theatres of the Body* is a significant contribution to the psychoanalytic conceptualization of the relationship between psyche and the soma. In *The Many Faces of Eros* (1995), she sets out to explore the inherently traumatic nature of sexuality and its many facets, and in *Plea for a Measure of Abnormality* (1993), she aims to "challenge the idealization of theory" (McDougall, p. ix). In a way, the titles of her books are far more provocative than some of her actual writings. There, we often encounter conservative conceptualizations of homosexuality that are, in fact, infantile theories of sexuality: homosexuality as defense against symbiosis, as attack against the parents, as denial of sexual difference, as confusion over identity, and as having a particular character structure. The gap between the openness of her titles and her conservative view already suggests a conflict involved in the framing and the context. I would like to look at this conflict as ushering in a change of mind.

In her account of her work with Mia, McDougall writes about being moved by her patient's pain upon separating from her partner, a separation

that followed the patient's depression, creative inhibition, and suicidal ideation. The analyst describes her "shock" upon learning that Mia's mother was
dying of AIDS, which she had contracted through blood transfusion, and feeling that the two losses, Mia's mother and the loss of Cristina, were related in
a particular way. Cristina, McDougall suggests, is a maternal figure for Mia.
We learn that before Mia's birth, her mother gave birth to a stillborn child,
and that from the ages of 9 to 16, Mia's father was frequently absent due to a
post some distance from their home. McDougall comments about Mia's keen
sense of her father's absence, her need to support her needy mother, and her
uncontrollable sobbing upon her father's death, which occurred immediately
upon returning from a trip, in her late twenties.

McDougall describes how the early phase of her work with Mia was
around unacknowledged dependency feelings and separation anxiety, which
became noticeable through the transference. Mia would have anxiety dreams,
would become de-invested in her creative work, and would manifest somatic
ailments upon the analyst's impending departure. McDougall feels that her
patient's transference reaction to her absence led Mia to slowly become
aware of this connection to her physical symptoms and "question seriously,
for the first time, the emotional events that may have surrounded her birth and
her place in the family." McDougall talks of her patient's dreams and fantasies
of a "dead child" and of her patient's initial "total denial" of the importance of
the dream, which the analyst sees through the patient's insistence of knowing
she was her mother's favorite. Mia tells McDougall that she could have never
told her father about her homosexuality. That, she tells her analyst, "Would
have been too much for him to take."

McDougall hears her patient's worry as an acceptance of a link between
her lesbian identity and her father's death. She goes on to describe one of her
patient's dreams about a dead child. In the dream, a child is killed, and the
patient is charged with murder. McDougall feels an urge to ask her patient if
the dead child was a little boy or a little girl but restrains herself from asking,
and later learns that her patient had found out from her older sister that her
parents were certain that the stillborn baby that came before her birth was a
boy and that her father, upon learning of Mia's gender, was devastated and
saddened.

The analyst feels that she and her patient came to understand Mia's fundamental phantasy:

> We also came to understand that, under the pressure of the unconscious
> belief that she should have been a boy and that she was sup posed to
> play her father's role to her abandoned mother, she had fought all her
> life for her right to be a girl.

McDougall also believes that her patient's repression of "all knowledge
of her childhood pain and confusion about being born a girl to parents who
desired and expected a boy" (p. 13). She also repressed her envy of her sister,

and comes to understand Mia's love for a girl at the age of six as "an attempt to give to another what she desperately desired for herself, as well as trying to resolve her pain around the birth of Sue."

The details in McDougall's paper provides the reader a frame with which to understand a number of the analyst's hypotheses about the origin of Mia's gender: guilt over not fulfilling the parental wish for a son and a wish to replace her father and take care of her mother. McDougall believes that her patient had to fight all her life "for her right to be a girl." The reader also finds, however, a sense of deep intimacy in McDougall's depiction of her relationship with Mia. Mia trusts McDougall, asking her analyst what she would do if she lost, as the patient did, her "identity card and passport," a plea which McDougall hears as a child's call for help, perhaps to recover lost parts of herself.

The author, we might propose, feels that her treatment of Mia was successful. We learn, for example, that Mia gets through her writing inhibition and finds a new lover. But the analyst also speaks of a strong countertransference when her patient, upon completing an autobiographical novel, decides to destroy it. This, for the analyst, is an aggressive attack on their therapeutic relationship and sends the analyst into a kind of rage: "Mia's novel was akin to a literary baby that we had created together and here she was preparing to abort it!" (p. 16). The patient understands her decision to be driven by a fear of co-workers, mostly men, finding out that she is gay. McDougall writes about helping her patient "examine these projections from all angles" (p. 16), which softens the patient's anxiety, and she decides to publish it.

McDougall then recounts a patient's dream in which she dreamed about the analyst for the first time in a long while: the analyst is entertaining people in her home, "a magnificent manor with exquisite gardens and trees everywhere." Someone who is *supposed to be* the analyst's husband is looking after things. The patient breaks a beautiful plate. She is looking for the analyst to give her the broken pieces that she is holding. The patient cannot recall the end of the dream but tells McDougall that she knows it ended with hope, "as though, in spite of my having broken the plate, this would be a peaceful matter between us" (p. 17). The patient then has a recollection of breaking four or five plates while helping her mother set the table at the age of six. When her father comes to help, pressing her mother to see that she was only trying to help, her mother remains adamant.

McDougall interprets the recollected scene as her patient's phantasy of responsibility over the death of the stillborn baby and her manic triumphalism. But she also considers the dream as a wish to mend the parental couple: "Could the happy couple also represent your own parents? And perhaps your feeling that the broken plate was not catastrophic may express a wish for your parents to be a loving sexual couple" (McDougall, 2001, p. 19), and a sign of integration, a mending of the self. The significance of breaking the plates, she seems to suggest, is the attempt to separate from the mother and from the idealized relation to the analyst. As if the patient is saying "someone who was supposed to be your husband" and she might as well add "and it should have been me!" The patient, McDougall suggests, is also able to use the analyst to integrate feminine and masculine elements and "was now flooded with ideas for further creative works" (p. 26). I read this idea of integration of femininity and masculinity as both metaphorical and literal. The analyst feels that her patient has more characters to play with, greater capacity for separation, and a creativity that involves both reception and aggression. Something opens for both analyst and patient through their relationship.

McDougall notes her patient's experience of what she terms a "memory spasm" in the final phases of her treatment, just as she is about to present her biographical novel and becomes unable to talk. Mia associates to her father and to the feeling that the disclosure of her lesbianism "might have killed him" (p. 25) and then, for the first time in her analysis with McDougall, is able to speak of an affair her mother had after her father's death. The patient's capacity to speak of the affair is taken by McDougall to represent another dimension in the patient's capacity for integration: "new heterosexual and homosexual Oedipal elements began to appear on the analytic stage."

In her final note on the case, McDougall quotes the opening lines of Mia's autobiographical novel, emphasizing to the reader that it was Mia who allowed her to use her notes and tells the analyst, as a "by the way": "I wish you could be my translator if ever my book is accepted for an Anglo-Saxon edition!" McDougall goes on to quote three passages from Mia's novel. The novel describes a reimagining of the biblical story of Adam and Eve. Banished from paradise lost and seeking to re-find this place of "absolute," "but it was never more than an oasis, a tamed volcano, violet-hued water haunted by sharks. Ersatz." The second is the patient's reflection of how she had followed in their footsteps she re-finds "childhood anguish." The last quote that ends McDougall's paper is poetic: "And the little girl who sleeps in my memory has taken the same pathway. No one had explained anything to her. Of course. Does one ever explain such things? Can one ever truly know what one is seeking."

Is the patient, by granting her analyst permission to use the material of her case and her novel, showing triumphalism per excellence? Does the analyst's inclusion of the excerpts show a demonstration of admiration for her patient's capacity to write novels? Is the last quote an address from the patient to her analyst? No one had explained anything to her. Is she saying, "all my analyst's efforts to understand me are for nought?" McDougall does not really talk about why she includes those passages. She does not comment on these passages or share her thoughts with the reader. The quotes leave meaning as mystery, and the reader is now sitting with an enigma.

The capacity to sit with not knowing is a negative capability (Bion, 1965) that both leads to and depends on an open mind, and in this sense McDougall's paper on creativity is also a study of the reception of history and the emotional susceptibility to the ideas received, which limited her capacity to imagine her patients differently. She writes about how, over time, she comes to realize that the impasse she experienced in the past with her homosexual patients belonged to her own resistance to change her mind. Part of her resistance, she feels, was due to a history of her education, the way in which in her psychoanalytic training she was being subjected to "bad theory." She credits a number of factors as playing a part in bringing about a change of mind, including her experience with patients over the years, her own analysis, and the growing criticism of the ways psychoanalysis has been deployed in the service of a reactionary and normative stance:

> As the years went by, my increasing experience, both with my ongoing self analysis and what I learned from my lesbian analysands, led me to conclude that the generalisations I had proposed in my lecture were inappropriate and applied only to the analysands quoted in that paper.

She begins her paper by reflecting retrospectively on the way she was subject to bad teaching and was "inundated with bad theory" (McDougall, 2001, p. 7). She goes on to write:

> At least I can comfort myself that, at the time I wrote the paper, in spite of being inexperienced and inundated with bad theory (our analytic teachers of that period regularly referred to homosexuality as a "perversion" and a symptom that should be "cured"), my countertransference was apparently not too noxious for the three analysands quoted therein. Two of them still keep in touch with me; both assumed homosexuality as their orientation, one has herself become a therapist and the second is a gifted artist. The third patient married a man who shared her ambiguous feelings about sexual desire, but both very much wanted children—and I get news of these grown-up children from time to time.
> (McDougall, 2001, p. 7)

McDougall believes that her analytic work with her gay patients was not affected by her history of bad education and her views on homosexuality. Her viewpoint returns me to the interesting question of the gap between theory and what actually happens in the clinic and invites analysts to consider the tensions between their own traditional education and their practice: how does the analyst navigate the changing culture, the clinical encounters with what Kristeva (1997) terms "new maladies of the soul": new dilemmas, new medical and technological possibilities, changing cultural imperatives, and changing attitudes among analysts? An added question can be asked: What deadens creativity in psychoanalytic training?

Reading McDougall's case, I imagine the analyst's efforts in her realization that theory is insufficient to understanding. The constraints of her education that created rigidity to the ways she saw her patients also ushered in a change. It is not her lack of experience, she tells us, that led to an impasse in her thinking about homosexuality but the failure of theory. There is a tension that is depicted in theorizing her case—simultaneous holding to theory and a letting go—that is involved in her own evolving understanding of female homosexuality. The tension also exists between the singularity of the case and its usage to develop broader theoretical insight. She no longer thinks that she should generalize from a case, because that, she suggests, created the rigidity that prevented her from listening differently.

McDougall's case leaves us to consider the question of how, when we are in a situation, we often cannot see our emotional susceptibility to a historical position that is also received. Her paper therefore speaks to the difficulty of trying to think about something that has not been thought about before or has been defended against. As long as she was in this situation of reception, McDougall was unable to know the nature of what she receives or the fact that something has been received. At the same time, theory is not simply poured into the receiver. There is a psychical attachment—a libidinal attachment—to dominant ideology. The affect is "the welcome mat" for the idea. McDougall, in this sense, was a soldier for ideology. She "needed to believe" (Kristeva, 2009). The reader gets a sense of the dilemma involved in grasping a situation and the difficulty involved in psychic change. Britzman articulates this dilemma as the affective conundrum of education: the method of understanding cannot be separated from one's own libidinal history of learning (2022, p. 760).

On the one hand, one can read her paper as a search for a cause. We still hear echoes of infantile theories of sexuality that leans upon a very traditional Oedipal story: the equation of sexual difference with the capacity to mend the parental couple, the framing of unintegrated masculine and feminine elements as the patient's "attempts to keep 'her father and mother separate' in her internal world," as well as situating this hypothetical separation as cause for her patient's creative inhibition. On the other hand, McDougall's retrospective attempt to understand is also a threshold to change because she now is affected by her work. And while she may be convinced, theoretically, about the traditional understanding of gender and sexuality, in practice she attempts to relax her insistences and the omnipotent hold of theory. She remains curious about her patient and no longer tries to cure her. The tension between failure of theory and unpreparedness, in other words, moves McDougall beyond repetition compulsion.

The analyst's change of mind, we come to see, did not occur on its own. It hinged on "interference" (Freud, 1974): her capacity to be affected by her work and the force of her patient's experience, her self-analysis allowed her previous understanding to be disrupted. But her change of mind also occurs within a historical zeitgeist—a history called gay liberation—and in this way, her article is already a threshold to something new. She moves away from an attempt to cure her patient's homosexuality, which she initially saw as denial of difference, to the understanding of her theories as no longer able to account for her patient's creativity and capacity for separateness.

The case raises a paradox for the reader: theory can only tag along to the situation; it doesn't lead, and therefore it is always out of step with experience. Freud is masterful in this regard where he speculates about what he observes without being certain about the permanency of his observations. Revision, Freud suggests, leans upon the capacity to treat theories as speculations on things we do not know that, once we enter the clinic, may take a different turn. Revisions, however, are difficult to make, as we have seen, within institutional life.

Resistance to change

I was surprised to have found McDougall's reparative article in the *Journal of Gay & Lesbian Psychotherapy*, a non-psychoanalytic journal. Why hasn't a reparative article written by a psychoanalyst found its way into a psychoanalytic publication, one that would be read by analysts and have a greater impact? This perhaps best describes the dilemma of institutes: as long as we narrow our views down so that all we have is our camp, not much will be changed. McDougall's difficulty in publishing her revised perspective in a mainstream psychoanalytic journal exemplifies a broader resistance within the field to reconsidering entrenched views. This resistance is strikingly illustrated in Jacqueline Rose's interview with Hanna Segal, where we see how deeply held convictions about gender and sexuality can remain unchanged even in the face of new perspectives. Segal, who was close to 90 at the time of the interview, is tough as nails. One of the unmitigated defenders of Melanie Klein, Segal emerged out of a chaotic political situation in Poland. She is remarkably stable and static in her views on gender, which have not changed since she was an adolescent medical student in Poland. While she had written extensively on politics, freedom, war, and the arts, there is something very sticky and stubborn in her views about homosexuality. From reading the interview with Rose, one gets a sense that Segal feels as if her whole world would fall apart if she changed her mind.

Seeing photos and video footage of Segal, I was also struck by the contrast between her rigid views on gender and her appearance and mannerisms. She could be read as subverting conventional femininity, raising an interesting paradox. From a stereotypical vantage point, her mannerisms and looks give a strong impression of a butch dyke. If psychoanalysis is to truly engage with the complexities of gender and sexuality, should it not also reckon with such contradictions within its own ranks? This observation is an unanswerable enigma, as is the possible generational transference between the young Rose and Segal. Rose thinks that she could charm her. She presents Segal with a question about creativity and homosexuality and wonders if the artist is not subject to those laws of sublimation (repression) and if art is an example of a refusal to sublimate. She is leaning on Freud's discussion of da Vinci's "Michelangelo" to try to get Segal to acknowledge that homosexuality can also be a creative act that expresses both femininity and masculinity, and a capacity to conduct oneself that is beyond the constrictions of the functions of social cohesion. Segal, however, remains steadfast in her belief that the parental couple is the universal signifier, leaving Rose's suggestion without an entrance point.

There is a psychosocial dilemma in changing minds that we see through this painful interview, one that recalls questions about the ways in which the concept of gender has been engaged with—and resisted—within psycho-analytic thought. This difficulty touches on the capacity for acceptance that one's discourse is an effect of one's history. We cannot study the reception of history, only observe the effort of receiving it. This conundrum elaborates a paradox that pertains to the relation between theory and practice and the incommensurable gap between them. Yet if psychoanalysis is to remain alive to its own project, it must stay with these tensions. Freud placed its work within the psychic world—a domain marked not by certainty but by move-ment, opacity, and delay—a world that can be entered in the clinic but not secured there. To work within such a space is not to stabilize it but to bear its uncertainties, and to let our theoretical frameworks be unsettled by what emerges there.

5   Claustrum of theory

As part of our practice as analysts, we regularly read and write cases. In opening ourselves to the work of interpretation, we bring psychoanalysis closer to the history of its own thought—its repetitions, its resistances, its self-reckonings. Yet in reading an analyst at work, we confront a paradox: we can never fully know the unconscious movements that animated their concerns. We have, instead, the stories analysts tell about change, their narratives of encounters that have, in turn, transformed them. One such case is Stoller's famous account of Agnes (Stoller, 1968a), a case that has reconfigured my own understanding of his contribution to gender theory. To return to this case, then, is not only to consider its historical and theoretical implications but also to trace the conditions under which a psychoanalytic framework shifts. How does a prior conception yield to another? What constitutes openness to disruption?

Agnes presented with "normal" male genitalia and chromosomes but, at the age of 12, had begun developing breasts. She told Stoller that she had always felt herself to be female, that masculinity had never sat comfortably with her; that since the age of 17, she had lived as a woman. She had a boyfriend, Bill, who wanted to marry her, and to fully inhabit the life she envisioned, she sought vaginoplasty. Stoller, she believed, was her last hope. Yet beneath this unfolding clinical exchange was another, more elusive, tension: the analyst's use of the patient's story to confirm a theory already in motion. Stoller's early conceptualization of "core gender identity" (1964, 1968a, 1968b) rested on the assumption of an internal, stable sense of self, a hidden biological force shaping identity from within (Forrester, 2017, p. 130). But the case was not to remain so easily legible. Agnes, years into treatment, revealed that she had secretly been taking her mother's effeminizing hormones since the age of 12.

At the time, Stoller had been working in collaboration with sociologist Harold Garfinkel at the UCLA Gender Clinic—one of the first to provide trans patients with hormonal treatment and gender-confirming surgery. In the late 1950s, the clinic had positioned itself as a site of inquiry into the so-called etiology of gender identity disorders. For Stoller, his initial reading of Agnes's case seemed to affirm a biologically driven theory of gender identity, an endogenous force that prefigured lived experience. "Some drive energy for

DOI: 10.4324/9781003440758-8

gender identity," he theorized, was at work (Forrester, 2017, p. 131). But once Agnes's long-held secret was disclosed, the case took on a new theoretical significance. Stoller was forced to retract his earlier conclusions:

> When the subject of the biological force was first described in 1964, there were several errors in my thinking. The first was that one of the two cases used to demonstrate the point does no such thing. This patient, by revealing a secret which she had kept from me for years, has shown that she does not exemplify the presence of an endogenous biological force but rather the effects of rearing.
>
> (Forrester, p. 133)

From this reversal emerged a different formulation. No longer seeking confirmation of a biological substratum, Stoller instead emphasized the familial conditions that shaped gendered life. In his revised account, he suggested that the psychic structures underlying adult transsexuality were continuous with the early mother-son relationship—that a mother's adoration, in extinguishing the boy's masculinity, had produced a particular gender trajectory (Forrester, 2017, p. 132). In tracing his shift in thought, what becomes clear is not only how Stoller came to denaturalize gender but, more pressingly, how the act of psychoanalytic interpretation demands a willingness to denaturalize one's own theories. What the case of Agnes ultimately illuminates is that it is not gender itself that requires rethinking but rather the conceptual frames that seek to capture It.

Stoller's famous case of Agnes raises the question of transference embedded in the ways in which evidence is thought and presented. The question of transference is key to understanding current psychoanalytic responses to the dilemma of trans, as gender becomes permanently entangled in contemporary debates about age, nature, authority, agency, and objectivity. Such debates are also sites of resistance, where responses to transgender identity are already steeped in the cultural claustrum of ideality, confusing scientific "evidence" with psychological "facts." Revisiting Stoller's belated reflections on his case invites the reader to consider their own emotional susceptibility to what they have learned about gender—and its unmaking. At the same time, through this case, I present falling apart as the grounds for learning.

Stoller is frequently criticized for his biological theory of "core gender" (Gherovici & Steinkoler, 2022; Saketopoulou & Pelegrini, 2023) and for failing to engage with the complexities of gender as a lived experience (Joynt & Schilt, 2019). The case of Agnes, however, is generalizable in the way that knowledge emerges through errors and interruptions. The case brings into view the idea that a discipline such as psychoanalysis—which engages with unstable constructs, whose data is accessible only to the analyst, and whose conclusions cannot be subject to confirmation—cannot possibly be scientific. It challenges not science itself but the conceptualizations that render science intelligible, as Agnes is an adolescent who has engaged in an activity that actively constructs gender (taking hormones, stealing, lying, being seductive, and getting her way). To read Agnes as a subject of agency is to recognize that biology is always already an interpretation, rather than a fixed foundation. It is a testimony to science's failure to capture the singularity of experience and the inability of scientific observations to be teased apart from their structuring phantasies.

In the process of writing on how people change their minds, I am also reflecting on the ways I have changed in my conceptualization of gender. I became interested in the case of Agnes upon reading a chapter titled "Inventing Gender Identity" in John Forrester's *Thinking in Cases*. He is very careful in reading the case, considering how Stoller has been received and dismissed by contemporary theorists. What struck me about Forrester's reading is his subtle critique of how readers of case studies often assume they know more than the writer and focus on what the analyst "missed." This is partly how Stoller has been read, with the assumption that Agnes's revelation did not fundamentally alter his belief in the deterministic origins of gender but merely shifted its foundation from a biological core to a "simplistic and essentialist" (Gherovici & Steinkohler, 2022, p. 9) psychological explanation.

From Forrester's vantage point, however, this is a banal critique. Reading Stoller as a simplistic theorist or focusing on what he supposedly overlooked does not necessarily give the reader access to what they are confronting in reading Stoller. Forrester is addressing the reader as a subject implicated in the very processes the case attempts to articulate. The reader must tolerate what is given, rather than judge what should have happened—a confrontation that produces anxiety. There is a transference in reading, Forrester suggests, and what remains overlooked is the idea that Stoller is writing a case about what he missed. This, in turn, is an example of how to read case material—not from a position of knowability but with attention to the ways in which the writer, artfully or not, unfurls something that has already occurred. This pattern of delayed meaning, where something is first experienced before it is understood and later returned to with a realization of its significance, is a ruling trope for Stoller, as it was for Freud. The writer of the case, Forrester implies, already knows what has happened—but presents it as if it were still unfolding, inviting the reader to experience the case as a site of belated understanding.

It seems to me, therefore, a misstep to appraise Stoller from the vantage point of hindsight, as if the task were merely to measure what he did not know against what we presume to know now. Such a gesture risks enacting the very closure that psychoanalysis invites us to resist: the foreclosure of uncertainty, limit, and the historical conditions of thought. Following John Forrester's sensibility, it may be more fruitful to situate Stoller within the contours of his own conceptual dilemmas, to consider not what he failed to achieve but rather how he wrestled with the tensions inherent to his moment. What emerges, particularly in his reading of the Agnes case, is not only a documentation of a subject but the recognition that the case itself is under construction—that the analytic encounter does not reveal a fixed truth but participates in its assembly. This, I think, is Stoller's radical contribution: a shift from the authority of the analyst as leader to the vulnerability of the analyst as follower, one who is being moved by the subject's narration rather than moving the subject toward a predetermined telos. In this movement, the stability of gender is no longer his guiding premise; instead, gender becomes the very site of contingency, relation, and negotiation. It is here that Stoller, perhaps inadvertently, gestures toward a more indeterminate, and thus more generative, analytic position.

Peaches and cream

My reading of Stoller's case follows Forrester's pedagogical device of climbing inside the writer's head, not from the position of knowing the other, but in the sense of being affected by climbing into my own head and thinking about my transference to the case. In the process, my view of Stoller and the significance of his case has changed. Following Forrester's delicate notion of "climbing into minds," I consider Stoller's case of Agnes as an exemplar; an experience that stands for different things with the insistence upon the shakiness of speculation. Much like paradigms, exemplars are "what you use when theory isn't there." Like Freud's case of the Wolfman or the Ratman, Stoller's case of Agnes is an exemplar for the shakiness of speculations and the instability of explanation for a phenomenon. It exemplifies gender as a timeless construction and its refusal, the work of the "negative" (Green, 2000).

In reflecting on his encounter with Agnes and his theories of gender retrospectively, Stoller opens a way of conceptualizing a problem that is, in some sense, universal: our transference to knowledge and the problem of belief. Stoller finds it hard to believe that Agnes presents with a "sex disorder" as she presents convincingly as a biological woman: "The most remarkable thing . . . was that it was not possible for any observer, including those who knew her anatomic status, to identify her as anything other than a young woman" (Stoller et al., 1960, p. 44). His initial encounter with Agnes provides Stoller confirmation for what he theorizes as an archaic, biological "force," of which gender identity is its expression.

The idea of a biological force is a theoretical shift from Stoller's previous work in collaboration with John Money. Through his work with Money, who had introduced the concept of gender, with an emphasis on social roles, Stoller further developed the concept of "gender" by coining the term "gender identity," in part as a way to distinguish it from sex (Forrester, 2017, p. 130). Stoller comes to understand gender identity as shaped by three things: "First there was anatomy then came the upbringing of the child, the attitudes of the parents, siblings, and peers. Finally, what he called a biological force provided 'some *drive* energy for gender identity'" (Forrester, 2017, p. 131).

I find Stoller's notion of a biological force linked to a "*drive* energy for gender identity" to be interesting, because it raises a question of what is meant by biology, particularly as Freud (1915b, pp. 109–140) defines the word *drive* as "a need for work imposed on the psychic apparatus" by the organism, and as a "measure of the demand made upon the mind for work in consequence of its connection with the body." Thus, the concept of "drive" implies psychic work, not a biological force. There is no demand on biology beyond the situations of life and death. How, then, do we conceptualize a force that forms the basis of something like gender? The case of Agnes raises this challenge to the very conceptualizations that render science intelligible. As Julie Walsh (2020) observes, there is an underlying confusion "between biological, cultural, and etiological designation" of Agnes's sex and gender (p. 18), further complicated by its delayed temporalization. This failure, she suggests, is inherent to categorization, gender subjectivity, and writing of a case study, and in this sense the case study, much like narratives of gender, will involve a failed translation.

Reading Stoller's description of Agnes across the multiple papers in which he continues to make observations about her, one is struck by a tinge of creepiness. Something ghoulish haunts Stoller's descriptions of Agnes, and one gets the sense that he cannot see her in ways other than a little girl: "pretty young girl with a fine figure" and a "peaches and cream complexion" (1964, p. 224), a description so affective that it is also picked up by Garfinkel. Garfinkel, who was impressed by Agnes's ability to present and live in the world as a woman, joined Stoller with a particular question about phenomenology of theorizing gender: "theorizing the normal environment—that makes up her work of making it as a woman, given that she was raised as a man" (1980, p. 10). Both researchers find Agnes beautiful, and it is clear that they are taken by her. "Peaches and cream" may be a metaphor for Agnes's beauty but also resembles a cosmetic commercial and a romantic description of skin. And while the qualities of the researchers' transference to Agnes can only be hypothesized, their description gives us a sense of how the scientist's perception cannot be uncoupled from their desire; a dilemma that returns us to the question of the place of subjectivity in science—a basic Freudian insistence.

Stoller's description attests to how he was affected by his patient to the point where he was able to submit to her lies. Presenting herself as intersex, Agnes gave Stoller a phantasy. Her motivation was Stoller's capacity, as a medical doctor, to provide access to transitioning (hormones, surgery). A paradoxical structure lies at the heart of this scene: an unsaid expectation associates truth-telling with a certain narrative of self to make trans experience legible, so Agnes delivered a "deceitful" phantasy on such terms in order to get what she wanted and to arrive at the truth of her gender. The discovery that his patient lied about being intersex and that she was taking hormones all along gave Stoller pause. It moved him to see his theory of "core gender identity" as flawed. Yet another paradox emerges here: while Stoller used his theory to interpret his patient's phantasy, it was Agnes's "deceptive truth" that ultimately revealed the phantasmatic nature of the theory itself.

The case for thinking in cases

One of the questions Forrester poses across his book is how a case is used in a way that can be generalized. Does the particular lead to the universal? This is a central question for the human sciences that concerns the status of knowledge and how it is made. Forrester treats case histories as exemplars of how an analyst works—and of what limits that work. The strongest example of this possibility, for him, is found in Freud's "The Interpretation of Dreams." There, his theories are oriented by the question of how the *object* of dreams has come about rather than wondering where dreams come about. Cases, like theories, Forrester insists, are speculations of what cannot be talked about, and like dreams, all we have in our theories are stories. Our theories in this respect are overdetermined, and our knowledge will be made from errors (transference, identifications, projections, and displacements). "Thinking in cases" provides a reading practice that opens a new way of seeing something that is no longer stable, urging us to think of cases as "exemplars"; that is, as "compositions" subject to the logic of displacement and condensation, and to the temporal movements of anticipation and retroaction. Examples in this way are a threshold for something new. The instability of the case, Forrester suggests, is also inherent in Stoller's writing of the Agnes case. The writing itself is the author's encounter with a text implicated by the aftereffect of transference. Here the reader begins to wonder about how transference shapes the ways in which we theorize gender.

Forrester's stunning reading of the case of Agnes considers the reader as also subject to the *nachträglich* processes that the case is attempting to relate. By asking the reader to consider "How can this idea [core gender identity] be modernized?" (Forrester, 2017, p. 130), Forrester is iterating the case as an exemplar that gives us access, retrospectively, to the social, political, and emotional situation of gender. In his capacious way of reading the case, he is also posing the question of how a concept like gender may regain new meaning, by asking: "Why return to Stoller?" In Forrester's careful reading, the reason has to do with Stoller's addition of the term "identity" to gender. This addition, he suggests, provides something new and is "far more important than [Stoller] lets on" (p. 130). Stoller's attempt to distinguish gender from sex, paradoxically, paves a way of opening the question of gender to the polymorphousness of sexuality. The case of Agnes brings up the question of identity as a place of doubt, because we cannot establish whether Agnes is a hermaphrodite, a trans, or transvestite. It involves the movements of gender that can take many forms and be expressed through any identity. That is where identity becomes a container, or a prison house, to polymorphous identifications.

Along with Forrester, I read Stoller's case not as a commentary about his patient but as a commentary about his work that raises questions for the analyst: how do our minds change through our encounter with a new subject? How are we, who may be in a position of gatekeeping, to decide what it is we see? Stoller's article is retrospective, and it is only in retrospect that he, and the reader of his case, come to know Agnes as a trans woman. Retrospect is a *nachträglich* engagement, and this is why Chase Joynt's film *Framing Agnes* is compelling in its recreation of a *nachträglich* phantasy about Agnes's encounter with Stoller. Joynt's film, in a way, performs a countertransference phantasy in which Agnes pushes back against Stoller and Garfinkel, who are presented as persecutory in their intrusive questioning. At this point, Agnes is cast as a seductress, aware of her power and cynical in her engagement. She flirts with and plays with the "doctor" figure, reversing the analytic hierarchy.

Joynt's project is an act of historical reimagining, animating the unrepresented pain of the archive in an attempt to work through it. Yet the desire to overturn the power dynamic—to claim narrative control—carries an affective charge that borders on destruction, shaped by the psychic demand to undo the trauma of being thought about rather than understood. The traumatic consequences of such encounters, their residues, are what Stoller also engages in his return to Agnes's case, just as Forrester's reflections trace the *nachträglich* workings of the case study itself. At this point, my focus shifts: from how Stoller changed his frame of mind through the case to how we might consider the analytic frame as something itself subject to change. How might we think about new situations of gender? And how, encountering Stoller's case today, are we going to think with it?

Agency

The case of Agnes (Stoller, 1964) can stand as an exemplar of what people do to create "who they were not before" (Foucault, 1982), that is, the capacity to conceptualize our possibilities for being outside of prohibitive anxieties of heteronormativity. The possibilities of gender, Foucault suggests, are the promise of being "someone else [we] were not in the beginning" (Foucault, 1982, p. 10). Her actions move the reader's notion of gender from the dilemma of identity to the question of construction. Through a series of actions, an adolescent engages in an activity that determines gender. The question we may ask here is what kind of information does the patient give his analyst about his or her gender? There is already a difficult structure framed around the paradoxical idea that you just tell the truth, at the same time as what is expected is a certain narrative of self to make trans experience legible. In other words, one needs to engage in a phantasy to get what one wants, and here we confront the dilemma of the unreliable narrator and the conundrum of getting a piece of information on which the researcher did not count.

There is a dimensionality to the case that is very interesting and, I think, easily bypassed: Stoller was not only seduced by his attractive patient but also by his own theory. This dimensionality brings us back to Kristeva's (2009) incredible need to believe. It has to do with the very basic fact of humans as self-theorizing creatures (Laplanche, 1992), which means that we are also susceptible to other's theories. Our theories are also significant webs that we have spun and are caught in. The discovery that his patient had lied about being intersex and had been taking hormones all along gave Stoller pause. What he had taken to be a natural, biological process was in fact induced by pharmaceuticals, exposing his theory of "core gender identity" as a phantasy. He writes: "my chagrin at learning this was matched by my amusement she could pull off this coup with such skill" (Stoller, 1968a, p. 136). Agnes's revelation was a moment of transformation in Stoller's theory but also a scene of failure, a sudden impasse. At the same time, there is an unmistakable hint of pleasure, as if the exposure of failure is being savored. The amusement over being fooled is as if a tribute to an unconscious structure of learning: one learns from failure, but first, one's theory is susceptible to belief. Following Agnes's revelation, Stoller was forced to change his theoretical viewpoint. His patient's revelation led Stoller to see Agnes as transsexual, not intersexed, and moved from an origin story based on biology ("endogenous biological force") to a social one: "This patient, by revealing a secret which she has kept from me for years, has shown that she does not exemplify the presence of an endogenous biological force, but rather the effects of rearing" (Stoller, 1968a, pp. 83–84). After interviewing Agnes's mother, he describes the relationship between her and his patient as symbiotic: "Mother hen and baby chick" (Stoller, 1968a, p. 137).

Agnes's revelation created a paradigm crisis that exposed the limits of theory, but her case is also a threshold to the idea that biology is useless in determining gender because it is not transparent; it too is subject to interpretation. Her revelation crashes the system on which Stoller's views on gender were built, because if there is no essential biological core that expresses gender, then the "force" that brings Agnes to express her gender in a particular way is not biology but desire. Biology no longer explained what Agnes was doing; it rather became the pliable object of her desire.

The instability of categories is also inherent in the structure of the case study. Adam Phillips (in Forrester, 2017, p. xiii) notes that we never quite know what any given case is an example of. This instability extends to the frame itself, evident in its effect on the observers: Garfinkel is moved by Agnes's revelations differently from Stoller. For Garfinkel, the emphasis falls on social roles and on experience as the overdetermining factor. One question we might ask today is whether we recognize the extent to which we are reading gender through a history of gender reading (Gozlan, 2025, upcoming). His theory is already one of self-theorizing, in the sense that the human reads the activities of the other and treats them as meaningful. This notion of instability—where meaning requires symbolic interaction—underlines Garfinkel's interest in the ways we signal our desires to each other. There is, therefore, phenomenological meaning to Agnes taking her mother's hormones that does not shift for Garfinkel that idea of her femininity. Through symbolic interactionism, the mother's own capacity to take feminizing hormones already signals femininity as interchangeable. At the same time, Garfinkel focuses on Agnes's "passing" and the "management of appearance in daily life" (p. 133), rather than gender. Agnes, in Garfinkel's view, is a woman because she is observably "normal." Her legitimacy as a woman, in other words, depends on her capacity to produce a certain narrative of self that makes her experience legible.

Despite the differences in the ways in which each was affected by the case, there was something disturbing for both Stoller and Garfinkel, and that was their theories. Their theories, they found, were insufficient in addressing the question of biology, sociology, and etiology, particularly given that Agnes's presentation is affected by the hormones. Walsh describes this conundrum aptly when she wonders when we define Agnes, given the "circulation of hormones that subvert the possibility of providing any clear-cut notion of gender as 'natural'" (Forrester, p. 136). "Do we designate her at birth," she asks, "at first glance; before or after surgery; before or after her confession; before or after talking with her mother? And what of the question of historical variation?" (Walsh, p. 17). Categories are defunct from the outset because they are not outside of the frame of the 'psy' professions, legal or psychoanalytic apparatus, and are based on speculations, compromised formations. They are an attempt to provide the mechanisms of inquiry, and as such, they are still subject to a failure in translation. It is through this instability that Forrester reads Stoller's "core gender identity" (1964) and considers its potential futurity.

Bisexuality or core gender?

Through Forrester's discussion of Stoller, the reader encounters a complex thinker who, like other mid-century psychoanalysts (Loewald, Modell, Sullivan, and Kohut), took a transdisciplinary approach to his subject matter, working with psychologists, sociologists, and philosophers, and thinking through anthropology, literature, phenomenology, and psychobiography. Looking at letters exchanged between Stoller and the philosopher William Simon (1988–89), one gets the sense of a theorist who, much like Foucault, is interested in the construction of human nature. If for Foucault the question of sexuality moves from the problem of identity to the problem of what people do (activities), the case of Agnes moves the reader to the question of activities: Agnes is an adolescent who engages in an activity that determines gender. And while Simon critiques ideality in science, which, along with Kuhn (1962), he believes requires a community of agree-ers—a critique which he also directs at Stoller's "observation-driven theories" (p. 59)—the case of Agnes is generalizable in the way in which knowledge is made through errors, because we do not know what we are observing, and the way we proceed is error by error. Stoller's deep commitment to serious work, Forrester suggests, involves the understanding that as a discipline engaged with unstable constructs, whose data is accessible only to the analyst, and whose conclusions cannot be subject to confirmation, psychoanalysis cannot possibly be scientific.

The question is not what gender is but what gender does to theory. Agnes's story interrupts the demand for gender to be intelligible. In that interruption, something happens to Stoller. He lets himself be affected. And it is only in retrospect—only in the echo chamber of delayed understanding—that he comes to recognize his own submission to the phantasy of certainty. The case challenges the conceptualizations that render science intelligible, rather than the subject of science as such. Forrester's idea of "thinking in cases" speaks directly to this question: how something may appear comprehensible until it is no longer intelligible. The problem with the paradigm crisis is that errors are made from the basic way that scientific knowledge is created—as a function of agreement—and then, theory supplants it. In other words, an Oedipal structure to knowledge produces a tension between science and its object of study.

In Stoller's case (1968a), Agnes's revelation acted as this third. Stoller is aware of the psychical qualities of scientific knowledge when he responds to Simon's critiques of scientific observation. He quips:

> Granted all observation is theory driven, nonetheless, certain observations lead to bridges that do not collapse, atom bombs, larger chickens, and shoelaces that take longer to wear out. . . . Of course, there is no such thing as reality, and of course there is no such thing as free will. But of course, I consciously choose to believe that I exist and that I can choose to choose.
>
> (1985, p. 9)

"We are doomed," he adds, "not only to be chasing our own tail but to have forever caught it and never have known to let it go" (p. 63). Stoller's comment brings into view a notion of analytic objectivity that does not take into account intersubjectivity. Such a notion is a situation of failure In a sense that it is grounded in ideality, and what remains obscured is the transference whose leitmotif is presence-absence, a relation that is also incommensurable because it is made from the stickiness of libidinal investments and the passion to eschew anything that one is unprepared to receive.

Stoller's response also threw into relief his capacity for uncertainty along with the ability to play. Stoller, after all, is a psychoanalyst, not a biologist. He is a very creative physician and theorist who listens to speech acts, rather than looking at cells. Though he had one foot in a normative way of thinking about gender, we can read him today very differently, in ways other than being the enemy of transgender. That is how Forrester reads him and that is how I am reading his theories in this book. While great discussion exists on Stoller not changing his mind, I am struck by his experimentation and the disciplinary approach he has taken in his attempt to figure out the nature of gender. The question of whether he fails is secondary, because, like the reader, Stoller is also a creature of history. Nonetheless, through being affected by Agnes, Stoller's frame of understanding also changes because he must ask himself how he had come to know. His process marks a slowing down that occurs through what Isabelle Stengers (2017) describes as "the presence of something that provokes hesitation and brings about another way of thinking, feeling, and imagining" (p. 10). This hesitation suspends determined ways of thinking and creates an aperture that makes us susceptible to the assertions of possibilities we have not considered.

Agnes's boldness gets at the idea that at a certain point the social is so oppressive that something has got to break, and the only way to break into its defensive shield is to be outrageous; to shock, to perform the horror of what is experienced.[1] What the case of Agnes breaks through, Forrester suggests, is the stability of gender. Forrester is able to get at how the concept of "core gender identity," initially used by Stoller to describe a biological determinant of gender roles, as separated from sex (genitalia), was unhinged from the challenge of the deceptive act on which it was founded and considered its fate in scientific discourse, in popular culture, and in political life. It is of course the case that a concept of "core gender identity" can be read (and is often read) as a concept denoting gender as innate, static, and immutable. Forrester, however, orients us by looking at the history of reading. One of the questions we might ask today is whether we understand the way in which we are *reading* gender through a history of gender reading?

From the question of history of reading, we may see Stoller as responsible for a rigid concept, but through Agnes's case, we may also understand how this concept came about through the story of accidents. This is a very psychoanalytic story that involves deception and a crisis of ideality through the wish to believe (Kristeva, 2009) and an investment in theory. The term "core identity" has a deceptive history but was strategic for some people in articulating a demand to the medical professionals. It has oriented the ways in which trans and intersex and gay individuals talked about themselves as having been "born into the wrong body" or the common narrative of gay individuals as being "always this way," a premise which has been deemed oppressive or liberating depending on who uses it, in what context, or for what purpose. It is an example of a traveling theory that has also slipped into gender identity disorder and now dysphoria.

With Forrester, I approach the Agnes case with the question: how would we think about the implications of the case today? How would we think "core gender identity" as a concept that helps us understand "what milage is there still to be got out of Freud's concept of bisexuality?" (Forrester, p. 93). To consider Stoller's concept of core gender identity as connected with Freud's notion of psychic bisexuality and its potential for modern mobilization may seem rather odd if we read him as an essentialist or reductionist. In Forrester's careful reading, however, Stoller's addition of the term "identity" to gender provides something new. He views Stoller's separation of sex from gender is a strategy that, paradoxically, moves us to think of the phenomenology of gender. Stoller, Forrester writes:

> wasn't altogether happy with the word gender. In 1973 he writes: 'The word "gender" is not very convenient, for usually it has been synonymous with "sex." So, uneasily, I added "identity," which implies an organization around life-long themes which add up to one's sense of self.'

(Stoller, 1973, p. 313)

It seems to me that Forrester is reading that statement of Stoller as almost incidental and apropos. At that point, Forrester adds: "I think identity is more important than he lets on" (p. 130). Forrester considers Stoller's addition of "identity" as a second thought, but he also seems to suggest that Stoller wants to make claims about the phenomenological experience of being oneself, which includes having a gender. Putting a social category of "identity" next to gender, Forrester implies, destabilizes the very notion of a static, unmovable core, because it now has to be recognized as a social category, subject to experience. Oddly, Forrester notes, Stoller argues for a "variable and indeterminant biological force of which 'gender identity' is the psychological expression" (p. 130). As the case unfolds, however, what we witness is not the force of biology but a psychological force. There is a drive seeking an object, a drive seeking satisfaction. In other words, we encounter Agnes's drive for change.

Separating gender identity from sex moves gender from the fact of anatomy to the emotional world of identifications, psychical positions, and interpretations. No longer a biological fact but a social "system" that can be disputed and that requires an army (cultural signifiers, hormones, surgeries, clothes, etc.) to prop it up. It is from a capacious understanding of the "choice of the object," not as an identity of a fixed position but as a question of desire—the social positions we take in gender, or our styles of loving—that I understand Forrester's attempt to modernize the concept of psychic bisexuality. Conceptualizing gender through a notion of a libidinal relation that is essentially a phantasy destabilizes any notion of orientation or identity as timeless or fixed, because here, femininity and masculinity are no longer known entities or oppositions.

While a change of frame does not necessarily translate to a change of view, Stoller's social explanations for transsexuality remain focused on origin stories—such as a dominant mother or an absent father. However, a new framing allows for retrospective possibilities. From a contemporary vantage point, Stoller's move allows us to consider social explanation not as points of origin or causes but as involuntary situations that are subject to interpretation and that push for creative solutions in gender. Stoller's writing of the Agnes case allows for a different interpretation of gender. With the realization of Agnes's agency arise questions of desire and libidinal investment. Once we enter the topic of Eros, we inevitably turn from questions of deficit or origin to phantasy. The question of agency offers a way to think about the patient's actions in ways that privilege breadth—understood as the dispersal of affect—over depth—what lies behind. This mode of thinking is of interest when distilling the temporality of the analytic situation and the interplay between internal and external conflict. Unconscious temporality involves the dilemma of unpreparedness: in learning, experience precedes understanding. It is within the gap between receiving and learning that also allows for new translation.

The contemporary use of the term *bisexuality* is overly saturated, referencing the question of object choice, where the attributes with which masculinity and femininity are burdened are mistaken for something essential and known. Freud's focus on the "psychic aspect of bisexuality" (Freud, 1901, (42), pp. 446–448) moves us to the question of integration of feminine and masculine elements. In *Civilization and Its Discontents*, Freud adds a footnote on gender: "while anatomy can distinguish between male and female, psychology cannot" (p. 43). From this vantage point, bisexuality resists categorization, emerging instead as a tension rather than an observable or easily distinguishable trait. The footnote is significant because it conceptualizes femininity and masculinity not as oppositions but as a tension that allows for conceptualizations beyond normative social representations. Gender turns from a "location" or an identifiable "thing" to experiences that instill in oral, anal, and genital development a capacity for constituting something like masculinity and femininity, as elements (soft/hard; passive/active) that comprise "gender."

The tension between sex and gender is a conceptual problem that cannot be settled. Sex can only be greater than gender if we imagine something besides normativity. In Forrester's question about the contemporary utilization of the concept of bisexuality, I find an attempt to hold on to an enlarged version of sexuality through the notion of a generalized polymorphous perversity. The separation of gender from sexuality means the departure from focus on the necessity of reproduction to pleasure, the desire for more. The retrospective significance of the Agnes case allows us to consider the enigmatic qualities of gender because it puts into question the idea of "core identity" through the problem of choice. The question of Agnes's agency—her active decision to take hormones and lie—along with the question of unconscious desire, is suggestive of gender as a field where choices are made from unconscious and enigmatic situations of seduction (Laplanche, 1992). Stoller's recognition of Agnes's choice underscores that gender cannot be stabilized or traced back to a singular origin.

Points of condensation

While Stoller's psychological theories on transsexuality may still exhibit some rigidity, his case studies reveal a highly creative thinker engaged in broader academic conversations beyond psychology. Stoller, like Freud, remained open to the unsettling pressures that clinical work could place on theory. His writing on Belle—the daughter of a Hollywood actress and a film director—makes this tension vivid. Belle brings to the analysis a series of erotic daydreams: not simple content to be decoded but charged scenes where humiliation and excitement fold into one another. In one such phantasy, Stoller (1979) recounts Belle imagining herself ravished by a stallion, while a director stages the spectacle before an audience of expressionless men, masturbating as they watch. The stallion is replaced, suddenly, by "an old dirty man" (Stoller, 1979, p. 71). What is staged here is not merely phantasy but the shifting structure of desire—and the analyst is already caught in its frame.

The men in the audience are not there to please her but to torment her; their arousal stems from Belle's unbearable excitement.

Reflecting on this case, Forrester (2017) highlights the inseparability of theory and transference in Stoller's study of sexual excitement. He approaches Stoller's analysis of Belle as an observer, acknowledging his own voyeuristic fascination with the case. Forrester's reading conveys the sense of intrusion into an intimate space, emphasizing how deeply the analyst is affected by his work. Throughout the retrospective analysis, Stoller occupies multiple roles in his engagement with Belle—analyst, observer, voyeur, narrator, and writer. Like an actor in a play, he follows Belle's direction, stepping into a role within her phantasy. He comes to realize that Belle's sexual excitement in her daydreams is intrinsically linked to the act of directing him. In listening—and in the stirrings of his own arousal—he is drawn into hers. Yet, what takes shape is not mere repetition. Her infantile sexuality stages a *fort/da* movement of power and return—roles shift, refusal becomes command. No longer the one sent away, she now positions the analyst, directing him into the role of observer, yet not one untouched. The scene does not resolve. It leaves both caught in its tension—and leaves its traces in the writing that follows.

Stoller's ability to be ruthlessly self-critical is evident in his recognition of the limitations of his initial theory, which framed Belle as merely a victim of childhood trauma. As the work unfolds, Stoller allows himself to follow Belle's lead—a movement that demands relinquishing more control than he may have intended. In leaving her excitement unimpeded, another shift occurs: the helplessness staged in her phantasies begins to loosen. But this too is a reversal of appearances. Belle was never wholly helpless; she had always occupied the director's role—guiding, shaping, positioning the other. The analytic scene takes on a new dynamic: her phantasies tilt away from humiliation toward the exercise of teaching the other how to bring her pleasure. This scene does not remain separate from the analysis itself. Within the transference, Belle instructs Stoller, crafting the terms of engagement. She is no longer simply the analysand on the couch, no longer only seducing but actively shaping the very story being told.

Reading the cases of Belle and Agnes, we see in Stoller a receptivity to change. It hinges on recognizing his patients' subjectivity and acknowledging that his understanding of them cannot be separate from the transference. In writing about Belle, Stoller cannot remain outside the scene; the text draws him—and the reader—into its voyeuristic pull. He begins by tracing the phantasy's content back to Belle's childhood, positioning himself as observer, but the frame does not hold. Within the phantasy, Belle, like her parents, occupies all positions—and presses him to do the same. The effort to locate an origin cracks; what emerges is not a linear history but the recursive life of the phantasy itself—one that continues to stage its demands within the analytic encounter.

In this process, he is, in fact, being recruited to be directed by his patient—Belle repeats her excitement over abandonment and its reversal, shifting from victim to director. To remain with this would require Stoller to turn a ruthless gaze inward—not to master the scene but to bear his own loss of control. Such a movement unsettles the frame of the analytic encounter, pressing most acutely where his own responses are stirred—where excitement, unease, and the unpredictability of transference slip beyond his grasp. Rather than seeking a definitive origin, Stoller's approach acknowledges that the phantasmic script of the patient is inextricably embedded within the intersubjective transferential field.

I have turned to Belle's case to illustrate how Stoller reconfigures the therapeutic endeavor through the question: "Who is Belle?" This question does not center on an underlying conflict but rather positions Belle's sexual excitement as a point of condensation—a scene that amalgamates "multiple inner people and multiple scripts" (Stoller, 1979, p. 177). A turning point occurs when Stoller realizes that he is not external to Belle's sexual phantasies; rather, she positions him within them as a directed participant. This realization marks a movement away from a theory of attachment toward a theory of dispersal—one that allows for a conceptualization of sexuality beyond pathologization. The analyst is no longer tracing an origin story tied to childhood trauma but is instead observing the dispersal of a fundamental phantasy, one whose core cannot be located or cured. What can be discerned, however, is the way it plays out in social relations—whether Belle's seductive femininity functions as a way to contain a phantasy of abandonment. Real events, phantasies, "phony victories," "reversals," and affects coalesce into a sexually exciting dream. Yet, as Stoller notes, the patient is the author of their phantasy while simultaneously refusing ownership of it.

What strikes me in reading Stoller's cases is his willingness to be affected by his patients and to revise his views accordingly. He takes Belle's directions and similarly allows himself to be swayed by Agnes's presentation until he is confronted by what he did not know. The case of Agnes dislodges any stable sense of origin once Stoller recognizes his patient's active production of gender. In both Belle's and Agnes's cases, the question of agency becomes central, offering a framework that prioritizes breadth—the dispersal of affect—over depth, the search for underlying causes. The temporality of the analytic encounter unsettles the relation between past and present—what is remembered, what is staged anew. In Stoller's engagement with Agnes, the question of gender begins to loosen from the grip of origin. With the recognition of her agency, another movement gathers force: desire, drive, and phantasy overtake the search for explanation. Subjectivity emerges here as a fantastical construction—not a coherent rewriting of history but a staging of worlds, driven by what Eros demands and refuses.

I read Stoller's case not merely as a commentary on his patients but as an exploration of the analyst's work—how they navigate and think through the analytic material the patient presents. What is striking about Stoller's approach to both Agnes's and Belle's gender is that, in each case, gender is fundamentally mediated by phantasy, although these are not surface-level fictions but scenes of unconscious investment, what psychoanalysis would call phantasies. What matters is not the restoration of intelligibility but what becomes possible in its absence—where new forms of livability can begin to take shape. Gender here is not a selection to be made, nor a choice in any simple sense; it is a process influenced by the libidinal qualities of making a choice—a movement where the very act of choosing is saturated with phantasy, desire, and loss. Agnes's revelation not only introduces a social dimension to gender but, from today's perspective, also challenges the meaning we attribute to the notion of a "core." When Forrester invites us to reconsider the concept of psychic bisexuality, he suggests that a contemporary reading of Stoller's case might expose a definition of "core" that is too restrictive. Returning to Forrester's compelling idea, we might view Stoller's notion of "core gender identity" through a modern lens, we might view Stoller's notion of 'core gender identity' through a modern lens, one that is no longer essentialist or static but aligned with the polymorphous expansiveness of psychic bisexuality.

The language of "identity" dislodges gender from the claim of nature, pulling it into the register of experience—where what is lived remains layered with phantasy and loss. Yet, here another tension surfaces. In separating sex from gender, Stoller's work draws gender ever closer to the field of sexuality—not to secure its meaning but to expose its instability. Encountering Agnes's case today, we are prompted to consider the ways in which gender cannot be easily extricated from sexuality—not as biology but as an instability, a sexuality akin to Freud's notion of drive and tension. In taking hormones and shaping the narrative that would allow her surgical transition, Agnes acts—not to reveal a stable core of gendered identity but to insist on its becoming. For Stoller, this encounter displaces any simple appeal to biology or psychology; Agnes's movement fractures the notion of core itself. What unfolds is not the securing of origin but the staging of gender as an ongoing negotiation—desire, phantasy, agency always in motion.

The question of "choice," here, edges closer to the terrain of drive: less a decision than a compulsion that cannot be fully accounted for. In this light, the "core" is no longer a point to be located but a pressure—deep, unstable, unreachable—that animates gender's construction. What surrounds this core is not explanation but the symbolic work of enveloping what cannot be fixed. Perhaps akin to Balint's concept of a "basic fault," we may envision this core as an inescapable and unreachable fundamental bisexuality. This is not a matter of object choice but rather a way of describing feminine and masculine elements as conflated and not easily separable—polymorphous perversity that allows for kaleidoscopic expressions, whose variations depend on multiple outcomes.

Permeability

Changing one's mind is not an unusual idea in psychoanalysis, but there is an added context of collaboration in Stoller's work, especially in his co-writing with Belle. This collaboration opens up a new dimension of psychoanalysis, where Stoller shares his writing with his patient, invites her to edit the material, and even allows her to decide whether it will be published. Beyond the ethical concerns or the usefulness of the technique, this collaboration carries a unique potential: Stoller and Belle write the new narrative together, exposing themselves to the unknown. This act is not only analytical but erotic, positioning an enigma or a question as an analytic opening. Forrester suggests that this opening reflects Stoller's willingness to learn from his patients, even at the risk of making boundaries permeable. He is energized by his patients, allowing himself to be educated by them, employing a wide and flexible range of methods, such as collaborating in sadomasochism and interviewing porn stars and directors (Forrester, p. 81). The collaboration also touches on the creative aspects of transference as an intermediate area, both real and unreal, where theories emerge as aftereffects belonging to both patient and analyst: "Neither analyst nor patient is likely to believe that the feelings are 'unreal'" (Gabbard, 1994, p. 1086). In this mutual reality, the transference neurosis becomes a genuine case of shared creation.

This creative process is evident in Stoller's approach to Agnes. Just as his work with Belle allowed for the creation of a new narrative around gender, Stoller's engagement with Agnes leads him to a radical reconsideration of biology. Agnes's ability to create her own gender offers Stoller a new lens through which to view the question of biology, which he ultimately deems irrelevant in defining gender. Once Stoller recognizes that Agnes is making a choice, he can no longer stabilize gender in any fixed or biological sense. To assert that someone possesses X or Y chromosomes is to describe a situational fact but not the essence of gender itself.

The case of Agnes touches on the contemporary conundrum surrounding gender, particularly the question of agency, which has become central in debates over children's and adolescents' capacity to make choices regarding gender transition. Concerns over autonomy, development, reproductive capacity, and the future of children and adolescents have complicated discussions about gender, flattening the possibility of thinking about gender as a question of desire. What Stoller's cases suggest, however, is the inseparability of sexuality from psychoanalytic understandings of gender—through questions of livability, erotic pleasure, and agency. While chromosomes may be the biological conditions of the body, they also carry psychical meanings shaped by the myths we construct around them. In this way, gender remains an enigma, always a problem of interpretation. The body, in psychoanalytic terms, is also the unconscious: experiences are metabolized by the body and, in turn, give meaning to it.

Reading these cases today, I see gender not as tied to an underlying problem or origin but as an inevitable consequence of being human. As a psychological experience, the biology of sex difference is always entangled with phantasy and requires interpretation. Unconscious phantasies can be imagined as the core around which gender wraps itself to become gender as such. Phantasy is atmospheric, shaped by conditions of the self—encounters, libidinal investments, affects, pleasures, and sufferings—that accrue multiple meanings over time to create the situation of gender. These structuring phantasies, to which we are all susceptible, form human "soft spots" in our psyche. The model for the self's process of becoming, in this view, is the dream.

Arriving at one's singular interpretation of gender is an affective process, shaped by desire and libidinal investments. This is not a dilemma confined to a few. It circulates—through institutional life, through analytic education, through the analyst's own uncertainties. As Laplanche suggests, traces of enigmatic messages, such as those related to femininity and masculinity, are implanted in the child. These traces do not remain contained; they drift toward the scenes of gender, sexuality, and love—where what marks difference and what encodes loss are never fully settled. In this movement, gender difference and the phantasy of castration are refracted through registers far beyond anatomy, troubling what the body is asked to signify. Indeed, what is unavoidable for the human is being born, encountering the Other, and experiencing separation and loss. However, the capacity to interpret these "enigmatic messages" (Laplanche, 1995) is also shaped by the symbolic codes available to us. And yet, isn't it equally unavoidable that we can transcend what we inherit?

The gap between what we are given and the space of interpretation relates to the concept of freedom: we have the internal capacity to imagine ourselves as Other to what we receive. In the late 20th and early 21st centuries, this freedom is increasingly elaborated through gender. Exploring the meaning of gender for a particular individual may be a key part of the analytic endeavor, but gender itself remains mute. We can never definitively say what gender is—only that it functions as a screen for projections. These are not neutral spaces. The traffic between individual experience and cultural discourse does not mirror the intersubjective space of the clinic; it disturbs it. In this field, adolescents appear—sometimes recklessly, sometimes with fragile hope—drawn toward what exceeds established forms of knowing. The cultural shifts surrounding gender do not simply call psychoanalysis to adapt. They unsettle the analyst's position, asking whether we can remain open to being changed by encounters that do not fit our accustomed frames of interpretation. It is not a question of how we choose to situate gender but of whether we can bear its dislocation—within theory, within the clinic, within ourselves. Stoller's cases offer a way to think about the human not in terms of depth but rather in terms of breadth (Cooper, 2022), where gender takes on a *nachträglich* (retroactive) structure: the phantasies and elements that accumulate over time create a particular, yet malleable, framework—one that can only be brushed against after it has been enacted.

Productions

Agnes's transitioning relies on mechanisms of production: surgeries, pills, cosmetics. Stoller must take the case of Agnes as an indication of gender as cultural production, deeply influenced by what Forrester (2017) calls "consumer-led science" (p. 138). The conceptualization of gender as something constructed and produced also challenges its earlier categorical stability—ideas like the negative or positive Oedipal, for example, fall apart in this new framework. "We have traveled a long way from Freud to inhabit this new gender system," writes Forrester (2017, p. 138), as he contemplates the downfall of gender as a fixed category. It is strange, indeed, to think of the body as a borderline space, shaped not only by phantasies and cultural mythologies but also by political movements, where the boundary between psyche and soma is blurred—although we act as if it is not. If gender is an enigma, it is something that cannot be known in fixed terms, and therefore must be constantly constructed.

Freud himself, in his exploration of gender, had to imagine a spaceman "from another planet" (Freud, 1908) to consider what it would be like to observe the differences between the sexes among humans.

> If we could divest ourselves from corporal experience, and could view the things of this earth with fresh eyes, as purely thinking beings from another planet, nothing perhaps would strike our attention more forcibly than the fact of the existence of two human beings, who, though so much alike in other respects, yet mark the difference between them with such obvious external signs.
>
> (Freud, 1908, pp. 211–212)

Freud did not have a framework for considering cultural production, but he was interested in the mental aspects of understanding, presentation, and perception. To imagine a perspective outside of corporal existence, he envisioned someone from outer space contemplating the hegemony of the gender binary as a narcissism of minor differences. Indeed, we have come a long way from Freud. We no longer need visitors from outer space to imagine the experience of inhabiting a new gender system; today, we have a medical establishment that turns gender into something one can acquire—something we can produce for ourselves through the mechanisms of surgery, hormones, and other technologies.

If gender were only lodged in biology, there would be no subject to think, no scene for psychic life—only compliance. What Forrester (p. 137) points to in speaking of gender as production is this collapse: "nobody can really tell the differences between sex and gender any longer. . . . Choice is all that marks the difference between being designated man or woman." The categories of gender that once promised a pathway to knowledge of the subject—within the framework of patriarchal structure—no longer hold. And yet, even as this scaffolding crumbles, gender exerts a new kind of grip: less a hierarchical system than an individualized demand. What sustains it now? What compels its continuing force? This is what Forrester appears to be asking in the title of his chapter on Stoller's case of Agnes: "Inventing Gender/ Identity." There is now something beyond patriarchy that upholds gender, he suggests—something found in the 'psy' apparatus, the medical apparatus, and the legal apparatus, even though these systems often do not think of themselves as structuring principles in the production of gender "technologies." Forrester offers a critique of the 'psy' professions, particularly the psychoanalytic imaginary: if gender is only conceptualized as compliance with dominant discourse, rather than as a choice, we risk trapping ourselves in an adolescent viewpoint marked by hatred of aging, continual dissatisfaction with ourselves, and subjugation to stereotypes.

The "hypnotizing effect" (Gozlan, 2023) of gender becomes particularly apparent in the popularity of the Barbie doll. Barbie, initially created as an adult doll to teach young girls who and what they can become, was intended to symbolize the perfect woman through play. However, the Barbie doll has a fate of her own, and this unpredictability takes us beyond mere compliance, moving us into the realm of agency. As the recent Greta Gerwig film demonstrates, Barbie is played with in unexpected ways—she experiences an existential crisis, wears Birkenstocks, and is accused of being a fascist by the girl who was once forced to play with her. This example reveals that production is never without agency because the fate of the doll—how she is played with—is unpredictable.

The inheritance of gender, in other words, is open to interpretation, and in this regard, Agnes is legendary. What Agnes shows us is that gender resides in meaning: whatever one inherits—socially, psychically, or biologically—is inherited in a particular way. There is always a gap between the two poles: what we are given by parental and cultural pressures, and what we receive in the act of interpretation. The gap between what is said and how it is received unsettles the very ground of interpretation. Laplanche (1992), in formulating the "anthropological situation," insists that discourse never arrives intact: it carries within it the inevitability of miscommunication. What is transmitted is always in excess of itself, giving rise not simply to misunderstanding but to the stirrings of phantasy—an emotional elaboration that both answers and distorts the message of phantasy. Far from being a passive subject to what Perelberg (2018) imagines as a new mode of (capitalist) production, which "takes over the production of the body itself," Agnes's triumph over the medical system demonstrates that such modes of production, because they "are there for consumers to manage" (p. 137), are also spaces of agency—spaces where choice can emerge. No matter how profoundly we are influenced by the discursive production of gender, it is in this moment of agency that the polymorphous perversity of sexuality appears.

Note

1 This bold move is echoed in John Fryer's, who as a closeted gay psychiatrist at a time when the *Diagnostic and Statistical Manual of Mental Disorders* (DSM) named homosexuality as a deviant mental illness, addressed the American Psychiatric Association, wearing a mask, to disclose his homosexuality.

6   A question of dreaming

I have turned to McDougall and Stoller as exemplars of thinking about gender. For McDougall, the conceptualization of gender emerged through her transference to her lesbian patient, whereas for Stoller, it was shaped by a loyalty to theory—a learning that came too late. What I have encountered in their writing of their cases is the limits of their clinical work and their wish to exceed the limit. Yet as a reader, the limit of the case is also what I am left with and the question of how I am engaging with the text. Writing is always a *nachträglichkeit* temporality, a representation of something that has already occurred, and in this way, it is close to the narrative of a dream and follows the uncanniness of deferral, presence, and absence where "the moment when it happens is not the moment when it acquires meaning, implying that for psychoanalytic thought, meaning is not so much linked to immediate experience as to a retrospective interpretation of it" (Green, 2000, in Britzman, 2024, p. 32). These conditions make reading and writing into a "twilight zone" (Britzman, 2024, p. 73), where the reader encounters gaps, resistances, wishes, confusions, and distortions that arise both from their own history and the writer's. Reading, Shoshana Felman suggests, involves the "constant struggle to become aware" (1987, p. 15). The analytic reading—of a case, of the patient's narrative—is always a reading of difference, and hence of displacement: a reading into and beyond what is said (Felman, p. 21). In psychoanalysis, reading is never neutral. It is an affective engagement, an intersubjective event that binds the reader to the problem of interpretation and to the problem of self. My own reading of cases is often marred by anxiety, by uncertainty, by the pull of identification.

Reading a case stirs identifications. Not always transparently, not always comfortably. We read toward the patient and toward the analyst—sometimes in search of ourselves, sometimes through the analyst's own shadows. And then the text: another temporality, another uncertainty. This is the rhythm of afterwardness—not comprehension but a movement with what resists holding. Reading, here, is a kind of listening—akin to listening to a dream, where each return leaves something ungrasped. It is with this sensibility that I approach Danielle Quinodoz's case of Simone. The narrative unfolds not as a

DOI: 10.4324/9781003440758-9

clinical success, nor as an interpretive resolution but as a scene where gender becomes legible through what exceeds diagnosis—through the dreamwork of the analytic relation. By 2002, Quinodoz rethinks an earlier formulation—one that located her patient's "madness" in the confusion and hatred between femininity and masculinity. Simone appears now as more coherent, organized through a differentiated relation to sex, stabilized through a phantasy of mutual recognition. But this stabilization is fragile; it mirrors larger uncertainties in how gendered subjectivity is being imagined, disciplined, and defended. It is the trace of an analyst transformed, rethinking the meaning of an "illusory solution," even as it remains entangled with the acting out of gender's enigmatic demand.

There are many aspects to Quinodoz's discussion of her case, her views on her transference to her patient, and the changes she observes in her patient and in herself. I will limit the focus of my discussion, however, to the two dreams she describes, as an entrance to the way gender is presented. Quinodoz begins by orienting the reader to the first dream. We learn that it occurs in the context of Simone's fear that the analyst would "tire of the analysis and not wish to go on with it" (p. 788). A few sessions back, Quinodoz describes a session that "hit [her] like an earthquake." In this session, Simone tells the analyst that she would be missing sessions because she has made an appointment with a surgeon to further feminize her: having her Adam's apple shaved and other cosmetic procedures. The analyst feels slapped in the face (p. 786) and that "everything was collapsing" (p. 786). For the analyst, the patient's turning to actively change her body was a sign of an analytic failure and a hostile betrayal by her patient. She states: "Simone was abandoning me, slapping me in the face, administering the most violent aggression ever: there was putting everything back on a concrete level, on the external appearances, whereas I had thought that she was now in search of a more internal, psychic, sense of identity" (pp. 786-88).

Dreams

> There was an extraterrestrial disguised as a man. He had a little head and a long neck. He had escaped and I managed to locate him. I was trying to understand how to subdue him. The police came. I could not bring myself to let go of him; no one could take him away from me. But he was someone who could be tamed. I could then let go of him and he would not go away. He became a person. I stopped subduing him and trusted him instead.

And then an elaboration . . . "I am discovering certain activities with Sven (male partner). . . . I feel as shocked as if it was the first time" (pp. 787-88). The analyst's interpretation is attuned to symbolism: "So the penis is an extraterrestrial who needs to be tamed? Even the operation could not take it away from you." She understands the dream as an expression of the loss of the penis, a loss that Simone experienced, Quinodoz theorizes just as she discovered "value of the male sex" that is discovered retroactively.

Quinodoz discusses another dream that "brings back things from the past" (p. 791):

> In the dream I am a little boy, as I once was; and I feel very persecuted. I am being chased by a pig of a psychiatric male nurse. (Yesterday I saw a stupid film that caricatured a psychiatric hospital.) The more I defend myself, the more inhumane the nurse becomes. There are two people inside this person, a monster and a human being. The human being gains the upper hand and I take him home to my parents' house. I find my way to my room. I had hit this man who has been sent to kill me, in the face. The main thing in the dream was that I had to find a balance between the violent and the affectionate sides of this same person.

Quinodoz interprets the dream as the patient's struggle with and integration of persecutory and frightening male parts:

A: In the same way as you are now considering the possibility that your masculine sides might be loved after you need to hit them to defend against what you felt to be their violence (p. 792).
P: (Laugh) You might also say that my masculine side was persecuting me like the male nurse!
A: You are never quite sure which comes first: do you bash him one because he is a dangerous monster, or does he become a monster because you hate him?

There are many ways of approaching a dream. Quinodoz approaches it through her countertransference, shaping her interpretation around a perceived struggle between masculinity and persecution. But as a reader, I have no access to the writer's private anxieties—only to the ways she narrates them. All I can do with a clinical case is ask how I engage with the text and where I encounter its limitations. As I read this case, I find myself questioning its assumptions: how are femininity and masculinity constructed here? Why does Quinodoz express such certainty in her observations? What if the dream is a commentary on the transference itself? Could it be, after all, that Simone experiences the analyst as the male nurse—someone who assumes phallic knowledge, is intrusive, but can also be tamed? Quinodoz does not go there. Here, we are left not with the material evidence of a case but with an emotional situation that raises more questions than it resolves.

Difficulties in the case are initially framed as the patient's inability to distinguish between femininity and masculinity, with her desire for transitioning seen as delusional. From this perspective, Simone's identification as female entails, for Quinodoz, a psychotic element. What we have access to is a threshold to infantile theories of gender. What does the analyst's view of surgery as a hostile enactment tell us about her conception of gender? How should we understand Quinodoz's insistence that Simone's "experience of time is regular, like a man's"; that she "did not have a woman's variable sense of time rooted in the rhythms of the body"? This is where meaning breaks down for the reader, as the analyst's descriptions begin to rely on rigid, biologized notions of gender. When femininity and masculinity are symbolically equated with body parts, the analyst's capacity to see the demand for physical transitioning as anything other than a hostile destruction becomes obstructed. What is avoided is the question of countertransference: to what extent, we may wonder, does it stand in the way of the patient's free associations?

For the reader, the dilemma of the case—as Britzman suggests, using Freud's term—is that what remains is but a "torso" (Britzman, 2024, p. xxiv). What I confront in my reading, then, is my own identification with the case, which fuels my countertransference. My countertransference as a reader leads to a sense of panic because I recognize in Quinodoz's writing a defended pedagogy that feels all too familiar. If reading case material communicates breakdowns, it also offers strategies for repair. In Quinodoz's case, this repair is tied to her admission of her own fear of madness. In trying to understand her patient, the analyst must tolerate her own divergent "antithetical tendencies" (p. 794)—both tenderness and aggression toward a situation that initially feels inconceivable. This process challenges the analyst to reconfigure her relation to an experience she has not previously encountered. It is decentering, because it has not yet been thought. One might even read Quinodoz's text as a kind of day residue, a lingering trace of her own process of dreaming her patient. From this vantage point, castration anxiety, feelings of mutilation, and violence are not merely themes in Simone's material but also affective traces of the analyst's own struggles with the madness of gender. The need to know, the difficulty of not knowing, and the fear of meaning collapsing in the face of unintelligibility all animate this process. Yet this decentering experience is also generative—new ideas can emerge. In Simone's dreams, femininity and masculinity come together in ways that lead Quinodoz to see her patient as capable of accepting paradox. The reader, in turn, witnesses a loosening in the analyst's own thinking; she is now able to conceptualize sexual difference in terms beyond the concreteness of the body. She comes to understand the importance of the analyst's ability to "trust in the force of psychic reality as against the ineluctability of concrete reality" (p. 794).

Simone's dreams—bridging past and present, violence and affection—are taken as signs of a greater capacity to "distinguish between the sexes" (p. 793). However, this distinction is no longer based on the recognition of bodily reality alone. Quinodoz now perceives Simone as capable of acknowledging her sexual desires and recognizing homosexual tendencies within herself (p. 793). This psychic transformation, occurring for both analyst and patient, is facilitated through dreams—where previously split-off elements do not simply integrate but remain in a state of dynamic tension, forming a third space. Importantly, Simone's newfound psychic unity is no longer, in the analyst's mind, in opposition to her surgery. Instead, it is expressed through her capacity to tolerate her sexual desires, including her desire for men. For Quinodoz, this shift signals a deeper psychic differentiation: moving from a universalizing treatment of men as potential aggressors to an awareness of the variability of experience. The reader observes a transformation in the writer's capacity to consider sexual difference as something internal, rather than fixed in external bodily signifiers. This shift is also tied to the analyst's evolving recognition of the patient's otherness—the right to secrecy, "the right to conceal her past" (p. 793), without having to conceal it from herself.

Change of minds

Reading McDougall, Stoller, and Quinodoz's theorization on gender, we encounter three enigmatic objects—transference, theory, and dreams—each playing out in the clinical material in distinct ways. These elements create a third space—a space where gender drifts toward abstraction, where its meanings unfold through relation and association rather than position. Yet such movement is fraught. The need for certainty, for a stable ground, presses against it, threatening to foreclose what might otherwise remain open. This same tension shadows the act of reading: an encounter where the wish to know collides with what remains unreadable. Felman suggests that in reading the discourse of the other, one is simultaneously reading one's own unconscious; what is understood hinges on the reader's unconscious involvement with the subject matter (p. 23). Reading is always a 'return of history' (Britzman, 2024), where the act of interpretation is shaped by residues of past experiences—both lived and unlived. For Britzman, residues of love, fear, and choice do not settle neatly; they arise within the ambivalence of what is lived and what remains unlearned—what is misrecognized or never fully known. Transference, too, does not stop at the clinical scene; it threads through education itself. What we have learned—and failed to learn—shapes the ways we come to relate and resist relation. Transference, Britzman (2024, p. 23) writes, is "our means of relationality but also of resistance to that connection." To be affected by the limits of one's experience is no simple matter; it demands a capacity to endure the destabilization that changing one's mind may bring.

Analytic thinking evokes what I call a "wondering mind"—open to ambiguity, receptive to what resists symbolization. Such a mind does not arise in isolation; it carries the impress of the analyst's own history of education and socialization. Psychoanalytic thought takes shape within these pressures, working through the difficulty of giving impressions and reactions a tentative form in speech. Recognizing this history does not prevent meaning from breaking down. In the session, sense-making may slip, and the analyst confronts a paradox: the mind shifts, yet something remains unmoved—the unconscious.

The unconscious gathers like a lint collector—indiscriminately, insistently—pulling in fragments of phantasy, part-objects, stray remains. What it collects resists order, and in doing so, presses upon the scene of listening.

For the analyst, to shift perspective is not only an epistemic demand; it is an ethical task. One must bear the presence of what cannot yet be made sense of, without retreating into the comforts of sedimented knowing. And here, no analytic intervention is free of risk; its consequences remain unknowable, its effects unfolded only in time. The helplessness this invites is not to be denied. It is part of the very openness psychoanalysis demands—a practice turned toward the enigmatic, toward what thought cannot pre-empt. In listening, we do not always know what we are meeting. And it is in that not-knowing that thinking may yet be transformed.

Part III

Matters of concern

This section turns toward those affective intensities that gather in the margins of thought—where something presses, unsettles, insists. These are not always recognized as gendered, yet they take shape in gender's idiom: as worry, attachment, aversion, and the feeling that something matters too much or not at all. Across scenes of therapy, scientific inquiry, ethical surrender, and animated phantasy, these chapters trace the middle registers of agency—the in-between states where knowledge gives way and thought takes shape in another register. Together, they ask how gender becomes a site of concern not because it admits of resolution, but because it continues to move us, unsettle us, and demand a different response.

DOI: 10.4324/9781003440758-10

7   As dialogue

Through reading clinical cases, we enter scenes of vulnerability, uncertainty, and transformation. These scenes are not merely descriptive; they are epistemological provocations, staging the failure of translation as central to psychoanalytic thought. Such failures—whether in language, affect, or the presumed coherence of origin—are not simply impediments to understanding but part of the very structure through which psychic change becomes possible. The failure of origin refers to the collapse of a unifying narrative that would retroactively make sense of the self. What emerges instead is a fragmentation of beginnings, a recognition that what we take as foundational—gender, desire, identity—is already marked by displacement and contradiction. One way to approach these failures is through the concept of "mutual analysis"—not in Ferenczi's literal sense of switching places on the couch but in a more subtle and textual register. Here, mutual analysis refers to an analyst writing their own position into the case—not as master-narrator but as a participant who is also being analyzed by the process of writing itself. What is analyzed, then, is not just a patient's experience but the analyst's shifting location in relation to that experience: how one's thinking becomes interlaced with another's thought, how phantasy and reality blur, and how analytic writing becomes a scene of erotic risk.

Stoller's collaboration with Belle on the writing of her case is an example of this kind of mutuality. Their joint authorship becomes a way of staging analytic intimacy—an intimacy that, as John Forrester suggests, brushes against the experience of sexual intercourse. The case becomes not just a narrative *about* gender or desire but a scene of transference enacted through writing:

> Adopting the position of watching the watcher, thus having the watcher unaware of being watched, is ensuring the director not abandon her. Stoller, in writing his case history, enacted this fantasy for her. Not only did he not abandon her, but he asked her to go over every word of every one of his sentences—she truly became the watcher watching the watcher.
>
> (Forrester, 2017, p. 83)

DOI: 10.4324/9781003440758-11

To have not published the book, Forrester suggests, would have been a failure. It would have been a foreclosure, a refusal to bear the ambiguity and risk of meaning-making in the open.

How strange, and yet how illuminating, to think about analysis as an act of co-authorship between analyst and patient. It challenges the presumed asymmetry of clinical work and writing, destabilizes its singular voice to introduce instead relationality as a site of conflict, endless revision, and erotic charge. Forrester describes Stoller's collaboration with Belle as transformative not only for the patient but also for the analyst. The collaboration between Belle and Stoller proved surprising in its capacity to give birth to new insights and to creating the very conditions for Belle's agency. Belle, Forrester suggests, transforms Stoller into "someone that knows about sexual excitement" (p. 82). Through their collaborative writing, erotic daydreaming is rekindled, and the book becomes a theatrical stage on which the patient's and analyst's "scripts," the erotics of watching and being watched, are replayed but with a newly found retroactive capacity of observing, questioning, and examining the ways in which reality is conspiring with fantasy.

That is also the extent to which erotic charge is linked with the reader, who is affected by the efforts, the striving for completeness, and the "raw material" (Freud, 1937b, p. 258) of what might be called a textual transference. What corners of sexuality become thinkable through this co-authorship? What is revealed about the limits of understanding when analysis is lived through a shared, erotic, and textual space? These are the questions this writing opens for me. If Stoller and Belle stage the scene of mutual analysis, Sedgwick's *A Dialogue on Love* (1999) extends this inquiry beyond the clinic—into a space where understanding itself becomes erotic, uncertain, and transformed by desire—by staging psychoanalysis not as a treatment bound by the frame of the consulting room but as a relational and aesthetic experience that unfolds in everyday life, language, and love. The text is built from her own therapeutic journey, but it is not a case history—it is a hybrid work, part memoir, part poetic experiment, part theoretical meditation. What makes it move "beyond the clinic" is how Sedgwick refuses to reduce analysis to a professionalized or medicalized exchange. Instead, she opens up the analytic process as a site of queer attachment, epistemological risk, and aesthetic invention. The very form of the book—fragmented, vulnerable, lyrical—mirrors the affective complexity of transference and intimacy but outside the boundaries of a traditional clinical setting. She treats understanding itself as a libidinal activity, one that is inextricable from desire, from not-knowing, and from the need to be recognized, thus moving psychoanalysis into the realm of literature, friendship, pedagogy, and mourning. In this way, *A Dialogue on Love* becomes not just about therapy but about how thinking, writing, and relating can all be forms of psychic transformation.

Where Stoller and Belle's collaboration enacts a transference captured within the institutional and medical authority of the case history, Sedgwick's work dismantles that frame—refusing fixed positions of analyst and analysand, expert and patient. The contrast highlights two modes of psycho-analytic writing: one oriented toward stabilizing meaning, the other toward inviting its undoing. *A Dialogue of Love* presents a mode of address that communicates an evolving relationship between a patient and her analyst. As a text, it might be introduced in a classroom as a way to explore how the therapeutic act is represented, opening spaces for rethinking the education of the therapist.

On one level, *A Dialogue on Love* invites students to consider what clinical work entails; on another, it highlights how reading itself can be an experience of affective transformation. If change occurs through making contact in ther-apy, Sedgwick's memoir suggests that change is also produced through the act of writing and reading—through the movement between affect, language, and thought. Sedgwick wrote this memoir at a moment of crisis, when facing a diagnosis of breast cancer while at the height of her career. In this context, reading and writing are no longer supplementary to her analysis but become its very medium. Writing becomes a space where she can hold together the fear of death, the ambiguity of love, and the complexities of identification. The page offers a transference object of its own—responsive, fragmentary, and open to misrecognition. Her writing, always marked by sophisticated self-reflexivity, takes on a new urgency, turning therapeutic experience into a scene of textual becoming, where understanding is not achieved but pur-sued through repetition, citation, and address. In illness, reading and writing cease to be theoretical tools; they become ways of staying alive to desire. Unlike Stoller's work, where analyst and patient co-author a case study, Sedg-wick constructs her own analysis, reflecting on her encounters with a thera-pist who exists outside her intellectual world. A pioneer of queer theory and anti-homophobic thought, Sedgwick's long-standing preoccupations with identity, desire, and power contrast sharply with the analytic reticence of her therapist—a man whose emotional reserve and distance from her intel-lectual and queer lifeworld generate a dynamic tension. Their exchange does not form a co-authored text in the sense of shared construction or mutual agreement. Rather, *A Dialogue on Love* stages the failure of co-authorship—or more precisely, the impossibility of shared language—as its central drama. What emerges is not a jointly crafted narrative, as in Stoller and Belle's col-laboration, but a record of writing across silence, of negotiating meaning in the face of emotional and epistemic asymmetry. Sedgwick's act of writing absorbs, interprets, and reorients the gaps left by her analyst's minimalism, transforming them into an erotically and intellectually saturated text. This is not co-authorship but literary transference: a solo inscription marked by the other's presence, absence, and inassimilability.

Yet, despite their differences, Sedgwick and her analyst enter into a kind of mutuality. In choosing a therapist in a small town, outside the circuits of academia, she may have sought anonymity, although her decision to write and ultimately publish a book about their work seems to contradict such desire. This decision enacts a paradox: the private space of therapy becomes a public text, inviting the reader into an intimate process of meaning-making. The memoir stages the way differences between them are played out, revealing how transformation emerges through the sustained engagement with tension, desire, and the limits of understanding. In this way, *A Dialogue of Love* positions the therapeutic encounter as a site of inquiry—one that mirrors the very process of reading, where knowledge is produced in the interplay of urges, seductions, and sustained questions. Sedgwick invites us into a scene where the analytic and the literary become entangled and where reading becomes an act of mirroring and being mirrored, of recognizing oneself in the text's vulnerabilities and elisions.

My interest in Sedgwick's memoir centers on how change occurs through reading and writing. If *A Dialogue of Love* positions the therapeutic encounter as a site of inquiry, it also invites reflection on the ways in which textuality itself can be transformative. Writing, Derrida suggests, is always shaped by the writer's libidinal investments, and every text carries the author's fingerprints—as a *dynamic* (Derrida, 1978) that implicates the reader, who remains an obscure object in the author's mind. At the same time, my own attempt, as a reader, to grasp the erotic fingerprints of the author is necessarily inflected by my own erotic and affective investments. Projecting my affects to the author's intentionality may, in fact, serve as a defense against reading. As Forrester points out, psychoanalytic writing "is not just about psychoanalysis; it is writing subject to the same laws and processes as the psychoanalytic situation itself" (p. 65). In this way, my own writing about *A Dialogue on Love* is exemplary of the failures of translation—failures to convert affect into concept, to render erotic attachment into academic language, to match Sedgwick's stylistic intimacy with theoretical detachment. These failures are not errors but symptoms—marking the place where the text touches something in me, where reading becomes entangled with desire, with loss, with the limits of my own understanding.

As an analyst, imagining a collaborative project with a patient fills me with a strange mix of anxiety, paranoia, and curiosity. Worries about breaches of privacy, unconscious exploitation, and the constitutive power imbalance between analyst and patient leaves me both disturbed and in awe of these writers' courage and willingness to tolerate uncertainty. The analyst cannot predict the aftereffects of such a writing encounter but can only assess the capacity of the patient to withstand its fate. Stoller's response to this dilemma in writing about Belle was to invite her into the process, allowing her to read, edit, and respond to his text. Sedgwick, too, writes from within analysis, yet her voice resists the role of patient, staging instead a text where transference saturates the page. Yet, writing always entails a form of disguise. What the reader encounters is never a transparent transmission of thought but a surface shaped by omissions, projections, and unconscious compromise. The author reveals more than they consciously know—not because the text emanates directly from them but because it bears the imprint of what cannot be said otherwise.

Reading Sedgwick's carefully arranged emotional scenes, I encounter fragments of writing—lines of poetry, journal entries, transcribed dialogue—that
resist narrative closure. Placed in proximity, they form a new configuration of
what might have happened and of what it means for a reader to receive and
be altered by that happening. By recognizing that I, too, am implicated in the
scene—affected, even *infected*, by the writing and by my own sublimated
voyeurism—I take up an ethical stance, or what Forrester calls the analyst's
"epistemological position" (p. 86). Like Stoller, I find myself in the position of
a participant willing to be transformed by the experience, even if it means tolerating not knowing. In entering *A Dialogue of Love*, I listen as if to a dream.
I witness emotional and transferential situations—scenes marked by dependency, susceptibility, and helplessness. When Sedgwick writes, "That's because
I'm talking. It's like the words are a plug," the analyst's silence becomes a
kind of pressure point, and her words both shield and expose a flood of feeling. The scene unfolds like a dream fragment: elliptical, emotionally charged,
suspended in the space between knowing and not-knowing. These are not
only mental states but libidinal states; they concern affect, phantasy, and
resistance to change as much as they engage conflicts of relationality, social
bonds, and cultural inheritance.

When Sedgwick confesses, "I'm afraid I've made myself too sad ever to
be loved," we encounter not just a feeling but a structure of attachment—
where sadness becomes both defense and desire, a psychic inheritance that
resists surrender even as it longs for repair. The movement between being
affected by emotional scenes and encountering the limits of understanding
reveals how the reader, too, becomes entangled in transference. In other
words, there is no outside to the transference. The reader is caught in the
same dilemma, negotiating the desire to know with the impossibility of full
comprehension.

What I want to underline is that reading, like analysis, is never outside
transference. Just as Stoller was drawn into the scene he tried to describe with
Agnes, so too does Sedgwick draw her reader into an affective relation that
unsettles the boundary between witness and participant. Several points of
convergence emerge between Stoller's and Belle's co-authorship and Sedgwick's uneven collaboration with her therapist. Through their orchestrated
scenes, both Stoller and Sedgwick explore the rough edges of existence—
phantasmatic sexuality, the masochism involved in trying to understand one's
sadistic relationship to knowledge, helplessness, and death. In their own way,
both must surrender the desire for knowledge and control to access something essential about the dynamic between self and other. Each co-authors
a book about therapy, and in both cases, a working alliance makes this collaboration possible. While both texts emerge from the analytic bond, the
difference lies in the structure of authorship and temporality. Stoller writes
retrospectively, retaining control even as Belle is invited in; Sedgwick writes
from within the transference itself, directing the scene even as she is shaped
by it. What appears as co-authorship in each case reveals not symmetry but a

tension between control and surrender, authorship and affect, where writing becomes a site of psychic negotiation.

The position of an analysand writing about her therapy differs significantly from that of a therapist writing about a patient. One key distinction between Stoller and Sedgwick is the sphere in which they operate. Both are educators in their fields—Stoller, as a clinician and professor at UCLA, collaborated with thinkers from multiple disciplines. Sedgwick worked in a much more public intellectual sphere. Unlike Stoller, who was bound by professional ethical codes, Sedgwick enjoyed more freedom in depicting her therapeutic process. Their differences in writing are not only structured by power—who frames, edits, and authorizes the narrative—but also by affiliation: Stoller writes from within the authority of institutional psychoanalysis, while Sedgwick writes from the rawness of lived experience, where meaning emerges amid vulnerability and aesthetic risk. In the latter's writing, the reader encounters intimate descriptions of her sexual fantasies about gay men, her experience of being fat, and her struggles with what she calls "raging depression." In one moment, she writes, "He doesn't say anything. I want him to say something that means he sees me." This line distills the painful asymmetry of the analytic relationship—where the desire for recognition meets the analyst's silence, and where meaning is sought not in explanation but in presence. In such fragments, Sedgwick stages transference not as concept but as experience—where communication is partial, charged, and transformative in its very incompleteness. Despite the differences between the two texts, both narratives illuminate core psychoanalytic concerns: asymmetry, influence, and the struggle to make meaning across emotional and epistemic gaps. In reading representations of analytic encounters, I enter not only the writer's imaginary but also the imaginary of psychoanalysis itself—a field shaped as much by phantasy and transference as by theory. This imaginary, as Britzman describes it, is not whole or coherent but a scene of conflict and longing, drawing on the margins of social life—spaces I can touch or brush against but never fully enter. This, too, is how I encounter my patients' imaginary: not as a destination but as a site of shared disorientation.

Sedgwick's *Dialogue of Love* exemplifies a phenomenological approach that expresses desire in ways that resist articulation—desires that can only be shown through embodied acts, such as a temper tantrum. The tension, between the inarticulable and the written, becomes part of the reading experience itself: we do not grasp Sedgwick's desire as content but *feel it* as disorientation, affective charge, and the pulse of what remains unsaid. This approach is particularly evident in a childhood memory she recounts, where an episode of distress becomes a moment of realization. She recalls being in a store with her parents and sister when her mother buys her sister a doll, then buys Sedgwick the same one.

Sedgwick, who describes herself as a "fat kid," did not want the same doll as her sister's because it was "too small." Overcome with frustration, she throws herself onto the floor in a full tantrum. Relief only comes when she realizes she does not have to accept what is offered to her. She does not have to choose between the options presented. The ability *not* to choose opens the space for an experience of the "depressive position" (Klein, 1940, p. 125)—a compromise. It allows her to let go of the fight and to surrender omnipotence in a generative way.

Sedgwick terms this capacity "a middle range of agency" (Sedgwick, 2011), where introjection (of an omnipotent wish) and projection (onto a frustrating other) are brought into relation. In this sense, the middle range of agency is also a process of libidinalization—a space where desire can be reshaped rather than foreclosed. Her response to the doll, then, is a symbolic act of refusal that opens up a new trajectory of desire. This movement from tantrum to desire recalls Raluca Soreanu's (2018) re-imagination of Ferenczi's *Fort-Da* game: not as a compulsive repetition but as a hopeful solution. As Soreanu suggests, "the child invents and appropriates space—he claims it away from stillness into the movement of his own imagination" (p. 43). Just as Freud's grandson was not the same child before and after inventing the Fort-Da game, the child Sedgwick describes—before and after letting go of her tantrum—is not the same, but it is also not the same Sedgwick who writes it. The self presented in this scene is already a construction—retrospectively assembled, narrativized, and filtered through the adult voice of the writer. What the reader encounters is not a transparent window into past experience but a textual reconstruction that stages psychic transformation through form, memory, and affect. In this sense, the tantrum is not only an event remembered but a scene rewritten—made legible within the imaginary of psychoanalysis and the reader's own interpretive transference.

Much like a dream, a screen memory is not simply a representation of unconscious desire but a new creation—a reconfiguration of identity positions: passive, active, and witness. Sedgwick's recounting of her childhood tantrum can be read as a screen memory in this sense: it stages a scene of overwhelming affect, yet what it remembers may not be the tantrum itself but a more diffuse and unrepresentable longing—for recognition, containment, or survival through disruption. No simple event: the anecdote carries layers that writing cannot settle. The tantrum holds something unspeakable, something approached and lost in the same motion. It is not just a child's rage but the trace of wanting—of the wish to hold, to know, to make meaning yield. The hunger is larger than what can be held, and with it comes the ache of what will not be satisfied. The memory also reveals a deeper refusal: not merely the rejection of the doll but a resistance to passivity itself—to being the one who only receives, who is given meaning rather than shaping it. The tantrum, in this light, becomes an image of condensation, where affect gathers without resolution.

Agency persists, bound up with helplessness rather than opposed to it. Images do not resolve; they linger in partial forms, holding what slips beyond grasp. The text moves through scenes of excess—rape, masturbation, sadism, masochism—yet coherence never arrives. Writing stammers and fractures, showing how desire exceeds what speech can contain. Failure remains in place. At the margins, pressure intensifies: the more peripheral the scene, the more insistently it returns. No single law governs here. Each phrase is shadowed by the unsaid, the unwanted, and the unpermitted until silence intrudes. What emerges is the wish to be enough—and too much—that refuses settlement. Yearning threads the text in broken grammar and charged turns, where love and its prohibitions surface in the gap between the sayable and the unsymbolized. This is not a settled theory but a pulse: a rhythm of attachment and loss that holds briefly before collapse.

Love

What I am concerned with here is the transformation that occurs through an encounter with otherness. Sedgwick is not only narrating; she is writing in the thick of transference, addressing not a neutral audience but a specific, psychically charged interlocutor—sometimes her analyst, sometimes the imagined reader, sometimes a lost or longed-for other. What distinguishes this form of writing is that the addressee is not outside the text but woven into its structure, shaping its form, hesitations, and intensity. This is not simply writing *to* someone—it is writing *with* their presence haunting the page. She is intervening in her own understanding of her experience in therapy, which she calls "a dialogue of love." But what kind of love? This is a complicated question, because love in this context is not a singular phenomenon—it is a structure of attachment and loss, of sexuality and gender, of self-presentation and self-erasure. It is shaped as much by Eros as by Thanatos: a love that consumes, a desire for fusion, a wish to disappear. What we encounter, then, is not a story about love but a literature of libido—a text animated by the drives, fantasies, and contradictions that love brings forth. Perhaps love is an apt way to describe the collaboration between analyst and patient, as they attempt to understand desire and the repetitions of earlier modes of loving. Love in this setting takes many forms: resistance, demand, the fear of taking in, and, in turn, a wish to swallow or be swallowed whole. This is the realm of transference—where projection, dependency, and the volatility of eroticism shape the analytic encounter. But writing about the erotic nature of therapy presents a paradox: writing itself is an effect of sexuality and cannot fully capture it. The act of writing about sexuality is bound by the very limitations that sexuality imposes on language. This presents an epistemological dilemma—one that echoes throughout Sedgwick's memoir. In attempting to articulate experience, we are simultaneously bound by the experience of expression itself.

A dialogue, however, does not necessarily mean harmony. Emotional scenes of frustration punctuate the text, highlighting the urgency of Sedgwick's desire to know—a desire that, paradoxically, obstructs her ability to be affected. Through animated depictions of doubt, disappointment, and her analyst's own admissions of inadequacy, Sedgwick and her therapist enact the dilemma of dependency: the desire to know without having to endure the discomfort of learning. Bion approaches such difficulty of learning as it manifests in arrogance, curiosity, and stupidity—three modes of engagement with truth that reflect our resistance to the fact that meaning exceeds grasp. This dilemma is palpable in Sedgwick's memoir. She watches him closely. The wish to be seen, to have her brilliance known—insistent, erotic, unrelenting. Each glance, each missed word, stirs disappointment, sharpens the longing. The scene turns. Recognition becomes discipline. She wonders: is her wish to "make people smart" a form of punishment? Is knowledge itself a kind of spanking—rhythmic, delayed, charged with dread and desire?

The phantasy will not hold still. It moves—between the therapy room and the classroom, between learning and being punished for learning. Freud's *Child Is Being Beaten* returns here. Submission, wanting, the force of being looked at and not seen. In Sedgwick's evocation, the pacing of therapy—the long waits, the delayed recognition—carries this same pulse. Knowing hurts. It arouses. It punishes. And beneath this, something more unstable: the analytic space as a field of charged gestures, words that pull and refuse, silences that overwhelm as they invite. Learning is not mastery here. It is ache, attraction, refusal, again. The beating phantasy itself is an orchestrated scene—an unconscious attempt by the child to transform a position of helplessness, jealousy, or unfulfilled desire into one of structure and control. In staging the phantasy, the child does not settle feeling. The scene strains—between too much and too little, between what can be held and what undoes holding. Sedgwick's memoir turns through a similar pressure. In the room, the struggle for recognition; in the writing, the attempt to perform what could not be fully seen. The wound remains.

Two people dreaming together—Sedgwick's phrase—yet the scene is marked by unsettled presence and the insistence of asymmetry. Influence moves both ways, though never equally, never clearly. The transference stirs at every point: the wish to affect, to be affected, to refuse. Progress is not the word. Nor capacity. The memoir circles a relation that never settles. There is deadness—"a cat playing with a dead mouse." There is alienation: "the unturbid current that must be his consciousness." And there is a kind of joining, fragile, unfinished: "our absolutely alien mental flows debouch so freely." But even this joining breaks open another division: "The space of Shannon is both me and not." The speaking, too, doubles—toward the other, toward oneself. Toward no final listener.

This dreamy notion of dialogue, to me, raises difficult questions about communication and influence in the therapeutic setting. The space between speaking to oneself and speaking to another is an intermediate position— one that oscillates between regression and transposition. It is a precarious and risky space, marked by the tension between finding and creating meaning—a space that easily lends itself to projection. Over time, the therapist is transformed—not because he or she becomes less "stupid," but because the transferential field shifts, and what was once felt as withholding or opaque is refigured through interpretation, mourning, and the uneven movement toward recognition—but also by developing a tolerance for his own stupidity, his or her own limits. The therapist is continually confronted with the demand to endure not knowing, to resist the rush to interpret to withstand the patient's ruthless attacks. What it means to give oneself over to the incompleteness of this work is a question that haunts analyst and patient alike. It is not a lesson that can be transmitted through psychoanalytic education; it emerges in the wake of failure. The erotic transference—the wish to submit to authority, the longing to be held, seen, punished, reassured—traces both the grounds and the limits of creativity. To theorize experience, here, is already to enter a regressive movement.

Chervet's (2024) discussion of Freud's psychoanalytic epistemology suggests that even the very act of understanding carries a masochistic dimension—for knowledge itself can be traumatic. To think is to return to the place where thought strains, not in order to master, but to bear its slips, refusals, and costs. Theory offers no shield; it circles the wound of meaning, lending structure yet never enough to contain it. In the face of experience, the mind moves unevenly, as identifications gather and pull, as idealizations harden and collapse, and as efforts to link are taken up, resisted, and abandoned. Ambivalence demands more than can be borne, and certainty beckons in its place, yet the work of analysis turns precisely here. To remain with what unsettles is no guarantee, for the pull to retreat is constant, and still the analytic task insists—not on resolution, but on staying close to what cannot be held. To understand this middle range, we must first examine the poles that structure psychic agency. From a Kleinian perspective, these poles are constituted by the paranoid-schizoid and depressive positions—between the longing for an idealized object and the impulse to destroy it. Omnipotence, Klein suggests, is not merely something to be relinquished through substitution (e.g., "Okay, maybe you can't own Mommy, but once you figure out substitution, you can own some other woman substituted for her; and if you get as far as substitution, you can have that same relation to a field of achievement" (Sedgwick, 2011, p. 19)). Instead, omnipotence is both desired and feared, as it poses a threat to loved internal objects and to the self. Sedgwick invites the reader to imagine an analogous situation: "Somebody who arrives on an overwrought scene you're involved in tells you 'It's not all about you.'" She critiques the ideality that underpins narrative structures, describing them as closed systems in which "what goes around comes around" (2011, p. 3). Yet, no matter how compelling our stories may be, our smooth articulations inevitably go "wastefully, farcically, 'off-course.'"

The narcissistic blow of not understanding plays out on both sides of the analytic relationship. Both patient and analyst are psychically structured subjects, and both are vulnerable to the phantasy of mastery—a phantasy that defends against the anxiety of encountering the unknowability of the other. The reader witnesses two complex selves struggling to articulate something. At times, Sedgwick describes therapy as a "strange form of address" that takes shape in her mind as a competitive scene of winning or losing. At other times, the therapist's office becomes a metaphorical womb—"wet," "calm," and "sheltered"—terms that evoke a sense of containment, as if listening to "a quiet, inside voice that is nothing" (p. 123).

What ultimately affects the reader is not just the content of their dialogue but the representation of their labor: their effort to create "a middle range of agency" (Sedgwick, 2011, p. 79)—a capacity to wait, to bear not knowing, to tolerate ambivalence and compromise, to allow for identification without renunciation. This position is beautifully articulated in an associative string of thoughts, underwent as she walks to her therapist's office:

> I can tune my mind today
> to the story I think I want to tell you;
> I can tune my eyes
> Already to your face, listening.
> As indeed I can.
> As I walk, I guess my little smile is enfolding a new thought: when I get inside maybe I'll put these words on a scrap of paper and see whether they look (as they sort of sound to me) like the possible start of a poem.
>
> (p. 123)

What stays here is not an argument but a tone—a quiet turning toward nothingness. Not to resolve, not to explain. A middle range, perhaps: the capacity to remain where no measure can hold, where affect slips the frame. This writing comes through illness, through the slow undoing of certainty. Buddhism moves beneath it—not as doctrine but as a practice of waiting, of not-knowing. To surrender here is not to fall away but to remain—inside obscurity, inside the spacing of time. No comfort in this. No promise. Only the work of staying with what unfolds, without grasp. Rather, it leans on the capacity to endure loss—to live with it, however painful and unforgivable it may be.

The middle range of agency is a fragile but hard-won achievement—a space beyond rigid binaries of dominance and submission, winning and losing. Agency here does not rest. It strains—between the wish for control and the fear of loss, between what can be chosen and what imposes itself. Sedgwick moves through this tension without seeking its resolution. The space is not free of domination or submission. It is marked by renunciations, by losses that shape what remains possible. To act without annihilating—oneself or the other—is not a stable achievement. It is something found, and lost, and found again.

What unfolds is not mastery. It is a field where uncertainty is not refused. Castoriadis writes of autonomy as process—unfinished, always touched by the unknown. For Laplanche, subjectivity itself is threaded through enigma—formed in relation to what cannot be fully known or claimed. In the clinic, this cannot be held as narrative. Loss undoes the hope of cohesion yet makes space for another kind of presence. To remain where contradiction stirs—to wait, to not know—is already a form of agency. Not control, but work: a bearing-with, a staying-near. Sedgwick's surrender here is not a conclusion. It is a movement toward reverie, as Bion would say: holding illusion and disillusion together, without flight into certainty. What comes is not a resolution. It is the chance to meet the past as it rises again, altered by its encounter with the present. The middle range is not about finding definitive answers but about making space for something more—for the quiet, unguarded moment when Shannon's face, Sedgwick's walk, the wetness of the air, or the calm space of the office become not just experience but poetry.

8 Coming to know

There are times when reality confronts us with the limits of what we can bear: aging, war, disability. These are not abstract conditions but deeply affective scenes—scenes of helplessness, where agency often collapses, and the psyche is left to metabolize what cannot be changed. In such moments, the choice is rarely between action and inaction. More often, it is a matter of how to live with what exceeds us. Eve Kosofsky Sedgwick's notion of a *middle range of agency* speaks directly to these conditions. It describes the capacity to hold competing viewpoints, to remain in the tension between control and surrender without collapsing into the fantasy of mastery or the despair of passive resignation. For Sedgwick, this is not a theory of compromise but a psychic mode of being—a way of surviving contradiction without demanding resolution.

To live within this middle range is to accept that understanding is partial and that agency is not about control but about *tolerance*: the tolerance of affect, of ambivalence, of the other's opacity. This notion resonates with a doubled experience of helplessness: first, the unsettling arbitrariness of suffering—its unpredictable arrival and uneven distribution; and second, the sobering realization that some forces—whether psychic or structural—remain unmoved by resistance, whether that resistance takes the form of protest, interpretation, or will. In such contexts, the middle range of agency becomes not a retreat but a method of staying with the world, however broken.

To think further with this idea, I turn to three emotional situations that call for a middle range of engagement: (1) our transference to science and knowledge, which is the focus of Chapter 8; (2) the possibility of reparation under extreme conditions, to which I turn in Chapters 9 and 3; and (3) our intersubjective relationship with the nonhuman, which is explored in Chapter 10. Each of these domains resists simple comprehension. In all three, there is something real—something that cannot be mastered—yet our relation to that real is structured through perception, phantasy, and transference. The challenge is not to *know* but to remain in a relation that does not foreclose knowing.

In both psychoanalysis and education, this means developing the capacity to sit with uncertainty. Freud models this stance in his theory of dreamwork,

DOI: 10.4324/9781003440758-12

where contradiction, displacement, and timelessness do not block under-standing but become its very conditions. The process of metabolization—of slowly registering what has happened and allowing it to take symbolic form—displaces the illusion of direct communication. Without this work, what remains is brute factuality, interpretation, and a flattening of psychic experi-ence into something overly explained, moralistic, or prematurely resolved.

One site where this flattening is especially acute is our transference to sci-ence. Here, Isabelle Stengers offers a crucial rethinking. In *Another Science Is Possible: A Manifesto for Slow Science* (2018) she asks: What makes science intelligible to the public—and why should it be? Her earlier work during the AIDS crisis takes up these questions with urgency, resisting the collapse into panic or passivity. Instead, she proposes *public intelligence*—a mode of engagement grounded not in certainty but in attentiveness to how knowledge takes shape—through time, experience, and the demands of a situation. Intel-ligence, for Stengers, is a matter of temporality. It requires slowing down, not to delay action but to allow ourselves to be shaped by the encounter with complexity.

Stengers describes learning as an aesthetic event—an act of "becoming able to" (2005, p. 1002). This suggests that true understanding is not immedi-ate but requires a shift in perception, a transformation in the ways in which we engage with knowledge. Crucially, she emphasizes that this process of learning is sluggish; it occurs when a situation forces us to slow down and respond differently. Without this slowing down, scientific knowledge risks becoming an empty consensus, where "scientific evidence comes to be equated with a community of 'agree-ers'" (Stengers, 2017, p. 57)—a state where agreement is mistaken for truth. In such a framework, the illusion of objectivity becomes a mechanism for silencing dissent, creating a "united front" (p. 32) that discourages critical engagement. Scientists, in other words, risk becoming *sleepwalkers*, moving forward unquestioningly in a system that prioritizes agreement over inquiry.

For science to take a different form, Stengers insists that it requires a pub-lic capable of independent thought—one that is not under sway, not brain-washed, and thus able to make decisions. She turns to Bruno Latour's concept of *matters of concern* to describe scientific evidence as it is reproduced in laboratory conditions, in contrast to the way it is often presented—as *matters of fact*. *Concern*, she suggests, calls for our imagination, doubt, and hesitation.

> [It] incorporates the notion of preoccupation and choice, but also the idea that there are situations that concern us before they become objects of preoccupation or choice, situations which, in order to be appropri-ately characterized, demand that "we feel concerned."
>
> (p. 21)

The framing of concern is also a way to approach the objects of scien-tific investigation as unconscious and our relationship to scientific inquiry as always bound up with transference—our perceptions, desires, and fantasies. Scientific evidence, then, is not a neutral or self-contained fact but something inherently shaped by the emotional and intellectual investments surrounding it. For instance, research on adolescent gender identity is often read less for its findings than for how it confirms or disrupts existing social narratives. This makes any claim to evidence an issue of dislocation: as soon as evidence is placed in the context of the arguments that led to its discovery, it ceases to be a fixed certainty and instead becomes a *matter of concern*. This destabilization offsets not only the supposed lucidity of matters of fact but also the coherence attributed to the epistemological frameworks of Enlightenment rationality—those ideals that promise transparency, certainty, and progress through reason (Phillips, p. ix).

Stengers is imagining another kind of science—one that remains open to what it needs in order to continually recreate itself. To return to Sedgwick, engaging in this new kind of science would require a *middle range of agency* because it moves beyond the binary of ideality (right or wrong) and toward relationality—the capacity to move in and out of experiences, to surrender to what is beyond our immediate grasp, to doubt, and to let oneself be unsettled by difficult ideas that provoke hesitation when things appear uncontestable. This requires a willingness to loosen one's grip on established paradigms, to imagine alternatives, and to resist the numbing effects of certitude.

Robert Musil's (1995) novel *The Man Without Qualities* provides an image of this resistance: at Diotima's reception, the scientific invitees "smile into their beards" (p. 156) politely, not to learn but to confirm what they already know. Stengers sees this as a gendered dynamic, where certainty is imbued with a phantasy of virility, a form of "masculine heroism" (p. 34). In her view, the rejection of questions deemed "nonscientific" or insufficiently evidence-based resembles the "phobic misogyny of the priesthood" (p. 36)— where doubt is endowed with a seductive, dangerous power that threatens to lead the scientist astray. Underpinning this anxiety is an unrelenting and hurried notion of progress, which feeds on contempt for hesitation or uncertainty, long feminized as signs of weakness, excess, or failure to decide. Any display of doubt is treated as a liability that could shatter confidence—not only in the evidence produced but also in the psychic, social, and political investments it sustains.

These investments operate differently across contexts: within scientific communities, doubt threatens methodological coherence and professional identity; in non-expert publics, it risks unraveling the phantasy of institutional omniscience. From a psychoanalytic view, this phantasy functions as a defense against uncertainty—where institutions are positioned as knowing subjects meant to contain collective anxiety. Against this, Stengers urges an "imperative to slow down" (p. 101). The *middle range of agency* is, in this sense, the capacity to interrogate one's situation—to hold space for a plurality of thought without the urgent need for blind acceptance or rejection in the name of fixed ideals. It resists the demand for rigid certainty, allowing inquiry to unfold as a process of continuous engagement rather than as an assertion of control.

The question of how we come to know what we know is not new to psychoanalysis. As Soreanu notes in her reflection on Ferenczi's proposition of epistemology, the question of what substantiates a social bond in psychic terms is inseparable from the kind of knowledge that allows for mutual vulnerability, rather than domination. This aligns with the middle range of agency: a mode of inquiry that neither clings to certainty nor collapses into disavowal but instead permits knowledge to emerge through sustained, affectively attuned engagement (p. 36). Epistemology, he proposes, is always a libidinalized affair, because the knowledge of an individual or a crowd, as Soreanu notes, "is a deeply political question" (p. 36). Ferenczi refers to the pleasure of analogies, the capacity to "establish a relationship of analogy between two elements that belong to distinct fields of knowledge and strata of reality, with the aim of discovering or going deeper into the meaning of certain processes" (Ferenczi, 1924, in Soreanu, 2018, p. 37). There is an erotic component to knowing, he suggests, because the capacity for objectivity in the attempt to know the other involves a creation of a symbol—an in-between, a shifting orientation that allows for oscillation between being affected by the object and taking distance from it. The creation of a symbol is an example of activating the middle range of agency because it allows for a relaxation from naïve possession or certitude. Here, the symbol functions not as a stable meaning or sign but as a psychic and relational process—a way of holding contradiction, born of disjunction, that invites rather than forecloses meaning. It is structured by a confusion of tongues that is not settled but generates a zone of desire and imagination.

I return to Stengers' conceptualization of and response to the current predicament of scientific discourse through the idea of a middle range of agency—not to repeat the concept, but to underscore its fragility, especially in moments of crisis. While it gestures beyond the binary of right and wrong so often attached to "evidence," this middle range is not easily sustained when public discourse demands certainty, reassurance, or decisive action. The COVID-19 vaccine debate, for instance, revealed how difficult it is to tolerate epistemic hesitation: doubt was quickly cast as denial, and urgency eclipsed the space for reflective, situated knowing. In such moments, the very capacity to think slowly—to imagine knowledge as provisional, affectively charged, and relational—becomes endangered. The *middle range of agency* involves an erotic aspect—not in the sense of an idealized wholeness but in the tension of relationality. It requires bearing with uncertainty, resisting consensus, and surrendering to possibility—to the unpredictability of the future.

For Stengers, *slow science* is not just about speed but about resisting the imperative to always accelerate, to never "waste time," to avoid hesitation at all costs (p. 101). A science that is not hurried, certain, or closed off to unknowability requires care, constraint, and commitment—all factors that involve the responsibility of making choices in the absence of absolute knowledge. The question of agency is embedded in the capacity to see the debates that gave rise to a scientific question as inseparable from how we understand the truths it produces. To regard these results as *matters of concern* rather than as *matters of fact* creates a middle range, one that offers relief from the false certainty imposed by evidence that is presented as self-evident.

This brings me to Stengers' call for *slower* science—the capacity to pause and ask how we have come to know something. The ideality of science within psychoanalysis plays out, in my view, in recent responses to developments in gender, particularly in current psychoanalytic discourses about the transgender child. The question then becomes: how can we have a conversation about *how* we are thinking about trans, as opposed to *what* trans is? This shift is difficult to make because the discourse is already situated within a cultural claustrum of ideality that conflates scientific *evidence* with psychological *facts*. This is particularly striking in recent psychoanalytic engagements with the question of the trans child and the underlying assumptions about the process of coming into gender. Questions about trans identities, especially when concerning children, remain entangled in debates about nature and received notions of the relationship between gender and biology. These debates have mostly been limited to scientific research that seeks *evidence* for and against gender-affirming care, particularly concerning the use of hormone blockers in adolescents.

Rather than entering into the vast debates on transitioning—discussions I have explored in depth elsewhere (Gozlan, 2018, 2022)—I want to focus on the question of transference embedded in the ways in which evidence itself is presented. The question of authority and objectivity are entangled in particular ways. I was recently struck by the way in which the Israeli Institute of Psychoanalysis, where I was invited to speak about transgender youth, framed their questions. Many began with axiomatic statements:

- "Developmental studies show that a basic sense of gender identity develops in the first years of life. Around the age of three, the child is already aware of gender, although before the age of seven, they do not understand gender as stable and tend to believe they can change it . . ."
- "Studies show that a high percentage of cases of gender dysphoria resolve on their own during adolescence . . ."

"Evidence shows." "Science proves." The grammar does its work. It closes the scene. No gap for uncertainty, no place for the question that stirs. The sentence lands as if neutral, but the wish behind it hums. A need for the fixed, the known. A way to still the unease that thought leaves behind. More deeply, they mask the affective and institutional investments that surround how questions are posed and how results are received. In this sense, they convey not only a passive grammatical structure but also a wish for authority—a longing for something stable to stand in for the messiness of thinking. As soon as we encounter the phrase "evidence shows," we enter the realm of fantasy—the fantasy that research can offer a neutral, uncontested truth. For Stengers, research does not simply show something; results are inseparable from what she calls "the enrollment of phenomena"—the ways a researcher's hypotheses, methods, and expectations shape the very conditions of what can appear, guiding inquiry toward some frames and away from others. Stengers argues that much of scientific expertise is "tasked with keeping the anxieties of opinions under control" (p. 31). The objective position of the expert is thus cast in stark contrast to the so-called subjectivity of public opinion. This binary—the split between scientific evidence and opinion—echoes what Kristeva (2009) calls an "incredible need to believe," a form of adolescent idealization in which objectivity is endowed with near-sacred value. In this framework, what is deemed impersonal—that which has no apparent relation to the self—is accorded greater truth.

Yet, as Stengers notes, this idealization of objectivity is not neutral—it is gendered. The authority of scientific fact, positioned against the perceived softness of subjectivity, is endowed with fantasies of control, strength, and dominance. Scientific knowledge, imagined as hard, fixed, and reliable, is contrasted with the formlessness attributed to subjective experience—a contrast long entangled with gendered hierarchies. The devaluation of subjectivity mirrors cultural associations of the feminine with fluidity and excess. Hardness still carries its weight. Certainty, control, mastery—what is claimed as strength—leans masculine. The porous, the shifting, the too-much are cast as feminine, as trouble. These binaries are not only epistemological; they are affect-fueled ideological machines.

Stengers' account offers a possible detour from these rigid oppositions. Rather than defending or dismantling scientific authority wholesale, she invites us to treat science as a *matter of concern*, especially in debates over gender transitioning. This means shifting the question away from *what is true* to *how truths are mobilized*, how concerns and facts co-constitute one another through transference, affect, and usage. In this reframing, we remain with Sedgwick's notion of the middle range of agency—a psychic and ethical position that resists the demand for resolution and instead stays with the textures of ambivalence, contradiction, and partial knowing. Applied to current debates around trans life, this middle range refuses the binary of affirmation versus skepticism, progress versus regret. It asks not what position one takes but how one listens: how one holds space for the difficulty of gender's unfolding without rushing to locate its meaning in either pathology or destiny. It is a stance that neither disavows institutional violence nor treats individual narrative as transparent truth, but lingers in the unsettled terrain between recognition and misrecognition, between desire and social legibility.

In my own approach, the middle range becomes a method of writing, thinking, and clinical listening. It is not neutrality—far from it—but a sustained commitment to what Sedgwick calls "non-sovereign" knowledge: knowledge that can tolerate not-knowing in advance and that resists the foreclosure of meaning. I do not ask what gender *really* is, nor do I seek to decode it as symptom. Instead, I treat gender as a scene—libidinal, aesthetic, phantasmatic—where the subject labors with and through form. The work is not to settle the truth of gender but to stay with its difficulty long enough that something new might emerge. Here, we resist the seductions of biological determinism without denying the real; we pause in the unknowability of what lies beyond inherited frameworks.

The drive to know, to bind, to stabilize knowledge presses insistently. Something harder presses beneath this: the early helplessness Freud evokes—a state not outgrown. When meaning breaks down, Kristeva (2009) points to the ache that follows. The need to shield against what disorients. Certainty, then, not as truth but as defense. A warding off of helplessness. Within this structure, belief becomes less a pursuit of knowledge than a defense against the intolerable uncertainty of not-knowing. Stengers locates this dynamic in group psychology, where certainty becomes contagious—where collectives of "agree-ers" gather not around truth but around the need for stability. In such formations, belief forecloses thinking. Transference is replaced with the demand for affirmation and inquiry with reassurance. And it is this foreclosure that psychoanalysis must resist—not by offering new certainties but by holding space for the anxiety that belief defends against.

This dynamic has implications for how we approach science. If slowing science means situating it within its broader milieu—the tangle of institutional pressures, affective investments, and cultural fantasies that silently contour what can be asked, known, or believed—it also requires understanding the political, social, and emotional structures that shape how a situation, such as gender, is framed beyond the explicit politics of its framing. John Forrester offers a way to think about science not as a fixed entity but as a series of activities, one of which is teaching. Teaching makes science appear clear-cut, but Forrester prompts us to recognize that what counts as science is historically contingent, and therefore, "subject to the gains, losses, and fortunes of history" (Forrester, p. 2). Science is not a singular method but a plurality of methods, and "thinking in cases" is one such approach—one that is central to psychoanalysis.

Thinking in cases involves taking account of one's own history of engaging with a case, a process that resists universalization. A case, in this sense, does not offer a general law but functions as a threshold—an exemplary situation that allows us to think differently. There is a dreamy, murky quality to Forrester's method, one that acknowledges the inherent ambiguity of the single situation and the temptation to arbitrarily foreclose it. In reading a case, we confront the tension between the singular and the universal, a tension that disrupts the certainty that group psychology craves.

Yet, with every choice, there remains a kind of pining anxiety—the fear of an unknown outcome—that returns us to helplessness. Helplessness is an easy place to regress to, forming the basis of trauma: the incapacity to act and the simultaneous loss of meaning. It reduces us to sheer catastrophic loss. In our helplessness, we may regress to what Laplanche and Pontalis describe as a "situation of impotence" (p. 189)—a state of total dependency on the other. In such moments, the authority of research and evidence can take on the force of omnipotence. This is not passive reception but a passion for ignorance, a refusal of the enigmatic, of what we are unprepared to receive. At that point, we become susceptible to materiality—as the reassuring solidity of what appears incontestable. Helplessness makes us vulnerable to belief, to the fantasy that something outside us can resolve what remains unformed within.

Science cannot provide us with reassurance, because emotional situations are irreducibly particular—they cannot be universalized without stripping them of their psychic complexity. Nonetheless, there is a tendency in clinical writing to sustain an authoritative viewpoint. For example, Roberto D'Angelo's (2025) paper concludes with a call for "caution" in affirming gender identity, while the case narrative subtly positions the clinician as the arbiter of meaning, often overlooking the affective complexity of the child's experience. As Forrester suggests, clinical writing often rests on a fantasy—that the analyst grasps the truth of the situation, yet this truth cannot be plainly explained. Instead, it must be staged through the unfolding of the case, preserving both authority and mystery. Forrester complicates our understanding of "the scientific method," not by opposing its foundational skepticism but by questioning how case-based knowledge comes to stand as a site of implicit agreement or normative authority.

"Thinking in cases" offers a relief—especially in light of new narratives of transitioning—because it shows that blind compliance is not inevitable. Something new can happen when inherited explanations no longer hold. Thinking in cases involves a threshold of waiting if one can remain open to a transformational moment in a case, which often manifests in the form of a failure, where an implicit assumption is brought to the fore and demands examination.

A case may offer us "thick descriptions, that are both evocative and informative" (Phillips, xiv), but cases offer us a third position beyond the binary often imposed by scientific paradigms—between objective law and subjective anecdote, because they are "rich in predictable and unpredictable context" (Phillips, p. xiv), and hence useful for analyzing unique and highly contextual phenomena. A case is the challenge to the conceptualizations that renders science intelligible. One has to surrender to a case to be startled by what is transmitted—by what it means and implies beyond conscious intention. Waiting always carries a tinge of uncertainty or helplessness, but it may open a situation in which frustration becomes tolerable, even modifiable. We can therefore say that thinking in cases enacts a middle range of agency in the sense that what is being thought is the importance of conflict, paradox, and incompleteness in the mental representation of an idea. What we recognize in cases are not the situation they describe in and of themselves but our own thinking—our habitual forms of meaning-making, as well as their naturalization.

Lydia Polgreen's article "Born This Way? Born Which Way" (*The New York Times*, December 1, 2023) provides us with an example of what it means to enact a middle range of agency. Addressing the issue of "regret" in the context of trans or gender "nonconforming" children, Polgreen examines the character of the decisions that should or should not be allowed—by children and parents—in gender-transitioning cases. The condition of regret has been intensely deployed in debates, including psychoanalytic debates, to raise concern or argue outright against allowing children or adolescent to make gender-transitioning decisions, such as changing their pronouns, taking hormone blockers, or having gender-confirming surgeries. The youth who come to gender clinics, it is often argued, are frequently characterized by high anxiety, social isolation, and symptoms of eating disorders, among other signs of distress. In these situations, the struggle for the right to choose one's gender is framed as the sole source of distress, such that any other form of suffering is subsequently interpreted as a consequence of that choice. How can the analyst know if this organization is a temporary container, a kind of a "shelter" from other psychic questions or predicaments? What is the justification for giving hormones and gender affirmation at an early age?

Polgreen approaches the question of regret by reflecting on her own childhood decision—not to join the swimming team despite being a strong and promising swimmer. She considers this as a choice she could have taken but didn't, one she sometimes regrets. Regret is ordinary. Children choose—sometimes with guidance, sometimes without. They regret. They move on. Some choices stay with them; others fade. There is no ground that makes choice safe. Nor is there a need for one. Polgreen's reflection stays with this: not every decision can be justified, and not every life must align with the logic of permanence—least of all in matters of gender, where the wish to fix meaning shadows every act. Gender, like choice, lives otherwise. It moves, turns back, and alters; it is never settled. The paradox embedded in gender's *nachträglichkeit* (or "afterwardness") gives it an ethical dimension—like many of our decisions, it is made without fully knowing what it will mean in the future.

And this not-knowing includes the subject themselves: the "I" who chooses is not the same "I" who will live with that choice. Autonomy, then, is always performative—it must be assumed before it is fully understood. What is it that we forgo when we regret a decision? As Polgreen observes, regret is not necessarily a catastrophe but often a road not taken, a place where we say to ourselves, if only I knew. When it comes to transitioning, we cannot predict regret any more than we can predict certainty. Regret does not necessarily mean that a wrong decision was made—sometimes, it is simply part of life.

Polgreen's articulation of regret underscores the impossibility of creating a framework to prevent it, because every case is particular. This returns me to Forrester's *Thinking in Cases*—an approach to science that resists universalization. Every case has its own trajectory, and we can never fully predict how someone will feel about a decision in the future. Even if discontent arises, its origins are not always clear, nor is it something that can be entirely prevented—just as contentment cannot be demanded. As analysts, we must confront the helplessness of our structural not-knowing. We cannot prevent future conflict; we can only listen to the present moment, attending to the suffering, doubts, and conflicts that unfold in real time. Psychoanalysis is not prophylactic. It does not promise certainty or protection from regret. Instead, it engages with the complex narratives of transition: stories of urgency, stories of fulfillment, stories of regret, and stories of defeat. But no story is final. Regret, like identity, is subject to time.

Thinking in cases offers a way of conceptualizing a middle range of agency—one that acknowledges the uncertainty and contingency of experience. Learning, in this framework, is always enigmatic: it is not a linear process but one in which experience precedes understanding, and where clarity is both temporary and subject to time. Thinking in cases demands containment—holding, tolerating, and above all, remaining curious. It also requires us to withstand attacks on the self and on the capacity to link ideas. These struggles are inherent to learning in all areas of life, because learning is always relational—it is a negotiation between the self and the other, between what we know and what we resist knowing. This is why gender, too, can only be understood relationally. It is not a fixed "attribute" of the self but an experience shaped by what is culturally available—by ideals of beauty, norms of desirability, and shifting social expectations. It is also shaped by age, illness, and disability. Gender is not an essence but a temporal and relational experience, one whose meaning can only be made in retrospect. In this sense, the understanding of gender—like the understanding of a case—resists finality.

Both Stengers' and Forrester's approach to evidence, I believe, is closely aligned with the psychoanalytic notion of transference. When problems become matters of concern, we are called to ask: how are we affected and effected by our work? In analytic practice, this is not a rhetorical question—it is a methodological one. It demands that we attend to the ways our own investments, resistances, and desires shape the encounter. This question does not seek to extract a singular truth but instead insists on staying with the tension between knowledge and its object—between what can be theorized and what remains enigmatic in the transference. Like Forrester's *Thinking in Cases*, this perspective resists rigid criteria for knowledge—not by refusing interpretation but by allowing for the possibility that something unexpected may disturb what the analyst thinks they know. For instance, a patient's offhand comment, seemingly unrelated to the analytic theme, may suddenly reorient the frame: the analyst is startled, not because the comment is shocking but because it touches something unformulated in the analyst's own listening. In that moment, the analyst becomes a participant in the uncertainty—not outside it, not master of it, but implicated. This is not a failure of technique but a mark of its ethical potential. It is an approach rooted in negative capability and imagination—an openness to uncertainty that acknowledges the unknowability of these situations and their future trajectories. This requires us to enter the cacophony of debates without immediately shutting them down through the desire to rescue, affirm, sound alarms, or assume the position of the subject supposed to know.

The concept of "middle range" agency offers a crucial framework here, particularly as it relates to analytic neutrality. Much like *Thinking in Cases*, middle-range agency resists extremes—it allows for a stance that neither demands certainty nor collapses into passivity. In the clinical realm, this manifests as the capacity to listen with a "third ear" to the suffering people articulate, recognizing that the sociocultural world—political, historical, and cultural valences that are presented as *facts*—functions as a kind of *borderline concept*. These are not pre-given truths that can be bracketed out but rather an uncanny space that is neither entirely "me" nor "not me."

To approach science slowly requires an awareness of how urgency is created—how time itself is structured within the drive for immediate action. This means inhabiting the uncanny space between knowing and unknowing, between the urgency to act and the unpredictability of fate. If our thinking leans on understanding how we are affected by our work, then this understanding is necessarily contingent upon the capacity to surrender to experience. In submitting to the uncertainty of experience, we must also recognize that we cannot safeguard against the future possibility of either happiness or unhappiness. This is particularly relevant when considering gender transitioning, where the impulse to prevent regret can overshadow the ability to remain open to what we do not yet know. If we become overly invested in rescuing the child from future regret, we risk losing our capacity to wonder. More than that, the very investment in protection shapes the field of decision itself: how the question of transition is approached—by the child, the family, and the clinician—is not separate from the decision's eventual outcome. The affective and epistemic stance we bring to the process co-constructs what becomes thinkable, permissible, and narratable as a "good" or "regrettable" choice. Within this tension—between encountering a new experience and the desire for certainty—we can begin to grasp, in retrospect, the limits of our social mindset. Only by recognizing these limits can we see how our own attitudes shape and potentially disrupt our work.

9   Hospitable enclave

What becomes of the mind when the world divides into a binary: destroy or be destroyed? These are the scenes I gather under the notion of a middle range of agency—not to resolve but to inhabit. In moments of psychic breakdown, the capacity to tolerate contradiction collapses. We are no longer in dialogue with experience but overtaken by its starkness. These moments do not permit slowing down or making sense; instead, they produce a stasis, where all movement—of thought, of feeling—halts. What was once complex now feels monolithic. And in that closing, another tension gathers—not easily settled: what remains at stake here and how might we stay with it? The idea of a "hospitable enclave" names a space—psychic or textual—where such questions might be sheltered. It is not a solution to breakdown, but a site where the enigmatic nature of experience is preserved. To treat an event as layered, as something not immediately legible, is already to resist its totalizing force. Freud's account of the dreamwork becomes instructive at this point, showing how meaning is displaced, condensed, and reconfigured rather than resolved.

Dreams unsettle the very idea of meaning as a finished product. Through displacement, condensation, and reversal, they suspend coherence and hold experience in transit—where what cannot yet be known is turned and set in motion. Here, the wish is not a directive but a trace—something partially formed, something to follow. In the wake of extreme events—trauma, loss, psychic rupture—this dream logic may be all that remains. Meaning fractures; memory pulls against representation. It is toward these states that Dana Amir turns. In *On Revenge, Pardon, and Forgiveness* (2022), she traces the psychic conditions in which the creation of a good object becomes nearly impossible. This is not a work that seeks quick repair. It hovers in the space where the wish for reparation meets the forces of psychic destruction—where the mind struggles to hold what has been broken. What haunts this scene is not simply loss but the difficulty of sustaining a sense of the ordinary when the world itself has turned against it. This question—of whether thinking itself can persist under conditions of extreme duress—offers insight into the horrors of catastrophic events. Unlike the romanticized narratives found in films such as *Schindler's List*, where heroism is foregrounded, Amir's work highlights a

DOI: 10.4324/9781003440758-13

different reality; not acts of defiance but the sheer devastation of loss. The horror is sharpened by the knowledge that no life stands apart from the reach of such events.

The kinds of losses Amir writes about are those experienced as irreparable and absolute. A stark example of such an event is the October 7, 2023, massacre perpetrated by Hamas, in which unspeakable forms of sadistic violence—including rape, mutilation, and the murder of men, women, children, and the elderly—were committed with apparent glee, documented by the perpetrators' own body cameras. In a "living diary"—a reflection "without perspective" published on an Israeli website for healthcare professionals—Amir frames such events through the lens of Jean Baudrillard's concept of the "absolute and irreplaceable event" (2004). These are moments that exist beyond the realm of meaning, where any attempt to explain or contextualize them remains foreign to their reality, diluting their raw horror rather than making them comprehensible.

Traumatic events such as murder and rape, Amir suggests, also attack the fundamental links between love, hate, and knowledge—a formulation that echoes Bion's concept of the disruption of thought. Such events not only empty meaning but actively *assault* the capacity to think. What is also under attack is the relationship to the loved object itself. Drawing on Kristeva's (1989) concept of *objectless depression*, Amir conceptualizes this broken link not as an incapacity to love but as the painful *palpability* of absence. In this state, "sadness becomes the object to which deep longing is directed"—a condition of *love without an object*, in which loss becomes all-encompassing. David Grossman's "Falling Out of Time" (2014) captures this experience vividly: it is a longing that does not seek reunion with the lost object but rather a reunion with death itself.

Building on her reflections on the effects of trauma, Amir turns to the question of how traumatic events are preserved and repeated in psychic life. In her paper "On Revenge, Pardon, and Forgiveness" (2022), she orients her approach to the dilemma of forgiveness around the dynamics of movement, arguing that "the enormous value of the ability to move, in both the intra-psychic and the interpsychic realm, between states" (p. 1112) is essential to psychic life. For Amir, what we care about in the psychoanalytic situation is precisely this capacity for movement—the ability to shift between different psychic states and relational positions. Yet just as important as transformation is the question of what resists movement. If movement is at the heart of psychoanalytic change, then the inability to move—psychically or relationally—reveals the profound effects of trauma.

To speak of such breakdowns, Amir draws on the concept of the hermetic narrative—first articulated in her work on traumatic testimony. She describes it as a

tight, saturated narrative impervious to any intervention, by internal or external forces, that might challenge its absoluteness. Its unconscious

objective is to preserve the traumatic event in its original state, keeping
it both unchanged and isolated from other psychic regions.

(Amir, 2022, p. 1114)

Such a narrative functions as both defense and enclosure. It wards off the disruptions—whether psychic or relational—that might unsettle its coherence.
But this preservation comes at a cost: transformation is foreclosed. The traumatic object, in this mode, does not loosen; it becomes an object that satisfies
by its very immobility—fixed, self-contained, refusing to be touched by the
passage of time.

For both victim and perpetrator, what is lost in the hermetic narrative is
the object of language itself—not as a means of distinguishing, marking, or
negotiating meaning, but as a tool of overgeneralization, erasure, and the
flattening of difference. Amir observes that "when both sides are trapped
in a hermetically blocked narrative, they are erased as singular narrators"
(p. 1117). This loss of singularity—a foreclosure of living dialogue—renders
encounter with the other unthinkable. Hermetic narratives seal themselves
against what might unsettle them. They do not admit ambiguity, nor the third
positions through which conflict might be mediated. In such scenes, absoluteness becomes its own kind of annihilation: not only of the other but of
what relation might yet be possible. This movement of hermetic repetition—
where events are recounted as fixed facts, where experience fractures into
rigid oppositions of "us" and "them"—is not confined to the clinical frame.
It permeates the ways we teach and remember history, the staging of trauma
in public pedagogy (as in Holocaust museums), even the cultural framings
of gender. Here, history does not offer repair. It preserves a kernel of aggression—one that continues to shape how the past is held and how we approach
one another in its wake.

Amir has long been engaged in developing categories for listening, thinking about discourse, and examining the collapse of meaning. Her work on
witnessing and the lyricism of the mind explores the dimensionality of psychic space, questioning both recovery and survival. Central to her inquiry is
the capacity to reanimate or recreate the good object that has been internally
destroyed. In her current paper, she extends these concerns by offering four
distinct approaches to understanding situations of hopelessness, particularly
in the context of political violence and the impasse between victim and perpetrator. Each of these modes of listening, however, carries its own inherent
limits.

The first position Amir traces moves in absolutes: the perpetrator as figure of
evil; the victim gripped by a drive for revenge. It enacts what Benjamin (1990)
names a "doer and done to" structure—where the field is split. Only two positions remain: submission or resistance. The space for thinking collapses; the
scene is lived as compulsion. In this position, both the victim and perpetrator
are trapped within *hermetic narratives*, in which the traumatic event is preserved in its original state—unchanged, isolated from other psychic regions,

and frozen in time (Amir, 2022, p. 1114). Dissociation moves through these scenes: trauma is recited in slogans, formulaic phrases, depersonalized accounts—speech that hollows out agency, leaving the subject untouched by what is spoken. The perpetrator's hermetic narrative—marked by justification, rationalization, or denial—finds its echo in the victim's response, which hardens in turn. Each side turns from the other's wounds. And in that turning, the impasse thickens—what cannot be faced returns as structure.

Amir's second position draws this movement sharply: banal evil on the part of the perpetrator, false pardon on the side of the victim. In banal evil, as Arendt (1998, p. 241) first traced it, acts of profound harm are rendered ordinary—spoken through the language of routine, bureaucracy, inevitability. The perpetrator does not deny what was done; the harm is made dull, stripped of moral force. What was unbearable becomes, in this telling, just another act among many—a move that disavows its psychic weight. Amir describes this as *screen confessions*—a dissociative form of testimony marked by a disconnect between explicit content and implicit meaning. The perpetrator speaks the event but in terms that strip it of weight—casting their actions as impersonal, inevitable. What passes for regret follows the same pattern: gestures of remorse that mask an attempt to absolve. The victim, caught in this structure, offers a pardon that does not seek recognition but works instead to close the scene prematurely. Here, confession and forgiveness play out as performance—gestures that forestall transformation rather than open to it.

Amir's third position is that of guilt and atonement—a dynamic marked by reaction-formation. On its surface, this structure offers the appearance of moral resolution: the perpetrator seeks atonement; the victim holds the power to grant or withhold forgiveness. Yet beneath this appearance, another movement unfolds. The guilt expressed does not lead toward true reckoning. Rather, it functions as a defense—an effort to undo the past, to escape its psychic grip, without fully inhabiting the harm that has been done. Likewise, the victim's power in withholding or granting forgiveness does not necessarily lead to transformation. Instead, both parties remain tethered to a shared perception of guilt—one that acknowledges harm but does not fundamentally alter the psychic structure of either victim or perpetrator.

The last approach Amir proposes is a particularly difficult position—one that I want to focus on as an opening toward a middle range of agency. It asks for something harder. Not apology. Not repair. A forgiveness that opens where harm cannot be undone. The movement is not symmetrical. The one who harmed must risk remorse with no guarantee. The one harmed must live with the wound and the question of whether to release what cannot be mended. There is no clearing the past here. No cycle to complete. To forgive in this way is to loosen the grip of the harm without erasing its mark. The risk belongs to both. Neither can know what will follow.

Amir's account of forgiveness extends beyond Julia Kristeva's (2012) notion of *for-giving* or *for-getting*. Kristeva suggests that forgiveness involves a necessary forgetting—not in the sense of passive erasure but as an active process of transforming past suffering by re-signifying it. I take this as an attempt at psychic reorganization: a struggle to render bearable what might otherwise overwhelm thought. However, Amir's framework pushes this even further. Drawing on Derrida's concept of *pure forgiveness*, she suggests that true forgiveness cannot be conditional—it must not rely on apology, reconciliation, or any form of moral reckoning. It unsettles the very terms of accountability. What would it mean to imagine forgiveness—not as the undoing of harm but as something that moves in relation to what cannot be forgiven?

To deepen this notion, Amir turns to Melanie Klein's insight that external catastrophes always produce an internal catastrophe as well. I see this as a critical shift: it moves us away from thinking of trauma as a discrete event and toward understanding it as a process that unfolds within the psyche. Amir's reading of Klein's *Envy and Gratitude* suggests that forgiveness, like regret, is not just a reaction to harm but something *a priori*, a potentiality that exists before any deed requiring remorse or pardon. This resonates with my own interest in how we internalize and reconstruct good objects after profound loss. If Klein is right, the ability to forgive is not merely about what happens between people—it is about the structure of the psyche itself, about whether we have the *groundwork of goodness* that makes recognition and internalization possible.

Deborah Britzman further elaborates on how Klein departs from Freud's notion of mourning, arguing that adult mourning must *resuscitate* the depressive position first established with the breast in infancy (Britzman, p. 54). I am struck by the way Klein describes this as a psychic process of reconstruction:

> The pain experienced in the slow process of testing reality in the work of mourning thus seems to be partly due to the necessity, not only to renew the links to the external world and thus continuously re-experience loss, but at the same time and by means of [loss] to rebuild with anguish the inner world, which is felt to be in danger of deteriorating and collapsing. Just as the young child passing through the depressive position is struggling, in his unconscious mind, with the task of establishing and integrating his inner world, so the mourner goes through the pain of re-establishing and reintegrating it.
>
> (Klein, p. 354)

I take Britzman's reading of Klein to suggest that loss does not simply happen *to* us—it is something we actively shape through the way we process and respond to it. In this sense, the loss of the breast, as Britzman notes, *creates* the lost object, which then gradually gives way to a new relation—one that makes symbols and an awareness of the other possible. This transformation is what interests me most: the shift from identification based on merging and sameness to an identification that makes space for difference. For Klein, mourning is not simply about Freud's idea of *letting go of the object bit by bit* but also about *rebuilding*—the capacity to enliven or recreate the good object that has been internally destroyed. This, I believe, is what is at stake in the possibility of forgiveness: not just the question of whether it is granted but the psychic work required to make it possible in the first place.

Klein suggests that external catastrophe unsettles the internal world—not merely destroying objects but leaving them emptied of meaning, held at a distance, or stripped of vitality. Amir turns to Klein's conception of reparation but presses it further—toward the difficult work of loosening internal objects from their omnipotence (p. 1280). This means relinquishing the idea that these objects are either the sole cause of suffering or the only possible source of salvation. In doing so, a person can develop a different relationship with the internal object—one that allows for comfort, rather than destruction. Reparation here is not a return to order or wholeness. It is the capacity to glimpse the possibility of goodness, even when violence has marked both inner and outer worlds. This is the foundation of hope: the capacity to see that, even when the external world is full of violence and loss, not everything internally must be annihilated along with it.

To enter Klein's ideas is to engage with a kind of mythology of early psychic development. But when we apply her insights to lived experience, we also encounter the question of selfhood—an ego that is no longer solely dependent on the breast but has the capacity for gratitude, for receiving help, and for helping others. However, Klein was not a theorist of world politics. Her framework centers on the need for internal reparation, the reconstruction of inner objects, rather than on questions of forgiving real-world perpetrators. What is forgiven, in her model, are the unconscious fantasies of destruction that fragment the internal world. And yet, as Amir demonstrates, Klein's notion of reparation remains deeply relevant to situations of political violence because what ultimately needs repair is *the shared human object* (Amir, 2024a, p. 78). This shifts the meaning of forgiveness: it is not merely about absolution but about moving from mutual accusation toward shared grief.

Amir provides a striking example of this kind of reparation through the story of Laura, a student from New York whose father, a rabbi, was shot in the head by a young Palestinian from a terrorist group while on a tourist visit to Israel. Twelve years after the attack, Laura sought out the man who had killed her father. Presenting herself as an American journalist, she entered his family's home, got to know them, and even formed an attachment to them. Eventually, she initiated a correspondence with the attacker. At first, his letters were distant, impersonal, and filled with ideological slogans. But when Laura asked him to share more about his personal life, something shifted—his responses became more intimate, and he confessed that he had come to realize that violence was not part of his true nature (p. 1130). This shift in tone reflected a deeper transformation: by inviting him into a dialogue that acknowledged his singularity, Laura pulled him out of the anonymity that had defined him as *only* a terrorist.

But the transformation was not his alone—it was hers as well. By seeing the human being beyond the act, she disrupted the rigid categories of victim and perpetrator. When the moment came to face him in court, she made an extraordinary decision: she revealed her true identity and asked for his release. Her act of forgiveness was not a passive surrender but an intervention—an unpredictable break in the expected cycle of retribution. Amir suggests that this act introduced a third space, beyond the familiar scripts of revenge or reconciliation. It was an opening—one that challenges our assumptions about what justice, responsibility, and reparation might look like.

In a mindset where the totalitarian erases the possibility of surprise, Amir shows how Laura's act disrupts this closure, opening agency where none seemed possible. In this fourth approach, the relationship between forgiveness and remorse is reconfigured. Here, the perpetrator's remorse is not a prerequisite for forgiveness; rather, forgiveness makes remorse possible. The victim's ability to forgive does not merely respond to the perpetrator's regret— it creates the conditions for it. Conversely, the perpetrator's remorse can also enable the victim's forgiveness. This reciprocal dynamic challenges conventional notions of justice, where remorse and forgiveness are expected to follow a linear trajectory.

What is forgiven here, Amir suggests, is not the individual but the fragile human capacity to remain human—even when humanity itself has been shattered. This is a radical and abstract notion, one that is not rooted in an optimistic vision of peace or reconciliation. It does not rely on seeing goodness in the other but instead insists on the ability to think, to hold both good and bad within the self, even in the face of devastation. By turning the gaze inward—rather than making forgiveness contingent upon the perpetrator's remorse—the victim engages with the broader human condition as the true object of forgiveness. I view this as the most radical form of ethics because it requires transformation within the victim that is not dependent on the actions of the perpetrator. In this third space, both forgiveness and remorse become possible, but neither is causally determined by the other. They emerge not from obligation or expectation but from a shift in perspective that allows both victim and perpetrator to exist beyond the rigid binaries of guilt and absolution. Yet, Amir suggests, forgiveness is also a form of revenge. She quotes Laura as saying:

> This, at the end, was my revenge. Not an eye for an eye and not turning the other cheek. I discovered a third way: complete change. Revenge is not always the elimination of the enemy. It can also mean a complete change in him or in yourself.
>
> (p. 402)

This perspective reframes revenge not as destruction but as transformation—a disruption of the cycle of violence that does not erase the crime but refuses to let it dictate the future.

The loss caused by murder differs from the losses that arise from life's contingencies. It is an intrusion, a violent theft of a loved one, leaving a void filled with terror and hatred. Laura's revenge is that she can let go of that terror. The best revenge, she suggests, is to say, *I forgive*. But this is not a naive forgiveness that erases the crime or its sadism. Instead, it is a forgiveness that halts the repetition of violence—the endless return of the death drive. Once an object is split into good and bad, and these parts are kept irreconcilably apart, Klein argues, what emerges is the logic of war. Splitting itself is an act of aggression, a force of destruction. But, as Klein emphasizes, the object is never merely a thing—it is always a *relationship*. Amir builds on this, arguing that the broken link of love is not only reflected in the loss of the actual beloved but also in the loss of the symbolic object of love. "Hatred," Amir suggests, "goes beyond the object. It becomes a sweeping, blind drift for which hatred itself—and no other goal—is its only horizon" (Amir, 2018, p. 45). In this sense, the vengeance one takes on another never truly provides relief. It merely feeds into the culture of the death drive, where violence perpetuates itself indefinitely.

The revenge of forgiveness, however, is of another kind. It is situated in a middle range between trauma and creativity: the ability to hold on to one's mind, to endure the intolerable injustice and the helplessness it brings, without surrendering to murderous rage. It is a refusal to let hatred dictate one's existence. It is, ultimately, the assertion that even in the aftermath of destruction, another way remains possible. The process of creating a good object from the devastation of loss, for Klein, hinges on the mind's capacity to sustain an internal object relationship. If this is a relationship, then the central problem becomes: how does one reconstruct a good internal object from the split between love and destruction? In such impossible conditions, this fragile link to symbolization endures. Amir recounts the case of an eight-year-old survivor of the October 7 massacre who recited a children's poem while hiding for 17 hours in a coffin near the murdered bodies of his parents and sister. The poem, *Anat Says to God in the Evening*, ends with the lines:

I'm so tired, and already under the covers.
And thank you very much from me and my whole family.

The boy could not say why this poem surfaced. Later, he spoke of it as a kind of protection—something that held him through the unendurable. Amir suggests that beyond the soothing effect of the words, the poem functioned as a kind of temporal anchor—a way of preserving continuity between the past and the possibility of a future. The memory of the poem did more than restore a lost good; it gave him a vantage point from which to look upon his own suffering (Amir, 2024b)—a way to hold what might otherwise have remained ungraspable. Addressing God—a parental figure—as a witness to his pain allowed him to create meaning in a situation designed to obliterate it. Through the "broken formations of thinking and speech," the boy established what Bion (1965) would call a *vertex*—a point from which he could observe himself. In Civitarese's terms, this act of speaking achieved "a spatial-temporal discrimination," allowing him to maintain a link between past and future. By turning to an imagined other, Amir argues, the boy not only reconnected with the lost parental figure but also carved out a space in which something human and alive could still exist.

Amir shows how the aim of such attacks is not only to harm but to saturate the world with pain—so overwhelming that it breaks the capacity for thought. This is what psychic destruction enacts: not suffering alone but the collapse of cohesion, the undoing of meaning. In the aftermath of unbearable trauma—and in the hunger for revenge—a deeper force stirs. It is not thought that is sought but its erasure; a hatred of thinking takes hold. And yet, thinking—slow, hesitant, unfinished—enables us to endure helplessness. The boy's repetitive recitation of a poem, addressed to an Other, evokes Freud's concept of the *Nebenmensch*: the nearby human figure, neither engulfing nor abandoning, who first helps the infant give shape to experience. As Britzman (2024) notes, Freud linked this figure to the origins of psychic life—the one who responds to helpless cries, incontinence, hunger, and bodily urgencies as if they were calls for meaning and love. The *Nebenmensch* is not a figure to be grasped; it is the first thread between need and symbol, between pain and the uncertain hope of recognition. Britzman takes up this early dynamic—the cry and its unanswered call, the wish for care that haunts the formation of psychic life. The *Nebenmensch* is not an idea to be held; it is a texture: a touch, a murmur, a breath in the dark. The boy's poem, like the *Nebenmensch*, offers a likeness—a rhythm, a continuity of human presence even when the world has broken.

Thinking with Amir's account of the boy, I'm drawn to Winnicott's idea of being alone in the presence of another: that paradoxical state in which solitude is possible only through internalized relation. Amir extends this into a new conceptualization of witnessing—not the literal observer, but the *internal witness* sustained through fiction, poetry, music. Here, the *Nebenmensch* becomes a shape in the mind, a trace of care located not in the actual but in the felt. For the boy, the lullaby-like cadence of the poem offered more than comfort—it became a way to hold onto life in the face of annihilation. The address to the Other folds into an address to the self. In reciting the poem, the boy improvises an internal witness, linking past and present, grief and survival. Amir calls this "a second chance of putting thoughts together."

The presence of an internal witness unsettles the scene—opening the possibility of a different relation to the self and the other. It interrupts what Scarfone calls the "deadly repetition" of Lacan's Real—that which evades symbolization and returns untransformed. The ability to sustain a relation to the memory of a non-persecutory other lays the groundwork for a new psychic object. This is not mere survival; it is the beginning of transformation. Improvisation enters here—not as aesthetic flourish but as a mode of psychic labor. The boy's unconscious retrieval of the poem becomes a symbolic act, much like the mother's voice transmuted into an internal object relation. Trauma arrests time—what Green called the collapse of temporality—turning into what always happens, what never stops. Yet the improvisational act—speaking, repeating, reaching—strains against this paralysis, unsettling the fixity without erasing it.

Amir invites us to rethink witnessing altogether. In the face of atrocity, what does one witness? What remains when language collapses? What becomes possible is not witnessing as representation, but the fragile maintenance of an *associative track*. For Bion and Klein, thinking itself is linking—between inner and outer, now and then, self and world. Klein names this movement between persecutory and depressive positions: the painful integration of fragments into something newly livable. Through the boy's recitation, we witness the formation of an internal *Nebenmensch*—a memory trace, a psychic echo, an improvised bond to continuity. The poem becomes a bridge, resisting rupture, holding suffering in a shared world. Scarfone (2015) shows that the Real insists, always returning unless transformed through symbolization. The boy's poem, like Laura's gesture, does not undo the trauma but inscribes a difference that makes thinking possible again. It links what cannot be reconciled, makes livable what cannot be undone. And here, improvisation—whether in the form of a remembered poem or a gesture of forgiveness—becomes a method of survival. These are not reconciliations with horror but refusals to collapse into it. They are, like Proust's Madeleine, fragments of the past that open a future. The cookie crumbles, yes—but in its crumbling, something is formed: a rhythm, a link, a path toward living with what remains.

10 Phantasm

I want to turn to a different social scene—our intersubjective relationship with the nonhuman, in a way that unsettles our assumptions about gender, desire, and representation—to think again about what it means to inhabit a middle range of agency. This scene does not take place in the clinic, nor in familiar spaces of Western psychoanalytic discourse. It unfolds through a specific genre of Japanese anime, centered on the figure of the Beautiful Fighting Girl: a stylized, often prepubescent, hyper-feminized character who becomes the object of intense sexual phantasy. The attraction to these figures—expressed through drawn images, dolls, and digital avatars—has given rise to a subculture known as Otaku, composed mainly of men, but also of women, who invest their desire in what is, ostensibly, a fantasy of unreality. Saito Tamaki, a Lacanian psychoanalyst and psychiatrist, takes this phenomenon seriously. In his remarkable book *Beautiful Fighting Girl*, he explores not only what these fantasies reveal about Japanese masculinity and sexuality but also what they teach us about the structure of phantasm itself. Saito's work refuses to treat this subculture as pathology. Instead, he opens psychoanalysis to an encounter with cultural phantasm, asking how desire attaches itself to the *not-quite-human*, and how sexuality can be lived in and through mediated forms that never quite touch the real. In doing so, he stages a version of psychoanalytic phenomenology—one that listens to gender and fantasy as they are lived through aesthetic detours, virtual attachments, and the refusal of adulthood.

Saito is also known for coining the term *Hikikomori*, which is also the title of his first book, meaning "withdrawal," to describe adolescents and young adults who retreat from social life, refusing work, school, or conventional relationships. He calls this condition "adolescence with no end." While it might resemble depression, it does not follow a linear trajectory of trauma or loss. Instead, it names a temporality of suspended development, where the social world becomes too intrusive, and the phantasm becomes a safer scene of self. Saito's writing brings together psychiatry, Lacanian theory, and cultural critique to ask a difficult question: what does it mean to desire without presence? And what kind of psychic survival is offered by the beautiful but untouchable figure of the fighting girl?

DOI: 10.4324/9781003440758-14

In his later work, *Beautiful Fighting Girl*, Saito extends this inquiry into another form of withdrawal—one that diverges from the passivity of Hikikomori through its imaginative intensity. Here, the figure of the Otaku emerges: not fully social, yet not entirely isolated. While Hikikomori withdraw into silence, Otaku displace their relational attachments onto animated worlds, cultivating deep affective investments in anime characters, particularly the beautiful fighting girl. This is not just escape—it is a form of sublimated relationality structured by phantasm.

The Otaku's engagement is immersive and highly structured: fan conventions, elaborate collections, even romantic identifications with fictional characters. What appears as detachment is, in fact, a highly charged erotic relation to an aestheticized world. The anime boom of the 1980s offered a phantasy architecture that held psychic life amid economic uncertainty and shifting gender norms. And within this architecture, the beautiful fighting girl emerged as a central figure—unmissable in her stylized blend of childlike innocence, androgynous sexuality, and supernatural strength. Often depicted as young girls with power that exceeds their adult male counterparts, characters like Sailor Moon and Minnie-May blur the boundaries of age, gender, and agency. Seventeen-year-old heroines are drawn to appear no older than thirteen. From a feminist perspective, this visual and narrative trope could be read as subversive: young girls who refuse victimhood, who transform vulnerability into strength. Yet Saito complicates this reading. He suggests that the uniqueness of the beautiful fighting girl lies not merely in gender politics or representation but in her function as phantasm—as a structure of desire that stabilizes the Otaku's relation to a world otherwise too fraught to inhabit directly.

For Saito, the true significance of the beautiful fighting girl lies in two realms—her reception and her autonomy—both of which highlight a deep connection between fiction and sexuality. She circulates as a figure of sexual fantasy—desired, consumed, produced in turn by the men (and some women) who animate her image. In some cases, the fantasy crosses into ritualized attachment: life-sized dolls modeled after favored characters are purchased, wedding ceremonies staged—acts through which the imagined relation is given bodily form. But Saito argues that the Beautiful Fighting Girl is not merely a reflection of women's status in society, nor simply an idealized fantasy of femininity. Rather, she functions as an autonomous object—her existence confined to specific media forms, such as anime, manga, and video games, without seamlessly transferring into literature or film. This containment, he suggests, reinforces her status as a uniquely constructed entity rather than a direct representation of real-world gender dynamics.

Otaku itself is a term that moves through fractured meanings. In some readings, it marks a distinct aesthetic and imaginative sensibility—a capacity to form new, often urban, communities (Eiji and Morikawa). In others, it is pathologized: a figure of withdrawal and arrested development, linked to the Hikikomori who retreat from social life in prolonged adolescence. Their pull toward childhood figures, coupled with their refusal of conventional social structures, stirs deep cultural suspicion. Here, Otaku becomes a condensation point—a figure through which anxieties about gender, sexuality, development, and pathology are projected. As Ortabasi (in Saito, 2011) writes, Otaku is both a lived identity and a media construction—a site where broader social fears crystallize.

Rather than focusing solely on the Beautiful Fighting Girl or the Otaku subculture that idolizes her, I turn my attention to Saito's relationship to the phenomenon and his mode of theorization. What I find particularly compelling in Saito's writing, at least in the essays and books available in English, is his method of engagement. Saito resists the pull to diagnose, to moralize, to close the scene with ready interpretation. Instead, he remains with Otaku culture in its strangeness—letting it press upon him without the scaffolding of familiar frameworks. What he offers is not an explanation but an opening: a way for readers to meet what remains foreign without rushing to domesticate it. This refusal to impose certainty or ideality is, in itself, a form of creating what I call a middle range of agency—one that avoids the defenses of regimentation or omnipotence and instead stays with the unknown.

Saito writes from a place of disorientation. The experience of Otaku unsettles his capacity to empathize, to locate a familiar psychic scene. What compels him is the force of a question that will not quiet: *How does arousal attach to what is not real?* His work is less an effort to explain than to remain with this disturbance—an inquiry into the forms of experience that resist immediate sense. To move from what is familiar to what is unknown requires a willingness to enter as a vulnerable subject, what Togashi (2019) calls the "psychoanalytic zero"—the capacity to surrender to uncertainty, to momentarily suspend context, and to resist the impulse to categorize. This position entails what Britzman (2024) describes as a commitment to *radical humanity*—a stance that Togashi articulates through his own clinical experience: "I had to accept the radical incommensurability between us—through which, ironically, we could become equally human" (p. 37).

Beautiful Fighting Girl, in my view, intervenes in the fraught discourse on Otaku by enacting this very stance. Saito's refusal to pathologize, his ability to dwell in uncertainty, and his insistence on describing rather than defining offer a way of encountering difference without reducing it to moral or diagnostic terms. In doing so, his work opens a space for thinking beyond binaries—between reality and fantasy, pathology and creativity, self and other. Saito shows a dimensionality to the situation of the fictional fighting girl. It primarily involves the Otaku, but, surprisingly, Saito also includes the filmmakers who present the scene of the fighting girl and the viewers who participate in it. Here, we could include ourselves, the readers. Rather than attempting to diagnose or define Otaku as an identity, Saito focuses on depicting its function. He reconstructs the origin of the anime character of the beautiful fighting girl as a traumatic moment for the animator Miyazaki, the creator of many of the animation works that feature beautiful fighting girls.

In Saito's view, Miyazaki's arousal response to the drawn figure became a primal scene and a source of anxiety, precisely because this arousal to an impossible, nonhuman figure happened against the animator's will. Using a Lacanian framework, Saito interprets attraction to anime as a response to the unanswerable question of sexuality, which is always felt as "other"—an irreconcilable difference: "what does the other want from me?" The impossibility of the anime figure, he suggests, "contained already within her the occasion of loss" (p. xi). It became, in other words, a source of repetition compulsion, as the attraction to this fictional figure echoes an unresolved tension. This, in Saito's mind, explains the proliferation of the beautiful fighting girl. He sees this structure of attraction to an object that 'threatens to dissolve into fiction' as a universal feature of desire. Sexuality, he suggests, always draws on fiction, a situation where the boundaries between reality and fantasy blur.

Reading Saito's book, I see a clinician who is able to engage with the imaginary in an entirely new way. By asking what it would be like to fall in love with a cartoon, Saito moves into the dilemma of the dynamics of desire: object relations, defenses, wishes, anxieties—all those things operating simultaneously and shaped by affect. Anime, he suggests, embodies an emotional dilemma—an overload of images—that is expressed culturally as an attempt to resolve it. It is a strategy by which the Otaku can experience and conceptualize desire in reflexive and performative terms. His approach to Otaku allows for a portrait of experience, capturing the dilemmas of desire and loss—a relation to the "impossibility of objects" (idealized objects of desire) that cannot be possessed or fully known, signified as "this woman I cannot even touch" (p. xvii). Beautiful Fighting Girl is an interesting example of how the uses of experience, by blurring fiction and reality, create an intersubjective realm.

From Saito's perspective, the fighting girl is not a reflection of reality but a way of investing in a new reality. Otaku, in this sense, do not struggle to distinguish fiction from reality; they do not treat their figures as real but as objects of use—images to be played with. They are able to see fiction, Saito argues, as a question of dimensionality and take pleasure in it. What Otaku's relationship to the figure of the fighting girl allows us to conceptualize is a notion of reality as always mediated by fiction. The Otaku's capacity to hold on to their "transitional objects" is instructive. Saito (2011) suggests that studying this phenomenon may help us learn "how to survive and flourish in our media-saturated (and now AI-drenched) environment" (p. xv).

A thin line

Fiction and reality do not stand apart in Saito's account. Their relation is one of entanglement, not opposition. Fiction, he suggests, is already a condition of reality, and the ideal of adaptation to "the world we live in"—often judged by how well we accept it—is perhaps psychology's greatest fiction (p. 22). This is not merely a provocative claim; it cuts to the heart of how subjectivity is structured. It is this entanglement of fiction and reality that psychoanalysis has always insisted upon, even if psychology at large prefers to forget it. I find this particularly resonant when considering how psychological narratives often rely on a notion of "adjustment" to reality, without accounting for how reality is structured by fictions of its own. The complexity lies in the idea that our mediated experiences may reveal something deeply real about us, even as so-called reality is always already mediated. The so-called real world is not a neutral backdrop but is already shaped by unconscious phantasy, symbolic mediation, and narrative imposition. This is not simply a question of theory. Saito gestures toward something more insistent: a condition through which psychic life must pass, again and again. Fiction's boundaries are only legible if we disavow the constitutive fictions underlying reality itself. Freud's notion of transference underscores this as the very ground of intersubjective life. From this perspective, fiction is not an escape from reality; it is reality's most rigorous expression. To insist otherwise is to cling to a fiction of stability far more fragile than we might like to admit.

In many ways, *Beautiful Fighting Girl* is a peculiar book. It includes letters from theorists who hold perspectives different from Saito's, as well as a chapter that presents an argument between Saito and another scholar who contests his observations. The book itself, in other words, has a polyphonic structure. It incorporates multiple viewpoints, and Saito positions himself as someone trying to learn—while also acknowledging the limits of his ability to fully enter this world. His study draws on both qualitative research in the form of interviews with Otaku and an analysis of the artistic work of Henry Darger, an outsider artist known for his obsessive drawings of sexualized children. Saito's interviews were an attempt to understand an emotional situation he found difficult to grasp. What he learned from speaking with Otaku was that their emotional attachment to their beloved figures differed significantly from what mental health professionals might term "obsessive" or "maniacal." The distinction Saito draws relates to the nature of their emotional investment. While an obsessive admirer idealizes, preserves, and "protects" their figures—often to the extent of refusing to sexualize them (e.g., seeing masturbation as a "dirty" act)—the Otaku, he observed, exhibit a more "dispassionate" attitude. As one interviewee describes, "Being an otaku means being able to play around a little with the works you like; if you sanctify and worship them too much, you've fallen to the level of a mere maniac or fan" (p. 37). Unlike an AI operating system, the beautiful fighting girl does not reciprocate affection, send emojis, or profess love. There is no echo that returns to the otaku.

What Saito's study also addresses, however, is the condition of learning about another's emotional situation. As Britzman, drawing on Adorno, insists, this process "begins by addressing subjective life at the level of intersubjectivity. Reaching the other must lean upon coming into contact with the fragile and creative aspects of intersubjectivity" (Britzman, 2024, p. 46). If the analyst is also affected by what they are trying to understand, then Saito's initial difficulty in empathizing with Otaku can be understood as a form of transference. His method—engaging in intimate interviews with individuals identifying as otaku and writing about the experience—becomes the closest he can get to understanding their world. In doing so, he seeks to grasp their sexuality without losing his own conceptual grounding. His "middle range of agency" (Sedgwick, 2011), then, might be found in his sustained curiosity about his own relationship to this situation.

If Sedgwick's concept of middle range of agency has multiple dimensions, one of them, I believe, is demonstrated in Saito's ability to pause and observe rather than anticipate or predict. His capacity to hold a transitional space without collapsing into the urgency that compels splitting is striking. As I read his book, I feel immersed in something that resists easy understanding. It activates my own desire for stabilization through diagnosis, alongside the frustration of passivity in *not* knowing and the urgency—or even hyperactivity—of trying to know. Yet Saito's writing reflects a keen awareness of the ways clinical discourse often attempts to force coherence where there is none. His sensitivity is evident in the way he works with ideas, resisting the impulse to use them as a means of stabilizing an experience prematurely. This tender approach is particularly apparent in his discussion of Henry Darger (1892–1973), an "outsider" artist whose life bore striking similarities to that of Hikikomori— reclusive, melancholic, and lacking ambition. Saito describes Darger's art as embodying a "naïve and self-authorizing innocence" alongside horror and unsettling sexuality. Yet, rather than pathologizing Darger, Saito's focus is on understanding the artist's sexuality. His approach invites a different kind of inquiry—one that allows for a *portraiture* of experiences of loss, exclusion, and oppression, particularly where translation fails. He asks: where do such experiences move? Where do they fall? What do they hinge onto?

Saito's writing animates an attempt to "climb" inside Darger's head through studying his writing and, especially, his drawings. The drawings, Saito observes, do not depict explicit sexuality with children, but in the scenes of violence, sexuality gets full expression: "atrocities committed on the little girls appear to be motivated by sadistic impulses." (Saito, 2011, p. 62). The scenes have clear fingerprints of pedophilia. The young girls in Darger's drawings have something in common with the beautiful fighting girl: they possess penises. Darger, Saito notes, clearly knew the anatomical difference between boys and girls and was never actively engaged in pedophilia in real life. His perversion, Saito writes, is "quite modest." To call Darger a "pervert," he suggests, "would not be very meaningful" (p. 76). What fueled Darger's capacity to create a new "realm" of fantasy, Saito argues, were sexual fantasies of his adolescence that were not far away from the brutality he had witnessed as a child: "He simply recorded the world as he saw it" (p. 79). Yet Darger's technique, Saito states, reflects a "simple faith in the possibility of using images to rival reality" (p. 74). What the youthful phallic figures reflect, in Saito's view, is Darger's own desire to remain a child; to stay forever "pubescent" (p. 75). His "adolescent mentality" (p. 76), he argues, did not only contribute to his difficulty adapting to adult life. It also "fueled his creativity."

We may describe Darger as someone who is attempting to preserve what Saito calls *"adolescence without end"* (Saito, 2013) or, as Otaku. But there is also a creative side to adolescence, which Julia Kristeva (Kristeva, 2009, in Gozlan, 2022b) portrays as "a time of heightened pliability, experimentation, creativity, and doubt." It is also tinged with obsessionality; what Saito calls "addictive quality" (p. 76) and magical thinking. To understand Darger's particular sexuality clinically, Saito suggests, we would have to study his life, and it is in this reading of Darger's work that he returns us to the question of the beautiful fighting girl as universal dilemma of relationality: the idea that we always think through fantasy in relationships. But the profound insistence that Saito makes is also one of randomness—"what happened to Darger, he suggests, could have happened to anyone" (p. 76). How anyone ends up a certain way is a question of randomness. Randomness, as Togashi shows—the capacity to "accept the radical incommensurability" (Togashi, p. 110) between self and other—that allows the analyst to imagine the other's situation, within the randomness of life, as one that could have been one's own.

Dispassionate stance

Saito, in my view, is not necessarily taking a neutral stance in relation to Otaku or Darger. He positions them close to Hikikomori and clearly understands the isolative, reclusive nature of their perverse, masturbatory relationality—or defense against it. However, what makes his approach uniquely human and closer to a middle range of agency is his capacity to treat difficult concepts like perversion with nuance. He acknowledges their negativity but also recognizes their generative potential. His ability to see Otaku's and Darger's sexuality, for example, as both creative and transgressive brings us back to Freud's notion of sexuality as inherently split: it can never be a unitary experience because meaning is always deferred. Its bi-phasic structure ensures a resurgence of infantile sexuality after puberty, allowing for a rich and complex sexual life. It also positions perversion on a spectrum rather than as a fixed pathology. In this context, the attraction to the fighting girl can be understood as a pure fantasy of phallic *jouissance*—a refusal to accept that an inanimate object is not alive. From this perspective, the attraction functions as a "badge" of perversion. Yet, the beautiful fighting girl is also an "as if" figure. As Saito's interviews suggest, the disavowal inherent in the Otaku's attraction is a momentary loss of judgment—an important mechanism for imagination. The momentary loss of reality is not experienced as a true loss.

Saito's depiction of Otaku presents sexuality as a kaleidoscopic scene: an attraction to a fictional figure is not necessarily a site of pathology. Rather, if we are willing to shift our perspective, we can recognize perversion as an inherent aspect of human sexuality. Sexuality, Saito insists, already has an "as if" quality. Is it not the case that sexuality is, in some sense, its own manipulation? If we pause to reflect, sexuality is a way of being alone in the company of another. In this way, it provides a momentary suspension of ordinary life. There is both intimacy and privacy, fantasy and willingness, excitement and tension. Orgasm functions as a perfect Freudian moment of the drive—it seeks release. But once we re-enter everyday life, that animation of the body is subdued. While we are also animated when experiencing fear, surprise, or pain, these are not the same as the pause that sexuality permits.

One way to read Saito, then, is through this kaleidoscopic lens: the spectrum of perversion experienced by Otaku, like other experiences of sexuality, should be acknowledged rather than pathologized—so long as it does not escalate into violence. Perversion is not outside psychic life; it is of it—animated by the force of our libidinal investments, which give it texture, pressure, and shape. To encounter a fantasy that seems foreign, such as arousal drawn to a doll or an animated child, is also to brush against the limits of what we can admit to knowing. For many Western readers, such attachments provoke discomfort, even disavowal. Yet this is not uncharted territory. As children, we have all known such scenes. Dolls, stuffed animals, cartoon figures, action figures—these were objects through which desires moved, where separation anxieties were calmed, where sexuality was tentatively staged. These early not-me possessions were neither fully other nor fully self. They held the space between wish and impossibility, reality and fantasy—objects one might abandon or reclaim without mourning.

Yet adulthood is often imagined otherwise: as a severing of these attachments, a demand that maturity be marked by the shedding of childhood desires, psychic bisexuality, and the polymorphously perverse. The psyche resists such linearity. Freud held that polymorphous perversity is not confined to childhood; it persists as a structure within human sexuality. The psyche does not map neatly onto the body. Sexuality exposes a deeper disjunction, revealing the subject as split. In this light, Saito unsettles conventional boundaries between perversion, fantasy, and desire—not as pathologies to be overcome, but as elemental features of psychic life.

The split in the psychical sphere of id, ego, and superego is one we commonly consider, but splits also emerge in the gaps between desire, limit, and reality. Winnicott's idea of transitional objects touches on this gap with the notion of an intermediate space between reality and fantasy, which allows a transition in relation to the object; a move from object relating (an aspect of perversion) to object usage ([1969] 2001). The shift away from the subjective object to placing the other "outside the field of subjective phenomena" (p. 87) occurs within what Winnicott imagined to be a third area of living between psychic reality and outside reality—culture—in relation to the transitional object. The area of culture is both created and found, made up of inner and outer reality, real and hallucinate: "it is real and would have been there even if it had been neither conceived of nor conceived. This is mad" (p. 58). The third space, Winnicott suggests then, is not continuous with the infantile space of the mother's "madness." It is an area of both difference and sameness, but there is a new formation that leans upon the capacity to play.

Psychical reality in this sense is not far away from illusions, phantasies, and cultural fictions.

If Winnicott's transitional space allows for movement between subjective fantasy and external reality, then we might ask how this applies to contemporary engagements with fictional objects. This brings us to the question of Otaku desire and the capacity for object usage. By asking, does the ability to get pleasure from a doll or a drawn character animate a capacity for object usage? Would it necessarily exclude the capacity to love other humans? And, is it really predictive of any particular form of sexuality one actually wants? Saito is focusing on the Otaku usage of the object—the cartoon character of the beautiful fighting girl. His intervention places Otaku "in a continuum with the rest of humanity" (Vincent, p. xv). For the "world to feel real," he writes, "it must be sufficiently electrified by desire" (Saito, p. xix). For Freud, the variation in sexuality is profound, even as "many people have their richest mental/emotional involvement with sexual acts that they don't do or even don't want to do" (Vincent in Saito, 2011, p. xx).

Saito's insights highlight how Otaku desire complicates traditional understandings of sexuality, particularly in relation to Freud's recognition of its variability. This raises a broader question: what does it mean to be libidinally charged by an imaginary object? To be libidinally charged by a cartoon is to be libidinally charged by one's imagination. While Otaku may use perversion as a way to enhance or "electrify" (Saito, 2011) their world by desire, their capacity for relationality (most are married and are part of a community) suggests that their sexually perverted expression does not make them perverse. Their detached capacity (the capacity to use and let go) toward the anime figure turns her into a dreamy object. Her fictional status, Saito insists, is also what makes the anime figure so great: she cannot be realized. The ability to be aroused by an impossible object is also a recognition of the fictional nature of sex, which, much like our dreams, induces variable interpretations.

If the Otaku's engagement with fictional characters blurs the boundary between reality and illusion, this has implications beyond fandom—it also mirrors the structure of psychoanalytic listening. The Otaku's borderline stance between fiction and reality parallels the analyst's position in relation to the unknown and affect. Illusion is what seems to hold one to bracket out the interpretation in Otaku sexuality. The uncanny position Otaku takes in relation to their characters—a borderline stance between fiction and reality—is perhaps what Saito feels is a lesson to us all. It describes the analytic process, not because psychoanalysis is not real, but because the fingerprints of subjectivity are always already all over it. Psychoanalysis, de Certeau (1993) proposes, "takes up the definition given to fiction as being a knowledge jeopardized and wounded by its otherness (the affect)" (in Britzman, 2015, p. 36). In the analytic field, this discourse is effective because it is "touched" or "wounded by the affect" (p. 36). Affects, Creatau suggests, are fictions affected by otherness, and here I think about the conditions that allow the analyst to be affected by inexplicability without the stopgap of interpretation—of having to know at all costs.

Just as Otaku desire requires an openness to the impossibility of its object, psychoanalysis, too, must remain open to what cannot be immediately understood. The willingness to be "wounded" by affect—to let go of fixed knowledge—demands a suspension of certainty, much like the suspension inherent in both play and desire. Since our "method of understanding," Britzman suggests, "cannot be separated from one's own libidinal history of learning" (2021, p. 90), the analyst may face a conundrum related to their education. The position of suspense is hardly natural for the analyst who is attempting to grasp situations that are experienced as inexplicable because of what they already believe they know. The capacity to suspend knowledge, to hold and wait, so that one may be affected by affect, involves an aesthetic risk: in the intermediate place between dispassion and immersion, one must tolerate the dangers of imagination to be profoundly impacted in unpredictable ways. To listen to desire—representations, inconsistencies, breakdowns, and vulnerabilities—one must be wounded by the otherness of affect. One listens to a dream.

The leap to gender

If phantasy is what renders reality affectively charged, then anime characters become more than visual fiction: they become erotic condensations, scenes of desire, sites where sexuality is stylized, displaced, and made visible. Insofar as she represents a libidinal attachment to a fictional object, she also challenges us to rethink our understanding of fiction itself. Saito's approach highlights that a libidinal attachment to a fictional object does not threaten Otaku's status as human but confirms it. This openness to rethinking what it means to desire leads me to another contemporary challenge for analysts: the experience of gender as a dynamic, often inexplicable phenomenon. By drawing on Saito's book, I am therefore making an intervention. The beautiful fighting girl allows me to enter into the dimensionality of sex and gender structures because there is a quality to the Otaku phenomenon that requires the reader to lose their mind—that is, to enter a phantasy. This, I believe, mirrors the psychoanalytic stance required to approach gender expressions and sexuality in the consulting room.

Saito is staying sane by being curious. His curiosity takes the form of surrender; by taking the "plunge" (Milner, 1950), what Marion Milner describes as part of a creative space: "one could sometimes do deliberately, but which also sometimes just happen[s], as when one falls in love" (p. 31). Taking a "plunge" is what I associate with Saito's capacity to take a position not from the omnipotent stance of attempting to know at "all cost" (Bion, 1965), but a position akin to what Bion terms "negative capability" (1965)—the capacity to tolerate the agitation of not understanding, to witness relationality to get a sense of a field of experience. It is dispassionate, not in the sense of lack of interest or complete neutrality, but in the form of surrender—witnessing an emotional situation from a new, unexpected lens.

Saito's *Beautiful Fighting Girl* does more than analyze a uniquely Japanese cultural phenomenon—it conjures a world. In writing about the emotional landscape of the Otaku, he does not merely observe their libidinal attachments; he invites us to consider attraction as a form of life, a way of being in relation. His work gestures toward a broader contemporary dilemma: how do we enter experiences, such as gender and sexuality, that are inherently unstable, marked by pleasure, pain, and the ever-shifting dynamics of desire? What if gender were not something to be known but an emotional situation mediated by fiction? Through Otaku culture, we glimpse a fundamental psychoanalytic tension: the moment we assume reality can be fully grasped, that what we see and what the other brings are one and the same, we slip into the realm of compliance. Saito argues that fantasy does not obscure reality—it animates it, shaping the very conditions of desire, recognition, and becoming. Perhaps through Otaku we can learn that the moment we think reality can be known, when there is no difference between what we see and what the other brings, we are in the realm of compliance.

At the center of Saito's method of study lies the capacity for relationality. The attempt to meet the unknown other in a way that resists pre-emptive preparation, no matter how many theoretical "banisters" we may use, requires a willingness to be unsettled. A capacity for a middle range of agency is a "feature of discovery" that moves away from the violence of splitting into good and bad (p. 130). Saito's work shows that attraction and fantasy are relational acts—ways of being in the world rather than fixed categories. This resonates with Winnicott's framing of "object use" as a space that neither colludes nor instructs but holds the possibility of experimentation. In this way, gender can function as a "good enough" placeholder, allowing for creative engagement rather than rigid definitions.

Otherness is not simple when it comes to perception. For Milner, it emerges when we accept that psychic creativity is pulled in more than one libidinal direction, a relation to what we do not know. Can the analyst loosen projections and idealities enough to encounter something genuinely new? I think here of Saito's "sway between otherness and likeness such as found in scenes of everyday life" (p. 13). It hinges on the capacity to contain our temper tantrums when we do not understand, or do not get the response we expect, so that we can listen in a way other than searching for causes, without abandoning curiosity in understanding conflicts, fantasies, and displacements. Milner suggests that true otherness emerges when we accept that psychic creativity involves multiple, sometimes conflicting, libidinal desires. For the analyst, this means disengaging from projections and expectations in order to encounter something genuinely new.

This, perhaps, is the ultimate challenge: to listen beyond the search for causes, to bear witness to the unknown without abandoning the desire to understand.

To listen in analysis requires more than understanding. It requires the capacity to stay with what unsettles, to hold back the tantrum that comes when meaning fails—when the response we imagined is not the one we receive. Listening here is not the search for causes; it is a form of waiting, where curiosity must remain even when no ground appears. Milner holds that true otherness cannot be met unless we accept the psychic life of multiplicity—of libidinal desires that pull in divergent, even conflicting directions. For the analyst, this demands a loosening of projections and expectations—an encounter with what cannot yet be known.

Otaku's sexuality brings us to this edge. Is it so distant from our own experiments with gender and desire? The wish to fix the Other, to frame or flatten them, to turn them into an object that steadies the flux of phantasy—this is no rare scene. We do it more often than we admit: reducing the Other to the sex doll, the image, the screen for our hunger. Sexuality unsettles the fiction of mastery. It returns us to that unbearable urgency—to know without knowing how, to be without knowing what being means. The space of sexuality is marked by superstition, phantasy, and a violence that belongs to interpretation itself (Aulagnier, 2001). Its force lies in what cannot be stabilized.

A sex doll—a blank canvas for projected desire—stages something fundamental, not only about sexuality but about gender's aesthetic experiments. Here the moral voice cracks; interpretation remains a wound. To enter the phantasy life of gender and sexuality is not an exercise in knowing—it is an exposure to what thinking may not contain. We do not always know what we do with our bodies. If we did, we might laugh—or collapse. The ego intervenes, not as master but as fragile organizer. It lends coherence where flux reigns, making even the genitals bearable, even beautiful—if only for a moment. Here, psychoanalysis offers something crucial—not an answer, not a cure, but an expanded capacity for life, for living within the aesthetic and erotic force of our becoming.

Part IV

The world of others

This section turns to the relational field—where psychic life meets the pressures of social life, and where gender becomes entangled with care, conflict, and collective life. Here, the question is not only how we become who we are but how we are shaped by others we cannot fully know and by histories we cannot fully claim. These chapters explore how listening, learning, and transitioning unfold in shared spaces—classrooms, clinics, memoirs—where the personal becomes political and the unconscious remains unfinished.

DOI: 10.4324/9781003440758-15

11 Second chance[1]

As the political right gathers force, and as the space for speaking about sexuality without persecution narrows, the work of care becomes more fraught—and more necessary. It is no longer clear where, or how, such conversations can unfold without risk. To care, in this climate, is to take up an ethical position under siege. We are living through a cultural war over sex education, sexual orientation, and gender identity—a war that is not confined to discrete arenas like the military or sports. It is diffuse, atmospheric, and saturates institutions: schools, the law, the police, the government, and the 'psy' disciplines. Across the United States and Canada, we witness attempts to police gender through the figure of the child, especially the pre-pubescent or adolescent, often treated interchangeably under the guise of *loco parentis*. The cultural figure of the trans or nonbinary child is gripped by polarized fantasy—where questions of nature, reproduction, autonomy, and regret return as projections. What unfolds here is not simply a matter of policy. It is a scene where adult anxieties about time, gender, and loss seek to take hold of the child. They are emotional situations—staged through the figure of the adolescent whose desire to transition confronts adult fantasies of protection, knowledge, and control.

The classroom stages this emotional situation with particular force. Saturated by institutional logics and group dynamics, it becomes a psychic and social theatre—one in which demands for recognition collide with scenes of misrecognition, projection, and affective excess. No one stands outside this drama. The teacher, too, is caught within its movements. As Deborah Britzman (2015) writes in *The Madness of Lecturing on Gender*, the classroom is a site where desire, idealization, defense, and the impossible demand to reconcile theory with lived experience all come to the fore. What makes gender so maddening, Britzman suggests, is that it precedes our consent. It is not a choice but an inheritance—embedded in unconscious life, sedimented through history, animated by the thoughts of others. To speak of gender is to speak of what is most archaic in psychic and social life. And perhaps, to do so is to seek not correction but the chance to remain with its unfinished conflicts, its unclaimed affects, its haunted repetitions.

DOI: 10.4324/9781003440758-16

Gender is first encountered, not understood. It is something we experience—bodily, psychically, relationally—before we have the language to name or narrate it (Gozlan, 2014). Perhaps gender provokes such intensity because it draws us back to what was always felt but never fully grasped. Now, as theories of gender move faster than its historical naturalization, another tension unfolds. Between what we can think and what we resist knowing, the emotional life of gender stirs—a scene where understanding and unknowing remain entangled. This resistance takes form in what Eve Sedgwick (2003) describes as "paranoid reading"—a defensive posture that refuses the instability of gender, disavows its psychic indeterminacy. In the classroom, such anxieties rarely remain abstract. They surface in the breakdown of knowledge itself: in moments when uncertainty provokes conflict, when ambiguity is met with moral certitude. What follows is a splitting of gender into right and wrong, masculine and feminine, legible and illegible These rigid binaries function as defenses—protections against deeper feelings of helplessness, dependency, and the fear that one's own position is more fragile than it seems.

The desire for knowledge always encounters its limits—frustration, the impossibility of mastery, and the loss of certainty. This struggle is central not only to education but also to gender itself. In both the classroom and the psychoanalytic clinic, learning requires an openness to ambiguity. Conceptualizing education as a space between knowledge and its limits allows us to better understand the current difficulties in addressing gender in teaching and therapy. One way to explore this link between learning, teaching, and gender is by examining the emotional dynamics of the classroom. Here, students' erotic attachments and transferences to each other—and to teachers as authority figures—are enacted through dress, mannerisms, and gaze, transforming the classroom into a carnival of gender. Clashing viewpoints on gender, which extend far beyond academic settings, expose deep anxieties about identity and embodiment. Debates over transgender and nonbinary students' access to bathrooms, participation in sports, and use of preferred pronouns often force a demand to take sides, reinforcing the emotional intensity of gender discourse.

How different professions handle these challenges often reveals a broader discomfort with uncertainty—something that the work of education and therapy inherently demands. The classroom, in particular, takes on an uncanny quality because it recalls something deeply personal: we have all been students before. Both teachers and students unconsciously reenact unresolved conflicts around truth ("Who am I?"), beauty ("Who am I for you?"), and belonging ("Where am I loved?"). These conflicts, shaped by gender, are tied to childhood ideals, super-ego demands, and repressed desires. Education thus constitutes a disturbance of memory (Freud, 1936), as Britzman (2015) notes: "Childhood looks different to those who are children no longer" (p. 143). In this way, the classroom becomes a site where early experiences of gendered socialization collide with the present moment, exposing the emotional weight of learning itself.

Education disturbs memory and unsettles language, making it difficult to articulate what is at stake in the experience of learning. The analyst's own education can itself become an obstacle to listening. In considering the emotional situation of learning, I am addressing something beyond the idea of emotional safety in the classroom or consulting room. Rather, I am referring to a deeper relational dilemma: the capacity for engagement without destroying the other. In part, this is a question of civility—of helping students or patients think about what is in their minds and where those thoughts break down. These conflicts, with their unpredictable vicissitudes, require a psychoanalytic lens as an ethical call to complexity.

In considering the emotional situation of learning, what I am addressing is something other than a notion of emotional safety in the classroom or consulting room. I am referring to a deep dilemma of relationality, the capacity for engagement without destroying the other. In part, it is a question of civility and involves the dilemma of helping anyone in the consulting room and the classroom think about what is in their mind and where it falls apart. The vicissitudes of these conflicts require, I believe, a psychoanalytic lens as an ethical call to consider their complexity.

Loss

At the heart of these conflicts is loss—the loss of certainty, the loss of coherence, and the loss of fixed meaning. Parents, teachers, and therapists are often confronted with something new, an experience of learning that resists full symbolization. In that encounter, gender emerges as an emotional situation. When adolescents share their wishes about their gender, the dilemma of how or what we are listening to is as much about them as it is about us—about the listener's transferences, fantasies, and theories of gender and sexuality. The ability to bear something we do not yet understand repeats the fundamental problem of the child's unpreparedness for the unconscious of the adult. What we do not understand returns as a loss. Bion (2005) captures this dilemma when he observes how, "when we are at a loss, we invent something to fill the gap of our ignorance—this vast area of ignorance, of non-knowledge, in which we have to move" (p. 2). In these moments, our ideologies and convictions about sexual difference and the masculine/feminine dichotomy converge with our theories about gender diversity. At the same time, as Britzman (2024) suggests, transference anxiety may be the plight of both the analyst and the educator: "loss and absence also begin quests for humane learning" (p. xxv).

It is with this idea of loss—as both an obstacle to understanding and an opening for something new—that I want to enter the discussion on gender. To do so, I will have one foot in the dynamics of the classroom, through dilemmas that shape teaching and learning in schools and psychoanalytic institutes, and the other in the psychoanalytic clinic. My focus is not on how teachers or analysts should intervene in these struggles but on what they do with their minds. My insistence is that we consider the intersubjective situation of the classroom or clinic not only as a response to the child's demands but as an encounter with our own otherness.

Adults teaching in schools, as well as analysts working in clinics and teaching in institutes, are themselves subject to fantasies, idealizations, desires for certainty, and conflicts with their own adolescence (Britzman, 2015, p. 73). In this sense, preoccupations with adolescents' gender often serve as a container for adult anxieties—about absence, intelligibility, cohesion, and recognition. The classroom and the clinic thus become spaces where our own histories of gender resurface, entangled with the difficulties of teaching and listening.

I want to begin by sketching the environment of loss that is central to the breakdown of sociality in discussions of gender and sexuality. In both the classroom and the clinic, we face a loss of certainty, an incapacity to know the fate of our work, and the vulnerability of communicating without knowing exactly how we are being received. At the same time, these struggles unfold within a broader political climate shaped by hysteria—one that plays out in particular ways in schools and institutes. The desire for knowledge, as it encounters its limits, frustration, and impossibility of mastery, is as much an affective reality of education as it is of gender. And because there is no education without relationality, transference always brings with it the complexities of care.

It is striking, in this regard, that the teacher remains a forgotten figure in psychoanalysis, despite the central presence of teachers in case studies of child analysts. This absence is all the more surprising given that the analyst is also a teacher and a supervisor. What is set aside in this forgetfulness is the need for a theory of learning—one that acknowledges how classrooms are emotionally charged spaces that return us to our own histories of childhood. There is a transference to education itself, shaped by the force of our own educational history, because new learning will always hinge on the reception of what came before. Disappointment, the failure of omnipotence, or wild success take the form of dreamwork: condensation, reversal into opposite, and symbolic equations. These anxieties play out in a particular way in the current situation of gender through group psychology, confusions of tongue, the aesthetics of care, and questions of risk—all dilemmas that highlight our susceptibilities to intersubjectivity.

These anxieties do not remain abstract. They press into the present—animating the conflicts now unfolding around gender and care. Lynda Polgreen's detailed discussion of the medical report evaluating gender-affirming care, in her essay "The Strange Report Fueling the War on Trans" (*New York Times*, August 14, 2024), provides a compelling example of how these tensions play out in real-world policy and discourse. Polgreen highlights how gender and sexuality remain caught in an uncanny position—something undefined, inchoate, unpredictable, and unstable, even as many attempt to control and regulate them. She exposes the double standard: hormone blockers and similar treatments, once routine for non-trans children, become suspect only when tied to transgender lives. The treatment has not changed; what shifts is the psychic and political charge surrounding it. How did an assessment report, "built on remarkably weak evidence" (Polgreen, 2024, p. 4) about the potential causes of gender dysphoria, become the basis for mainstream medical associations' decisions to restrict medications that "have been offered for decades to adolescents across the globe with few negative side effects or regrets"?

Polgreen exposes a hypocrisy that reveals how these debates are shaped less by reasoned argument than by anxious attitudes—anxieties that exceed opinion, let alone "scientific evidence." The report's central assumption is that adolescents lack agency and are incapable of consenting to treatment, leading to the insistence that adults must protect them from making irreversible choices about gender. Here, the figure of the "child" or "adolescent" (often treated interchangeably in such arguments) becomes a hypothetical universal, a vessel for containing adult anxieties about gender's instability. This reaction can be understood as a form of catastrophic knowledge—an attempt to resolve unknowability with rigid certainties. The report, as Polgreen shows, is no neutral assessment. It is a political text—one that diverts attention from transgender lives by staging anxiety in the name of protection. Its logic is already transferential: the very fantasy that regret must be foreclosed betrays an underlying panic about what cannot be controlled. As Polgreen notes, regret is ungovernable; life allows no such guarantees. The report enacts a wish to master what is unmourned in gender's instability—its unpredictable futures, its refusals to settle. What Polgreen's essay makes visible is not simply the incoherence of this discourse but the deeper difficulty: how to think gender without collapsing personal experience into the political demands that now seek to contain it. Moreover, her critique highlights how thoughts about gender often exist *without a thinker*—where the appeal to facts and the formation of group psychology become a contagion of hysterical symptoms. The proof does not matter when people refuse to believe.

Group mentality

What is clear from the preceding debates is that gender is an emotional situation that cannot be separated from its structuring fantasies, idealities, and the stickiness of transference—whose leitmotif is presence/absence: the glue of libidinal investments and the passion to eschew anything one is unprepared to receive. The certitude that stifles dilemmas of gender functions as a defense against the reality of not knowing what the other—in this case, the adolescent—is thinking. Instead, we draw upon a history of impressions that shape what we believe we are seeing. This returns us to the idea that theory is not simply an objective framework but a libidinal situation, saturated with emotional investments in commitments, loyalties, professionalism, and ethics. In this way, it becomes a question of group psychology.

The dilemma of being caught between the desire to know and the impossibility of mastery is a fundamental human condition, where conflicts of love and hate are transferred onto problems of knowledge (Freud, 1930; Klein, 1937). This is what ushers in a *strange education* (Britzman, 2024, viii): one that makes us subject to estrangement. Learning, in other words, is also a refusal of the unknown. The emotional situation of adolescence is particularly susceptible to regression, as students in schools and institutes may become subject to dependency, helplessness, and natality, where the subject presumed to know is the teacher. Students often want to be told what to do and expect to be punished for their ignorance. Yet adolescence is also a state of mind, an ongoing universal dilemma. Julia Kristeva formulates this psychic position as a syndrome of ideality (2009). Characterized by the *need to believe*—a state animated by splitting, hubris, loyalty to ideals, and strong convictions. This "need to believe," in turn, constitutes an anxious response to the ambiguity and instability of psychic objects.

Crucially, neither the teacher nor the analyst is immune to these dynamics. The capacity to invite uncertainty remains a challenge for both educators and analysts, yet their work inevitably involves unconscious impressions that escape their own notice: unfulfilled wishes, distorted and displaced anxieties. In the face of uncertainty, teachers and analysts alike risk responding with their own infantile theories of gender—mirroring, in a sense, the adolescent position. Much like their students, they may "[give] up being the child researcher he/she once was for the position of believer in the idea that perfection must exist" (Kristeva, 2009, p. 37).

Both education and talk therapy are not direct forms of communication, and there will always be a failure of translation. Something inevitably falls into the gaps, leaving both teacher and analyst to metabolize what they do not yet know. Freud noted that both professions produce "unsatisfactory results," and that learning to tolerate these limitations is itself a challenge for the professional. Bion (1965, in Gozlan, 2025) formulates this struggle as a constellation of curiosity, arrogance, and stupidity—an emotional defense against the helplessness of not knowing. An insistence on knowing the truth "at all costs" can become an obstructive object to the analyst's thinking (Civitarese, 2024, p. 236). Yet, the other aspect of learning is that education is always, at its core, a form of group psychology.

Classrooms, in many ways, are the best spaces to study gender because schools, as Ferenczi (1955) observed, are a "hothouse" for libido and repression. They are spaces of transformation, segregation, sexual exploration, surveillance, and critical interrogation. In schools, nearly everything is touched by gender. Through transferential relations, emotional ties, love, and identifications, group psychology produces stark distinctions between good and bad, us and them. This dynamic is particularly acute, as Britzman (2004) notes, when groups feel the need to defend themselves against change and new ideas. Under such conditions, internal doubt and ambivalence struggle to find expression within the group, even as individuals within it may experience them acutely (p. 111).

The analyst, too, is always confronting a kind of crowd, even in the intimate space of the consulting room, where the puppetry of the internal world is staged and given a second life in the intersubjective space of the clinic. The psychic boundaries between individual conflicts and group experience, as Freud (1921) suggests, are fluid and unstable. Every analysis, Bion observes, is a form of group analysis. In a certain way, the classroom, too, can be understood as a room full of patients—not in the sense of pathology but in the sense that students bring with them preoccupations and unconscious conflicts that remain unknown to the teacher.

The work of the psychoanalyst and the teacher differs in its form and purpose, yet the two professions are deeply linked—not only because both endure their own history of education but because, as Freud famously suggested, both professions are "impossible." Their impossibility lies in the way they demand that practitioners endure the helplessness inherent in their work—the difficulty of teaching, helping, and learning. What the adult learner resists is not merely the acquisition of new knowledge but the confrontation with their own history of dependency and helplessness. The effect of this uncanny encounter is that theoretical change can be experienced as a loss—at times even as catastrophic.

This same dynamic saturates the spaces of education and analysis, where projective identifications pulse beneath the surface. Some part of the encounter always resists translation—something slips, misfires, remains opaque. And it is this failure that unsettles both professions. Freud observed that education, by its nature, yields "unsatisfactory results." But it is the demand to endure such dissatisfaction—without fleeing into mastery or despair—that tests the limits of the professional's own capacity to learn. This difficulty is further compounded by what Bion describes as a mixture of curiosity, arrogance, and stupidity (Gozlan, 2025)—a common defense against the helplessness of not knowing.

Characters

To approach how group life shapes the dilemmas of gender, I turn not to arguments but to characters—not static types, but psychic and relational figures who circulate in the classroom. The classroom stages gender through scenes of education, just as the clinic stages it through scenes of transference. In both, relational life takes on form. These characters inhabit what we might call intermediate spaces—scenes of mind and body alike, akin to McDougall's (1989) evocative *theatre in the body*. They appear, as McDougall writes, because "we do not escape the roles that unconscious selves intend us to play, frequently using people in our lives today as stand-ins to settle problems of the past" (p. 4).

Freud, too, turned to characters to track the wreckage of success—to render how guilt, rivalry, and the wish for triumph collapse under the weight of Oedipal longings. Education inherits this structure: its scenes are thick with triangulation. Teachers, students, institutions, even the educational text itself—each becomes a site of transference and projective identification. What makes the classroom so vulnerable is this Oedipal texture. Schools and institutes invite a dreamwork of rivalry and repetition: scenes of sibling struggle, demands for recognition, refusals to learn, grandiosity, hatred of authority, pseudo-agency—all played and replayed.

Encounters with gender in these spaces move through similar currents: the insistence on certainty, the refusal of ambiguity, the retaliation that follows the pain of being misrecognized. Recognition is rarely simple. It often arrives first as demand—*this is who I am*—paired with prescriptions for how one must be addressed, theorized, received. Such moments spark disputes over rights, over language, over legitimacy itself. The wish to be seen on one's own terms carries a haunting expectation—that the other will fail to understand. In this way, the very demand for recognition may reverse an earlier hostility: a defensive certainty that understanding is already foreclosed. These struggles can be ruthless, maddening, at times unbearable. To step back, to imagine the classroom as a theatrical space, is to glimpse a haunting puppetry—a scene where characters emerge not as free agents but as carriers of psychic investments that exceed them. Gender, here, is not a lesson to be learned but a drama already underway.

These figures do not simply reflect individual identities but represent transferential positions—repetitions of past conflicts, anxieties, and desires. Among them, we meet the Soldiers for Normalcy—those who, often under the guise of *loco parentis*, assume the role of protectors, seeking to shield a hypothetical child from what they imagine as an unnatural disruption to development. They frame gender-affirming care as interference—as a deviation from what they take to be an essential trajectory of growth. Yet theirs is not only an argument; it is a defensive stance against the unknowability of gender itself. The more uncertain gender becomes, the more strenuously they assert its fixity. And then there are the naysayers—unyielding in their dedication to normative gender. For them, transsexuality is not merely inconceivable; it is unthinkable. The nonbinary elicits not curiosity but disbelief, as though the person before them were caught in a case of mistaken identity. These figures cannot disentangle gender from the projective scenes of persecution they stage. What they resist is not knowledge but the unsettling possibility of another's experience—one that threatens to undo the coherence of their own. Their position is shaped by a deeper structure: *"You cannot know me because of who you are."*

Elsewhere, we encounter the Soldiers for Trans—those for whom activism becomes an armor. They arrive certain of what they know, intolerant of metaphor, impatient with complexity. Their task is to instruct, to correct, to educate the teacher. Here, the adoption of gender markers—"he/him," "she/her," "cis"—becomes a sign of allegiance. But beneath this solidarity lies a more anxious demand: that identity must lead the way. Gender is split into "us" and "them," a field of clarity imposed upon an experience that resists it. And yet, the irony persists: those most fluent in the proper terms are often those whose gender is never mistaken. Nearby stand the Glossary-Keepers—those who cling to language with anxious precision. For them, no term may wobble, no word may drift. The slightest inflection feels dangerous. Words must hold, must fix, must ward off the enigma they name. But in this effort to anchor meaning, something of gender's strangeness, its capacity to slip, is lost.

It often appears that no term can be malleable in its use or enigmatic. Their vigilance stems from the broader psychic drama of certainty and mastery—a refusal of the unknown that mirrors the very anxieties at the heart of gender discourse. And we should not forget the "disbelievers," for whom terms like "contagion," "amputation," or "castration" are descriptors of gender, rather than libidinally invested objects of transference. Each of these characters stages gender as a site of transference, defense, and psychic investment—less a fixed experience than a scene in which unconscious life becomes tangled with cultural forms. Their presence in the classroom underscores how education—like psychoanalysis—is never a neutral act but rather a site of projection, resistance, and transformation.

One may also find, however, those for whom gender is a creative act—who are creative with gender. For these individuals, gender is neither essence nor argument but an errant gesture—something provisional, worked and reworked, a small revolt staged in the everyday. It resists being coded as less than human; it insists instead on fugitive aesthetics: a turn of fashion, an accent in speech, a demand to be addressed otherwise. What draws attention here is not an effort to make gender an object of conviction or proof but rather a relation—a way of holding tension, of staying with the uncertainty of where gender might lead, while still finding the impulse to move, however tentatively, toward change. Unlike those who arrive armed with certitudes, these figures do not seek to *convince* but to *engage*, treating gender not as an immutable object but as an object relation—an unstable scene of address, response, and reimagination. Theirs is not a politics of identity but of experiment—where meaning wavers in the space between self-invention and the inscriptions of the social. There is an aesthetic quality to this stance: an openness to ambiguity, a willingness to linger beside what cannot be resolved. Such a position, as I will later suggest, forms a precondition for care: a refusal of foreclosure, a resistance to the severing of psychic links.

But more than positions, what I listen to in the classroom are characters—figures who stage how the world wounds, invites, and resists us. For all their ruthlessness, these figures expose the fragility of intersubjective life: the labor of trying to become known, the bitterness of being unseen, the violence that misrecognition unleashes. And they return us to the predicament of learning itself—how it can collapse under its own conditions: preconceptions that stiffen into barricades, attachments to certainty that ward off the very transformations they fear. These scenes do not unfold on the level of thought alone; they are driven by the force of affect, phantasy, and the unconscious inscriptions of cultural life. What we encounter, again and again, are individuals caught within gendered structures they did not invent but must endure—structures that press on perception, that shape what can be thought and what must be refused. These are not external forces alone; they inscribe the very emotional conditions under which one begins—sometimes barely—to think, to bear the losses, ruptures, and injuries that social life demands.

Confusion of tongues

Together, these characters form a chorus of psychic intensities, composing a layered reality where the demand to be understood collides with the impossibility of perfect comprehension, often leaving in its wake the casualties of hurt feelings and pedagogical failures, as Britzman has written (2015). The emotional situation of gender—its melancholic residue, its ecstatic convictions—exposes its status as a site of contestation but also of deep longing. It is entangled with the formations of loyalty, the magnetism of ideology, the seduction of certainty. And here, again, we encounter what Ferenczi termed a *confusion of tongues*—the trauma that arises when the child's "language of tenderness" meets the adult's language of passion and command (Soreanu, 2018, p. 44, in Gozlan, upcoming). But this is not only a childhood predicament. Its aftereffects reverberate in all experiences of authority and submission. It is the foundational paradox of authority itself, one that reverberates in every scene of learning, where the teacher or analyst is both desired and resented as the figure presumed to know.

In the domain of gender, *confusion of tongues* manifests in many guises: in the dogmatic insistence on an ideality of selfhood, in the rationalist fantasy that knowledge can foreclose ambiguity, in the reactive postures of moral panic and rescue. We see it in the teacher or therapist who, in attempting to affirm, *cheerleads*—not out of care but out of an anxiety that cannot bear the child's suffering, a wish to dissipate distress rather than dwell in its difficulty. In turn, adolescent ruthlessness emerges as a total eschewal of what others have to offer. Adolescents, with their peculiar ferocity, sense these failures of containment. They refuse consolation that feels contrived. They turn ruthlessness into defense, eschewing what they suspect will wound. If they must be misunderstood, they will make themselves *unreachable*. This, too, is an impasse of knowledge, the fragile threshold where recognition slips and the risk of thinking together collapses into the silence of estrangement.

By listening to "characters," I am attending to emotional tableaux—psychic landscapes where the mind stages its peculiar idiom (Bollas, 1987), the signature choreography of vulnerability. Their clashes rehearse the inescapable uncertainty of intersubjective life, where frustration compounds upon frustration, thickening the atmosphere of the classroom and clinic with residues of prior injuries and preconceptions that thwart the elasticity of thought. These encounters are not merely intellectual debates but libidinal dramas, structured by affects, phantasies, and resistances to change. They speak to the ways in which subjects are both ensnared within gender's inherited architectures and yet called to improvise within its constraints. It is here, at the threshold of knowing and unknowing, that we glimpse the fraught and necessary work of metabolizing the pain of social life.

Passion, as an epistemic event, precedes understanding—it emerges in its own time, as both an excess and an enigma, something that resists smooth articulation. And yet, is there room for a second chance, a moment of revision in the life of thought? To pose this question is to step into the dilemma of thinking itself: to endure the agitation of inexperience (Waddell, 2018), a discomfort that arrives not as an internal reckoning but as an intruder—knowledge that refuses to behave, to submit to expectation. The mind, in turn, revolts. For Bion, new experience carries catastrophe within it.

What appears as instruction is also interference. For Anna Freud (1974), every lesson carries desire, transference, and anxiety at its edges. Anna Freud (1974) already warned us: no lesson is imparted without a residue of desire, transference, and anxiety—a tremor that disrupts the subject's fragile hold on certainty. To study the emotional situation of gender is, in this sense, to linger in its disturbances, to sit with the startles and frays that render thought porous, open to revision. And yet, this exposure to knowledge can feel like a kind of beating—the humiliating encounter with one's own limits, the sting of incomprehension. The classroom, then, is not merely an instructional space but a crucible: a place where theories collide, where attacks—real and imagined—leave their mark, where the possibility of thinking is always at risk of foreclosure. Klein (1921) emphasized this condition of psychical life when she observed how her efforts to convince her son, Fritz, that he could not speak every language, cook every meal or make babies, had failed. This led her to stop educating him and listen to his fantasies as communication of anxieties and desire. Fritz' inability to distinguish his inner reality from external reality foreclosed his curiosity at the same time it gave rise to incessant questions for which enlightening answers are not believed.

The refusal to believe, Klein suggests, turns on an unconscious question to which any answer will feel intrusive, ill-fitting, or persecuting. Even before the lesson begins, the scene is primed. The air hums with anticipation—a silent script already in play: battle lines drawn, characters armed, the teacher cast as omnipotent or ignorant, the analyst as an interloper in a drama decade in the making. Theories, like bodies, brace for contact. The anxious expectation of harm gathers its own momentum: a tit-for-tat unfolds, a scene in which no response can fully escape the repetition of injury. What is enacted here is not understanding, but the impossibility of a clean break from history. And so, the task before us is not to master, but to enter—to step into the scene of revolt with enough elasticity to sustain its ruptures, to hold the fragile possibility of play, and to wonder, still, about what the other is doing with their mind.

The aesthetics of care and the question of sexuality

The anxiety of turning to something unfamiliar may propel the analyst or teacher's readiness to join the other's repetition. They may decide that the other's experience is so other to them that they cannot respond to it, or use the empathy model of equation, where everybody is the same: the impossible quest of placing the self in the other's shoes, through affirmation or activist models of enlightenment. The third possibility is a new mode of understanding, one that is oriented by curiosity about erotic life. It leans on the psychoanalytic idea that relations between students and teachers are also transferential, and hence erotic, conflictual, intimate, and frustrating. Psychoanalytic vocabulary may allow us to think about the capacity to respond with tenderness to dilemmas we do not understand through the psychoanalytic entanglement of knowledge with desire and the charge carried by curiosity. Freud (1905) terms this capacity for discovery "sex research" (p. 209) and characterizes children as "little sex researchers," because, having nothing to go on, they create a phantasy of how something comes into being.

I use "sex research" to convey the human's attempt to understand emotional situations. It is the recognition that there is a poignancy to the problem of the subject and an attempt to conceptualize the tenderness of the learning and teaching. I imagine the analyst's or teacher's curiosity as the capacity to listen to gender experiments and to instances made from the student's "sex research"—their narratives of gender, along with psychical and physical elaborations—with "warm regard" for the theories at stake. There is something pitiful and vulnerable about the ways we learn and teach, whether we can do something about it or not. Demands for recognition, defenses, and infantile theories are real problems the analyst and teacher will face in making a relationship with the adolescent.

In the realm of pedagogy, Deborah Britzman (2024) describes this approach as an attempt to find our way to a "warm pedagogy" (p. 45) that allows us to respond with care for "inexperience." I imagine warm pedagogy as the capacity to attend to emotional situations of agitations and interruptions embedded in trying to know something we do not understand, with tenderness and curiosity. This is not a natural position for the analyst or teacher, as Britzman (2004) observes in her classroom experiences, while teaching Anna Freud's defense mechanisms:

> I tried to take their questions seriously, particularly those that seemed to ward off engagement or dialogue. This capacity to tolerate the detours of learning, perceiving, and interpreting the unfinished symptom without mobilizing one's own defenses may be one of the most demanding experiences for any teacher.
>
> (p. 79)

The students, she suggests, were unconsciously acting out the very defenses they were learning. Knowledge stirs love and hate.

The recognition of relationality as already fragile, tittering between love and hate, places that break and places that hold, invites a new way of listening to an emotional situation. One way of conceptualizing this fragility is through the notion that the characters in the classroom represent a set of narratives, sex research, and fantasies of reality. That is the power of a polyphonous understanding of sexuality and relationality, and in that sense, characters speak not *as* something but *with* something. In other words, I am witnessing a relation that together creates a field of experience. A warm pedagogy is not far away, in my view from how psychoanalyst and poet Dana Amir imagines ethical bonds made from the vicissitudes of loss through a position of "radical hospitality," elaborated earlier in the book. It is a concept borrowed from Derrida that leans on a relationality without any guarantee of reciprocity, to think about how people maintain normalcy in abnormal times. It conveys an attempt to understand what it is to pick up the pieces after devastation rather than seeing the aggression as representing something that requires our response.

Amir's bold position's objective is not reconciliation or redemption but a capacity to tolerate an aesthetic conflict: the uncertainty of interior life, of miscommunication and the conflated position of victim/perpetrator, as a condition for reparation. This is a difficult concept not only because psychoanalysis is an exemplar for that radicality—we invite people to come as they are and try to work with people whose worldview may challenge our very being. It is also difficult because we are in a political world that is totally bifurcated and split off into friends and foes. What is radical about Amir's approach is that it recognizes reparation from the place of psychic difference. The central point of concern is a state of mind as opposed to revenge—seeking or even seeking change!

If "hermetic narrative" (Amir, 2024, in Gozlan, upcoming) characterizes this absolute and clear distinction that frames situations of "tit for tat," "us and them," victim and perpetrator, then a "radical hospitality" hinges on what Sedgewick describes as a "middle range of agency" (Sedgwick, 2011, p. 79), where a space for thinkability, between the poles of ideality and destruction, becomes a feature of care. It involves the afterwardness of a collapse and a rebuilding of a relation. And here, thinking entails the capacity to not destroy this new relation with disparate anger and helplessness. It is a rebuilding that is not necessarily grounded in hope but a relationality that does not destroy the self. In reading Amir's modes of listening, I hear an insistence that in places of unbearable pain and in the desire for revenge, there is a hatred of thinking. Thinking, for Bion and Klein, involve putting things together, making links between inside and outside, past, present, and future, ideas and feelings. The question of care is embedded in this conceptualization of thinking because in bringing disparate parts together we create a broad perspective.

Care is central to thinking, because it concerns the very question of what the other gives birth to, that is, the capacity for a self, because there is an Other. Britzman and Amir's question of care allows us to consider the question: what kind of position would provide the greatest capacity for growth, to help students and patients think for themselves as the basis of being a subject with others and tolerate the conflicts that this otherness creates?

Their respective concepts imply that a "vantage point" (Amir, 2023, p. 42) is made through a relation to otherness; that is, to something uncertain. Listening without understanding creates a transitional area of play where concern about the future shifts to a question of care. And while the analyst or teacher may be a "magnet" for hatred (Britzman, 2006), their capacity to respond to ruthlessness with tenderness will be a tonic for the devastation that is the confusion of tongues, a potential softening of its hermetic qualities and a possibility for dialogue.

Yet, if care opens a space for thinking, it also confronts the limits of language, particularly in the context of gender debates, where language can become a battleground. The challenge is not only in sustaining dialogue but also in recognizing how language shapes, and sometimes forecloses, the possibilities of thought. Amir suggests that hermetic language is parasitic, in that it "performs a kind of double act of resuscitation and annihilation" (p. 25). This oscillating linguistic act becomes exacerbated in the discourse of gender when characters address the other on a topic that seems obvious and natural but actually implicates spectrum, age, biography, sociality, and law—all the tentacles we think about when we consider gender. If the confusion of tongues describes a mix-up of tenderness for passion and passion for tenderness, then parasitic language appears as an extreme interest in something only to destroy it. At this point, the discussion on gender—and in particular on transgender—collapses into a parasitic zone.

What I am characterizing as "parasitic" is not necessarily the relationship between the actual patient and analyst, student and teacher, but in the ways in which we enter language when attempting to represent—and thus potentially resuscitate and annihilate—the dilemmas of gender. It concerns the ways in which such debates are constituted on a "passion for ignorance"—Shoshana Felman's (1987) term for the difficulty of distinguishing the quest for knowledge from "desire not to know what one already knows" (p. 77). Amir describes a flattened, blocked, and deadened quality to the hermetic narrative that erases the subjectivity of both sides.

In the maddening debates on gender, we witness hermetic language in a split between attempts to protect the carefree child from social pressures (contagion, bodily harm, hormones, affirmation, or regret), so that they will not turn careless. The child or adolescent, as the assumption goes, will safely march into natural development if not disturbed by external forces. On the other side, we see a notion of activism, whose goal is to release childhood sexuality—imagined as unencumbered and polymorphous (Gozlan, 2024)—from the oppressive social. Both repressive and activist approaches assume that children and adolescents do not have agency, backed up by a theory of learning: children are passive puppets of culture who are susceptible to corruption.

Affirmative approaches, advocacy, or appeals for inclusion repeat another binary by placing a kind of imposition on discourse, this time with the idea that so-called proper knowledge—knowledge of freedom, inclusion, affirmation—will lead to a change of minds. The attempt to present sexuality as a conflict-free zone is the hermetic discourse of activism that is closer to the immediacy of the drive: a tit-for-tat desire for revenge. The notions of oppressor vs. victim, trans vs. cis, coupled with a strong desire, particularly among students, for role models create an amazing splitting and fragmentation of ideas based upon identities. What unites these seemingly opposite discourses is the incapacity to tolerate the urge to know, which will forever be frustrated by the insufficiency of knowledge. The eschewal of ambiguity in language, the insistence on the stability of bodies and sexual practices, and the deadening of curiosity through reliance on naïve understanding of cultural oppression (Britzman, 1998; Gozlan, 2008) are all forms of a paradoxical desire not to know. If hermetic narratives of wild affirmations and wild condemnations are both defenses against the internal and external forces that might challenge absoluteness, what becomes lost is the object of language and hence the possibility of livability: by refusing its otherness, experience becomes static.

Taking a risk

The capacity to disengage from our projections, identifications, and idealities marks a threshold to something new, but this act of suspension is hardly natural for the analyst or teacher. It is very hard to have an open mind, and taking a second chance with thinking involves taking a risk. I see the work of the teacher and analyst as meeting the trans adolescent who is taking a risk in gender. The capacity to see adolescents as sexual beings who have agency, can think, and risk an experience for something they want hinges on whether the teacher of analyst is able to risk surrendering their viewpoint, to see themselves as creatures of culture and then to consider their blind spots because of that fact. At that moment, when the worry over the possibility of death or regret is set aside, a space is made for relationality.

The capacity for risk, however, leaves us with the dilemma of trying to think about how to live with our choices. Risk, French psychoanalyst and philosopher Anne Dufourmantelle (2019) proposes, is always "beyond choice." The urge to risk is an act of seeking, and in this respect, "sexual research," an aspect of the unconscious that "solicits the future" (Dufourmantelle, 2019, p. 123). It is a capacity to abandon ourselves, to tolerate fate, while supposing that there will be someone on the other side to receive us. Making any choice, however, does not determine how it will be lived, and that is its uncertainty. Choice itself is not prophylactic.

Whatever direction one takes becomes in its afterwardness a choice (Gozlan, 2022c), and choices will often be disillusioned. This does not necessarily mean that it will have to be reversed or leave us helpless. Our agency, in this way, is not measured by our capacity to make a choice but is a consequence of making one. It is not so much a possession but a *position*, a negative capability to wait, to create, in a situation where we have to decide to submit ourselves. From this vantage point, thinking about what we are going to do or who we want to be are not necessarily situations of choice. It is a coming to terms with one's own decisions—rather than collapsing into the omnipotence of fantasy, where the boundary between wish and reality dissolves. The decision to take hormones, to change one's name and pronouns, or to have surgery are simply situations in which we take a risk and allow ourselves to enter risk with creativity. It references Winnicott's "intermediate area of experience," where gender is both "a discovery and a creation" (2014, p. 25), and in this regard, a "continuous achievement" (Gozlan, 2014, p. 25).

There is another stake in Winnicott's transitional phenomenon. It leans on relationality. For Winnicott, intermediate spaces of experience, Farley writes, "[are] made possible through a good enough environment that takes the side of the child subjective experience" (Farley, 2018, pp. 108–109). Precisely because our subjectivity depends on the other's recognition, we are reminded of how tender, tenuous, and uncertain is our claim to knowing who the other is. The capacity to receive the adolescent's self-theories of gender with warm regard will lean upon a surrender to the obscurity of an uncertain future. The analyst and teacher's listening in this regard requires a "leap of faith" (Gozlan, 2014, p. 76), to receive gender as an "enigma that rests on a belief" (Gozlan, 2014, p. 76).

A warm and hospitable position is a kind of waiting mechanism, a state of mind that bears a capacity to pause on over-excitement, to relinquish the fight, and to want something that does not lead to destruction. Waiting, however, does not necessarily mean deferring action. Suspension, Dufourmantelle tenderly suggests, is "not the arrested time that comes *before* something happens; it is the event itself—the passage into intimate time where, in reality, the decision has already been made but no one knows it yet" (p. 13). I conceptualize waiting as a third term that gets us out of the binary of thinking and doing. It is the possibility of tolerating our frustrations of not-knowing and modifying them when our aesthetic engagement, as imagination, interferes with our certainty. Together, Bion's "learning from experience," the idea that our learning occurs in the afterwardness of the experience, and Dufourmantelle's ethics of waiting offer a shared commitment: not to decide but to stay. Not to resolve but to receive. These are not only ethical postures between the poses of anxiety and curiosity but aesthetic ones—forms of psychic labor that make room for what has not yet become thinkable. The capacity to doubt, even for a moment, the mirage of identity is a potential for a reverie that forces us to "think more." In this intimate time, thinking becomes another form of waiting.

Note

1 A shorter version of this chapter will be published in Gherovici & M. Stainkholer (Eds.), *Routledge international handbook of psychoanalysis and gender* (upcoming).

12 From social condition to human event

Psychoanalysis has long been preoccupied with the question of how cultural life inscribes itself in psychic life. From Freud's reflections in *Civilization and Its Discontents* to contemporary debates over identity, neutrality, and ideology, analysts have returned—again and again—to the problem of how the social becomes internal. We are, perhaps, living through another such moment. As cultural and political ruptures intensify, so too does the analytic encounter with what these upheavals leave behind in the psyche. Across Western societies—and particularly in the American context—there is a growing recognition that unconscious life is structured not only by infantile fantasy but also by internalized mechanisms of inequality (Layton, 2020; Moss, 2021). Dominant ideologies about gender, race, whiteness, and ability do not stay outside the clinic. They arrive in transferences, in resistances, in the assumptions we bring to the work of interpretation. What is now being re-evaluated is not simply the analyst's neutrality but the fantasy of neutrality itself. These questions are now pressing themselves upon analysts who are rethinking how ideological structures—race, gender, class—permeate their presumed neutrality in the consulting room. As new demands emerge to account for one's social positioning, analysts are increasingly challenged to conceptualize anew the relation between the social world and the analytic frame. What happens to neutrality when the analyst is no longer imagined as a disembodied presence but as a gendered, racialized, and classed subject in a shared space?

At a recent panel of the American Psychoanalytic Association, "The Influence of the Social Unconscious," I found myself caught in a familiar tension: can psychoanalysis address social bias and structural inequality without abandoning its claim to neutrality—or is neutrality itself one more instrument of normative ideology? Preparing for the panel, I turned to the term *social unconscious*—only to encounter a field already unsettled. For Erich Fromm (1941), it names how dominant social structures inscribe themselves upon individual life. Hopper (2002) turns to *equivalence*: the unconscious conflation of present social realities with the traces of past group traumas. Layton (2020) moves further still, insisting that normative unconscious processes reproduce power both inside and beyond the clinic. No stable definition

DOI: 10.4324/9781003440758-17

emerges. What persists instead is the deeper question: How does psychoanalysis listen to the social, when the social is already inside us?

While these definitions diverge, they share a concern: the psychic life of ideology and how it manifests in the transferences, resistances, and institutional practices of analytic work. To qualify the unconscious as "social" is only misleading if we presume the social to be external to psychic life. Freud's work (1900, 1905, 1913, 1920, 1924) suggests otherwise: that the unconscious is not an interior sealed chamber but a site where speech, prohibition, identification, and fantasy—all borrowed from the outside—become internal dramas. Even the compulsion to repeat, for Freud, reflects an entanglement with trauma and symbolic loss, indicating an unconscious that is never simply internal but haunted by its encounter with the world (Freud, 1924/SE 18). The social does not arrive after the fact; it is already folded into the dream, the symptom, the slip. Rather than an addition, the social is the condition of the unconscious's formation. I therefore found myself returning to Dalal's (2001) provocative question: if the unconscious is inherently social, is it not misleading to qualify it as such? Is "social unconscious" a redundancy, or does it mark a new epistemological challenge? Freud's *Civilization and Its Discontents* already intimates this problem, tracing how cultural demands become psychic conflict, but it stops short of theorizing the unconscious itself as a social formation. What is now at stake is not only how the social is internalized but also how it structures unconscious life from the outset.

To my mind, the term *social unconscious* functions less as a conceptual advance than as a symptom of the field's anxiety about its exclusions. It marks not only a desire to acknowledge the structural realities of inequality but also a fantasy: that by naming these realities, we might overcome them. In this way, it risks becoming saturated with ideality—the belief that awareness of positionality or social content might substitute for analytic work. The danger is twofold: on the one hand, the term flattens the distinction between unconscious processes and ego-level defenses, suggesting the unconscious is educable, amenable to correction; on the other, it may foreclose the analyst's encounter with their own complicity, recasting moral awareness as psychic insight. Rather than reject the term outright, I propose we treat it as a borderline concept—a liminal space between the psychic and the political, between fantasy and structure, between desire and recognition. Like all such concepts in psychoanalysis, it is best approached not for its clarity but for its instability. Any account of the "social unconscious" that does not confront this opacity risks reproducing the very disavowals it seeks to undo.

This tension was not abstract. On our panel, the term *social unconscious* was used to describe the analyst's blindness to how social structures shape clinical encounters. But the questions it raised—about technique, positioning, inclusivity and moral responsibility—often relied on the very clarity the unconscious resists. How, for example, might structural inequality be reduced—defensively or prematurely—to internal conflicts? The chosen subtitle, "what is the clinician supposed to do?" conveyed a sense of urgency and moral pressure, which was soon followed by technical concerns: how can we operationalize neutrality, transference, resistance, and enactment in a world marked by inequality? Can we bring the social basis of prejudice into the room without becoming prescriptive? Are we working within a culture-bound or a culture-neutral tradition?

As Layton (2020) warns, "by limiting to the family context in which it views patients' conflicts, psychoanalytic therapy is one of the many practices that enforce the norm that unlinks the psychic from the social" (p. 37). But the inverse also holds: to over-link psychic life to social content risks reducing fantasy to ideology and listening to policing. This warning recurs throughout the field and underscores the double bind we face: too little attention to structure, and we reproduce the myth of psychic autonomy; too much, and we risk converting the unconscious into moral lesson. The question remains: how do we stay with this tension without resolving it? These questions cannot be answered through technique alone. They are aesthetic and ethical questions—about how we listen to what disturbs our frameworks.

Yet this focus on technique risks bypassing a deeper question: how are we thinking about the social as a psychic event, rather than an empirical fact? That is, do we treat culture and politics as knowable structures, or as enigmatic scenes of encounter? What remains unexamined, in my view, is the idealization of inclusion itself—our wish to have surpassed psychoanalysis's historical exclusions by virtue of our current self-awareness. The question that such appeals may inadvertently circumvent is this: how does our very desire to "do better" animate the problem we are trying to resolve? For me, the psychoanalytic unconscious is neither normative nor social in the ways these terms are often used. It is constituted by loss, repetition, and fantasy—not by the clarity of political insight but by the opacity of desire.

This raises a further dilemma: are we truly grappling with a "social unconscious" or are we encountering our own defenses, particularly the fantasy of having overcome exclusion through the mere act of naming it? What kind of unconscious is being imagined here—one oriented by fantasy, conflict, and displacement, or one amenable to moral correction and conscious insight? This confusion, I believe, stems from a broader theoretical slippage: the modern tendency to blur unconscious processes with ego defenses—as if naming bias or positionality could substitute for working through our own idealizations. Yet such gestures risk bypassing the disorganizing force of unconscious life itself. To take seriously the social in the clinic is not to affirm its content but to encounter it as an emotional situation—ambivalent, affectively charged, and overdetermined. What happens to our technique when our patient's suffering is shaped as much by history as by fantasy and when these cannot be disentangled? What's called for is not clarification but a capacity to remain with contradiction.

To ask what kind of unconscious we are invoking when we speak of the "social unconscious" is not a rhetorical question—it is a methodological one. Are we speaking of an unconscious marked by displacement, condensation, and the opacity of repetition? Or are we imagining a structure receptive to ideological insight and cognitive repair? This conceptual slippage risks replacing the psychic work of analysis with a politics of recognition, where awareness is mistaken for transformation. And yet, the problem remains: how are we to address the ways in which dominant ideologies—racism, transphobia, classism—do shape psychic life? The analyst is then tasked with holding not just material reality but unconscious temporality—with its distortions, deferrals, and repetitions.

This dilemma cannot be resolved through technique alone. It is an aesthetic and ethical one: to which world are we listening? The material? The affective? The idealized? Or the world structured by unconscious time? Do we aim to make the social unconscious conscious—or can we tolerate not knowing the work of our intervention or its fate? Following Bion's notion of negative capability, I propose four analytic orientations that resist translating social meaning into fixed identity: (1) *unknowability*, the excess and overdetermined nature of communication; (2) *unpreparedness*, a stance of analytic openness; (3) *the uncanny*, where psychic boundaries blur; and (4) *randomness*, the involuntary and nonlinear unfolding of subjectivity (Togashi, 2022). These are not interpretive strategies but ethical postures—ways of remaining with contradiction, of listening where knowledge cannot yet follow.

Unknowability

People enter the clinic with preoccupations we cannot fully know. As analysts, we are taught to listen—but to listen as doubters: to hear speech as compromise, as enigma, as something that cannot be rendered into accurate or complete translation. This is not a deficit of technique; it is the structure of psychic life. To remain open is also to be exposed—drawn into currents of dependency, fantasy, defense. No communication is simple. Every utterance carries an excess, a remainder, a trace of what cannot be said. I call this dimension unknowability. For Civitarese (in Cooper, 2022), psychic "truth" is unstable; it shifts, slips, and undoes itself. The analyst's task is not to stabilize this movement but to bear it—to resist the lure of early closure, the fantasy of clear understanding.

Unknowability saturates the act of listening, especially when unconscious life and cultural ideology collide. There are moments when speech becomes charged, unbearable—when its enigma becomes a site of conflict between what must be spoken and what cannot be thought. In such scenes, neutrality is no refuge. It is a fragile, compromised effort—haunted by the analyst's own unconscious investments, shaped by histories that cannot be undone in the moment of hearing. Faced with the unknowability of what is heard and what is transmitted, neutrality becomes strained. What does it mean to be neutral when the unconscious refuses to be? When language arrives already fractured by histories of race, gender, class? When each utterance invites us to take sides, to enter the scene? We know, clinically, how such moments seize the room—how difficult they are to endure, to think within, to hold without collapse.

In psychoanalysis, debates over gender have been especially charged, implicating the analyst's own education in both the effort and the failure to listen. Neutrality, then, is hardly straightforward. Analysis is held within a bulwark of unconscious framing—idealities, symbiosis, libidinal investments, and resistances—that belong to patient and analyst alike. These forces do not simply instruct; they unsettle. They awaken pain, dependency, loneliness, and the vertigo of not knowing. Out of such states come both curiosity and destruction, a haunting of how we meet the psychic realities of race, gender, and class. Neutrality is never a fixed position. It is a fragile labor: to remain open, to hold back, to listen through the thicket of one's own unconscious investments. Technically, it supports listening without certainty, but always under pressure—leaving us to ask how long this stance can be sustained and whether it is already compromised. Neutrality in psychoanalysis is often defined in shifting ways—sometimes described as benevolent, compassionate, or technical—but remains fundamentally an ethical stance, rooted in openness and self-awareness. Cooper (2022) describes it as an active, shifting stance—a working position grounded in ethical commitment and curiosity. He links this capacity to wait, rather than rush to conclusions, to the depressive position. Hoffer also ties neutrality to Freud's image of the analyst as a mirror or detached surgeon and raises a provocative question: is neutrality genuine or merely a mask worn during the analytic hour?

I conceptualize neutrality as something we *aspire* to, patient by patient, in the 45 minutes of analysis. What we aspire to is knowing when what is repressed in us has been touched by the encounter with the patient. Here I am leaning upon Bion's idea that the clinic is a place of the unknown, in a sense that every time the patient comes to the session, you encounter a different patient. A patient we cannot presume to know. What we cannot know or anticipate is the patient's and our own defenses as they occur in the moment, because our defenses constitute our ego, from which we cannot step outside. We do not know, for example, our splitting or the consequences of altruistic surrender as they occur. It is closely related to the question of time because it is only from a *nachträglich* vantage that we are able to assume a more distanced position of "unknowability"; meaning is never immediate but woven retroactively, after the encounter has already disturbed us.

My use of the terms *neutrality* and *unknowability* offers a way to think about listening to experiences that are socially devalued—such as those shaped by race, gender, or trans identity—which often provoke demands for adaptation or hyper-normality. Cooper (2022) links neutrality to Bion's idea of *negative capability*—a capacity for curiosity and not-knowing. At this point, the concept of the *uncanny* becomes useful, because it points to the force of psychic reality. A patient's conviction that their suffering is entirely due to being a person of color, a woman, or a trans person expresses something both real and unreal. These experiences are grounded in reality, but the certainty with which they are felt can function as a defense against the more unsettling truth—that we do not know what the other is thinking and that our histories of misrecognition and "confusion of tongues" shape what we come to know.

Psychic reality is essential for the analyst—not because they are outside it but because it obligates them to reflect on the origins and quality of their responses. In his essay on the uncanny, Freud grapples with using an unworldly concept to ground a psychoanalytic science rooted in reality. He explores how experiences of loss—of home, of bodily integrity—disturb our sense of what is real, as perception becomes shaped by projective identification. The uncanny unsettles the boundary between fantasy and reality, showing how events move between inside and outside, past and present, self and other. For Freud, there is no direct path to reality; it winds through the uncanny, through what returns in distorted, disavowed, or displaced form. For Freud, the path to reality passes through the uncanny. This brings us to Britzman's discussion of the "crisis of responsibility" (2021, p. 95), which emerges when the analyst, unsettled by uncertainty, seeks to impose premature closure. Rather than enduring the enigmatic nature of the analytic encounter, the analyst may fall into rigid interpretation or over-identification with the patient's certainties. For Britzman, this marks a failure of imagination—an inability to stay with the unresolvable tensions of psychic life and social reality. Like the uncanny, which unsettles the very ground of perception, analytic responsibility begins in resisting the pull toward foreclosure—in staying with what remains unresolved, ungraspable, not yet known.

Freud evokes this crisis through a moment of self-recognition: startled by the image of an old man, he realizes it is his own reflection. Every encounter, then, risks mistaken identity. As Dufourmantelle (2019) puts it, "perception dismantles thought" (p. 59)—each sensation equal to the judgment it unsettles. The fantasy of coherent perception cannot shield us from internal doubling. A similar doubling recurs in my patient's encounters with hostile, transphobic others. Though the scenes vary, the affective tone remains fixed. Repetition replaces the uncanny with certainty; the events are not strange but terrifying and true. In such moments, the analyst may feel drawn to affirm the patient's logic—to rescue, to confirm suffering. Neutrality, however, resists this pull. It asks the analyst to stay with the strangeness of repetition, to notice gaps where thought might re-enter. As an ethical stance, neutrality requires bearing separation anxiety, risking unfamiliarity, and waiting with what remains unnamed.

The struggle over neutrality—between repetition and the possibility of something new—presses most deeply in the presence of social prejudice, which moves not only through systems and institutions but also through the unconscious. Prejudice, as Young-Bruehl (1996) shows, is not simply a belief or attitude. It is "a constellation of processive affects and drives, impressions, imprints, projections, the acting out of ideologies" (p. 38)—a psychic architecture built from what cannot be fully known or seen. To study prejudice, then, is also to study the unconscious and, with it, the difficulty of thinking where thought is most needed. Young-Bruehl does not offer a map but an atmosphere: a way of sensing the diffusion of social and psychic life. Prejudice gathers in the air between people, shaped by transference, by emotional memory, by the unconscious effort to imagine the other. But this effort is never clean. The very tools we use to reach toward understanding—our perceptions, affects, identifications—are also the sources of distortion. Analysands do not bring us feelings. There is always something about the social scene that eludes us, not because it is hidden but because it is already overdetermined.

Patients do not simply report feelings; they compose scenes—and inhabit them. In the clinic, social and political conflicts arrive as dreamwork. They condense, displace, reverse, migrate. Racism, anti-Semitism, and sexism do not always declare themselves outright. More often, they surface as dread, shame, uncanny certainty—as the repetition of something that feels both familiar and unbearable. They enter the analytic field as atmosphere—sometimes voiced, sometimes enacted, sometimes disavowed—never entirely traceable to a single subject. These are not simply events to be interpreted; they are structures of feeling, lodged in the transference, enacted again in the space between analyst and patient. Young-Bruehl writes, "Trying to understand society is like trying to understand a madhouse" (1998, p. 209). But perhaps the analogy is exact. The social world, when it enters the analytic field, does so in fragments. And neutrality—if it has meaning here—may be the capacity to sit with this fragmentation, to resist premature sense-making, and to allow what is socially and psychically unformulated to find its shape in time.

To think about social situations through the question of something obscure is to suggest that neutrality is tightly bound with the capacity to bear with the transference as the "atmosphere" of psychic reality—a mechanism of gathering elements from which to imagine the other's situation, without taking sides. But this does not mean neutrality is the absence of bias or of being positioned; it means resisting foreclosure, resisting the impulse to resolve ambiguity prematurely in the name of certainty or righteousness. The analyst, much like the patient, is subject to unconscious processes, and neutrality, in this sense, is an ongoing struggle rather than a fixed stance. That is, listening to material situations of suffering—racism, anti-Semitism, sexism, etc. and social identities (black, trans, etc.)—is also bearing an echo of psychical reality. In intersubjective use, the libidinal investments and attachments related to social identity situate their function in object relations, defenses, wishes, and anxieties.

Following on Young-Bruehl's conception of the complexity of listening to emotional situations represented through political and social concerns, the idea (and ideality) that in being conscious of our biases we can somehow avoid the unconscious impact on us, defends against not only what the analyst may not want to recognize in themselves (e.g., racism, transphobia or misogyny). It is also a denial of the phantasmic qualities of being in the world under these conditions of duress and that such conditions are not only reinforced by the environment. They are also metabolized and absorbed, saturating conceptualization and representations. Political or politicized events, such as conflicts of gender, race, class, or religion are emotional situations and hence, they draw us in, and we are asked to choose sides. In our attempt to grasp deeply the emotional situation of others, in other words, I wonder if contemporary questions around equality or bias are truly able to be addressed without getting caught in the very defense that animates them. That is, these questions contain an unacknowledged ideality of having surpassed inequality by espousing a tacit belief that one can evaluate patients from a neutral position. And here we may also ask ourselves to think about how we might attempt to bracket out an ideology.

Unpreparedness

If Young-Bruehl helps us see how transference structures our engagement with social reality, Britzman (2025) allows us to consider how historical and cultural narratives shape our emotional investments in these realities, by analyzing how histories of trauma, education, and psychoanalysis shape subjective experience, influencing how we process and relate to the past in the present. As Britzman (2010) suggests in her work on *difficult knowledge*, history does not simply exist as an objective record but is continuously reworked through subjective investments, anxieties, and defenses. Our engagement with history is always affectively charged, marked by desires to integrate or reject unsettling knowledge. The challenge, then, is not only how we listen to political conflicts in the clinic but also how we allow them to unsettle us—how we resist the impulse to smooth them into coherence before their meaning has had a chance to unfold. If neutrality involves resisting foreclosure, it also requires tolerating the analyst's own discomfort in the face of uncertainty. But what happens when this uncertainty is experienced not just as a theoretical dilemma but as an affective, embodied encounter?

This emotional situation—susceptible to ideality, ruthlessness, and certitude—is where psychoanalysis meets the political world. The analytic endeavor is not a neutral contemplation of social "events" but an ongoing struggle to listen to human conditions: unpreparedness, uncanniness, and the randomness of experience. As Bion puts it, "whenever two people meet, they create an emotional storm" (2000, p. 321). If we cannot rely on what Keats (via Bion) called negative capability—the capacity to tolerate discovery without rushing to resolution—we risk collapsing into moral judgment, dividing experience into "good" and "bad" fantasies. This dilemma is not abstract. It takes shape in the room. It emerges in the analyst's effort to listen without foreclosing meaning, to hold the tension between psychic reality and the material world. To frame the analyst's encounter with political and social suffering—discrimination, violence, exclusion—as a clinical event is to suggest that psychoanalysis is itself a mode of conceptualizing human encounters.

Nowhere is this more apparent than in the work with G., a nonbinary patient who expects rejection from both trans and non-trans communities. A recent job on a trans-focused TV show quickly became a site of exclusion: transwomen colleagues did not see G. as "truly trans," while non-trans actors dismissed them as "weird looking." Outside of work, G. is regularly harassed, verbally attacked, and denied access to gendered bathrooms. In turn, they become combative, counterattacking perceived compliance with normative gender roles and expressing resentment toward those who seek surgeries to join what they see as "oppressive heteronormativity." Here, the material world structures psychic response. Suffering is experienced concretely and often defensively—through externalization and projective identification. The clinician, too, is pulled into this structure. In such imbricated scenes, the analyst receives an appeal: not only to witness the trauma but to affirm it, to take a position. Would I state my political views? Become a role model? Offer a corrective experience? Or would I risk recognizing the impact of structural inequality while refusing to reduce that inequality to intrapsychic origins?

As I listen to my patient's descriptions of their material experiences, I also hear something else: wishes for revenge, the *jouissance* of identity, an attachment to punishment, suffering, and pleasure. These encounters carry a demand, not only for recognition but also for the analyst to take suffering as literal truth. And here is the dilemma: if we assume suffering can be traced to an original cause—whether a childhood trauma or a social injury—we risk treating the past as deterministic, but causes are never singular. They arrive overdetermined—saturated with unconscious life, with the residues of history, with the urgencies of the present. Like dreams, they unfold through condensation, displacement, reversal. This complexity alters how we must listen—and reminds us that not all listening leads to understanding. Nor should it. The clinic is no place for clean comprehension. It is a space where uncertainty, frustration, and the contingency of relation flood the room. These forces do not ask to be solved; they ask to be borne. To remain within such a scene requires what Bion (1962) calls the capacity to withstand the disorienting force of the encounter. Without this, we will too quickly grasp for certainty, mistaking our own defenses for knowledge.

Yet psychoanalysis has often failed to sustain this openness. In presuming the nuclear family as its primary psychic scene, it has repeatedly reinforced exclusion. The historical pathologization of homosexuality remains one of its most persistent wounds. Not long ago, the DSM still named homosexuality as a disorder. For much of its history, psychoanalysis framed it as perversion, narcissistic pathology, or a failure of Oedipal resolution. The ideal was not recognition but conversion: to turn homosexual life toward heterosexual repair (Gozlan, 2022). This legacy continues to haunt the field, in subtler and more insidious forms—where the pressures of normativity still seep into the ways we listen and into what remains unspoken.

Yet normativity is not a stable structure: it is brittle, held together by the very emotional and defensive forces it seeks to regulate. As in G.'s experience, normativity is both an emotional situation and a site of anxiety and exclusion. If normativity is brittle, then psychoanalysis must return to its foundations—not to reinforce them but to rethink them. Conceptual work must begin not with the nuclear family as an unquestioned frame but with an openness to how the psychic and social intersect beyond inherited structures. Instead of taking gender as a given, we might ask: how do we come to know gender's emotional position? These are not abstract questions. They shape analytic listening. What I find myself grappling with in the clinic is not only how an analysand narrates their emotional situation but how my own interpretive framework shapes what I am able to hear. The question is not only what I should do but how I conceptualize the problem in the first place. How does my thinking about "culture" animate the dilemmas I encounter? Do I approach them as something I already understand, or can I receive them as enigmatic? In other words, can I try to understand my patient without fixing them—or retaliating against what they unsettle in me?

The political and historical are often felt as attributes of the subject. But psychically speaking, as Bion (1965) suggests, these are also properties of the intersubjective field—shaped by libidinal investments, projections, and introjections. They are inseparable from fantasy, construction, and anxiety. Intersubjectivity is always a space of miscommunication. For Laplanche (1992), what is conveyed by the other—whether social, cultural, or political—is always received through interpretation. This is the work of transference, whose leitmotif is presence and absence: the experience of trying to hold onto what is gone. In attempting to understand how my trans patient thinks about the world in their psychic life, I am not exempt from what Jacqueline Rose calls "the unconscious effects on identity of the pressure to internalize cultural norms and ideologies" (Rose, 1986, p. 12, as cited in Layton, 2020, p. xxiv). I, too, can feel the unconscious pull to repair or retaliate against what threatens my own ideals of gendered coherence. Rose (1993) argues that identity politics draws us toward experience, where we are seduced by its apparent stability and the illusion of continuity. Identity becomes something essential and self-evident. But one of the failures of identity politics, she writes, is its exclusion of self-difference. In assuming identity is fixed and timeless, subjectivity is compromised.

My responsibility in listening to my trans patients also hinges on how I theorize gender development. If I rely on normative psychoanalytic models—those grounded in positive and negative Oedipal development—without recognizing their inherent bias, how might this shape the way I hear a trans patient describe being shunned at a bathroom? The ethical stance, I believe, begins with asking how I am listening to a patient's experience of not having a place in the world. It involves wondering about my own normativity—about what I take for granted when I move through the world without being bothered. From this position, I must also consider how the world encourages such "taking-for-grantedness," sustaining a divide between what is deemed normal and what is cast as pathological. Listening for self-difference requires suspending the demand that gender make developmental sense. It involves tracking how a patient's gendered experience surfaces through affect, fantasy, metaphor—not only through conscious identity claims. And it requires an ongoing critique of one's own normative assumptions—not only about gender but about what counts as coherence, what counts as pathology, what counts as intelligible experience. To listen in this way is to hold psychoanalytic models lightly, allowing the patient's own symbolizations and uncertainties to orient the analytic encounter.

To take history personally is to recognize its living presence in the analytic encounter. Freud shows how history lives in our dreams—imprinted, unresolved, awaiting reinterpretation. The patient's suffering is entangled in both personal and collective histories, and so too must the analyst engage in a process of revision: questioning their own assumptions and the inherited frameworks that shape analytic listening. This difficulty—listening without imposing a preordained meaning—draws me toward what I call the *emotional situation of unpreparedness*: the strain of encountering the unknown without the shield of interpretation. Theoretical frameworks may orient us, but they cannot steady what arrives in the room. To listen here is to relinquish the fantasy of mastery, to bear an openness that no theory can fully contain. The emotional situation of unpreparedness refers to the fate of libidinal investments—our own and the patient's—over which we have no control. It also speaks to the nature of communication itself: fractured, enigmatic, never fully cohesive or transparent.

Here, Bion's (1967) call to listen "without memory, desire, or understanding" (pp. 30–31) becomes a challenge to our theoretical reflexes. It asks us to surrender to experience, to receive what the moment stimulates—consciously and unconsciously—so that, as Levine (2023) writes, we might "catch the most ephemeral wild thoughts" (p. xii). There is always a gap between experience and its emotional representation—between what is lived and what is known. This gap marks the problem of unpreparedness: the analyst's and analysand's shared struggle to bear something that is felt but not yet understood. As Freud and Klein suggest—and as Britzman (2022) articulates—each decision to take in an experience returns us to a pre-history (p. xix): an archaic inheritance of impressions without meanings, whose weight bears upon the present. This difficulty of tolerating unpreparedness is especially evident in clinical work, where the analyst must navigate between affect, fantasy, and external reality without prematurely foreclosing meaning. Layton (2020) offers a compelling illustration of this dilemma in a vignette where she struggles with the tension between open listening and the impulse to impose interpretation. I want to stay with this example, not only as a reader of clinical material but as someone trying to enter the intersubjective space it depicts—a context that resists understanding even as it demands representation.

Layton recounts a patient's dreams in the early days of the Iraq War. The patient, a woman in a same-sex relationship, wonders whether to share her political views with a senator. Layton resists splitting the psychic from the social and instead invites associations.

Dream 1: She sits in the backseat of a car. John Kerry, newly a presidential candidate, is in a wheelchair outside. She lets him in and wonders whether to speak politically.

Dream 2: She's fleeing with a group. She's told to start a fire by rubbing objects. It works, and she's surprised, pleased, then anxious it will destroy everything before they can choose what to carry forward.

Layton engages both the patient's and her own associations. A pattern emerges: the patient oscillates between omnipotent projection and self-blame, echoing a childhood dynamic—"I'll follow, but then you're responsible." This repetition, Layton suggests, disguises conflict around autonomy, especially in a political moment defined by helplessness. What distinguishes Layton's work is her movement across psychic, affective, and social registers. Rather than master the material, she stays in its vulnerability. Her question, "What would you say to the senator?" opens space not to explain but to think together. The question becomes a site of susceptibility, where affect and association precede knowledge. Reading this vignette, I find myself affected: "Kerry" becomes "carry." In the dream, he is immobilized. The second dream evokes sexuality—friction, ignition, loss of control. Perhaps Kerry symbolizes not only the political or paternal but the patient's vulnerability in the face of uncontained desire. Is there fear of being carried away, unless someone intervenes? The case foregrounds the analyst's helplessness—not as failure but as precondition for thinking. As Castoriadis writes, both analysis and education demand autonomy from subjects who do not yet possess it. To read such material is to confront "difficult knowledge" (Britzman and Pitt): not just socially or emotionally fraught but epistemologically unstable. The case does not resolve but invites the question: how do we think psychic life at the threshold between interior and exterior, between impression and interpretation?

A borderline concept

The status of exteriority—and its internalization—has been a central concern of psychoanalysis from the beginning. Freud's *Project for a Scientific Psychology* (1895), often considered the nuclear seed of psychoanalysis, grapples with a fundamental question: why do humans have a psychology? In this early text, Freud struggles to theorize how the external world imprints itself on the psychic apparatus and how psychic life arises from the organism's need to regulate stimulation, helplessness, and pain. Layton's clinical example, in this sense, brings into relief a central psychoanalytic tension: to what extent are our psychic struggles shaped by the force of external reality versus the unconscious processing of these encounters?

Freud emphasizes the infant's dependency on the other in moments of helplessness:

At first, the human organism is incapable of bringing about the specific action. It takes place by extraneous help. . . . In this way this path of discharge acquires a secondary function of the highest importance, that of communication, and the initial helplessness of human beings is the primal source of all moral motives.

(Freud, 1895/1950, p. 366)

Later, Freud insists that psychic life is grounded in the demands of the external world:

There is no question but that the external world is the origin of all major quantities of energy. . . . The system ϕ, which is turned towards this external world, will have the task of discharging as rapidly as possible the Qη̇s penetrating to the neurons . . . but it will in any case be exposed to the effect of major Qs.

(p. 890)

If psychic life is constituted through external impressions, then the boundary between the personal and the political, the psychic and the social, becomes blurred. Cultural, political, and social realities are inherently borderline—neither fully external nor fully internal, but psychically metabolized through fantasy, transference, and the response of the other. In Freud's terms, it is not interiority that inaugurates psychic life, but the infant's first cry—and the other's response to it. The helpless cry, carried on the first breath, calls for help; it is answered as though it were communication. That response constitutes the earliest ethics of care, a recognition of pain as a message. The world enters the psyche not just as violent motion but also as transmission. And the psyche, paradoxically, begins by trying to represent what cannot yet be known. These dynamics of inside and outside—and the psychic labor of metabolizing social realities—become vividly apparent in clinical work.

My work with D., a trans man in his mid-thirties, returns me to the question of what it means to hear the social through psychic life. D. says he is a "failed man" who "can't do anything right." The list is long: too slight to be hired for "masculine" jobs, unable to satisfy his partner without a "normal" penis, too indecisive, too emotional. What he wants is to be recognized. What he expects is to be dismissed. And when his boss recently referred to him as a "drama queen," D. lodged a formal complaint—not just against the insult but against what it meant: that his masculinity had been revoked. That his claim to being a man was always conditional.

I come to understand this moment not simply as a response to external transphobia—although it is that—but as a site where psychic life and social exclusion intertwine. If transference is where impressions register before they make sense, then this moment, for D., is already sedimented in feeling. He is helpless, but more than that he induces helplessness. I am cast as someone who cannot understand, whose very presence threatens to repeat the rejection. *No one treats me well. It's because I'm trans.* This is not just a statement of fact; it is an affective insistence, a truth too real to allow for curiosity, too painful to make room for anything else.

And yet, the scene is never only about the present. It carries with it the weight of history: a mother who withheld affection, a stepfather who demanded control. But those figures are not here. I am. And so, I become, in the transference, the terrible parent. The bad object. The one who can never get it right. In this sense, the "terrible parents" operate like a dream-image—condensed, displaced, always partial. The room becomes a space of haunted identifications, where the analyst is not interpreting from the outside but caught within the very fantasy they are trying to think. There are aspects of this reality that resist understanding. That may never be metabolized. But perhaps this is where the work begins: not in knowing but in staying—ethically, emotionally—with what cannot yet be named.

In the clinic, what I often hear are scenes in which people are caught in structures of gender, race, or class not of their choosing, yet ones that shape how they see the world—and how they are blocked from living in it. D. is deeply affected by these forces, particularly the ideals of masculinity and femininity, although they remain implicit in his suffering. Part of what afflicts him is the ideality of culture—the production of masculinity as something he must live up to but can never attain. But there is also the fantasy of the subject, the way his psychic life organizes and sustains this failure.

The scene D. presents is emotional, situated at the intersection of interiority and exteriority. This is a world where meanings remain unstable. On the one side, there is the question of what has happened; on the other, how this scene has become an internal structure—a way of knowing himself. I am listening, then, to both the generality and the singularity of masculinity: the cultural demands that define it as a measure and the way that measure becomes an unlivable ideal. But I am also listening to a transition that cannot yet be metabolized and to a failed relationality playing out between us. Perhaps, with time, the analysis can help D. construct a narrative that allows for more breathing room. For now, there is no curiosity—only the insistence of what has already happened. By shifting the frame of understanding away from causality—whether internal (repetition compulsion) or external (paranoia)—toward an attempt to imagine what it feels like for my patient to be a "failed man," I encounter the conundrum of unpreparedness. I am confronted with the experience of being affected before I can understand. In analysis, both analyst and analysand must bear the weight of an experience before its meaning can be known. Understanding, in this sense, comes as a deferral.

As I consider the multiple worlds shaping D.'s experience of gender, including the idealized masculinity to which no one can measure up, my listening is guided not by explanation but by proximity. Proximity here means not solving the riddle of D.'s masculinity but staying close to its affective pull—to how it organizes desire, fantasy, and identification, even as it eludes coherence. I hear in D.'s words not the effects of masculinity but his unconscious project of becoming something called "a man." This is a project oriented toward something unstable and ultimately unknowable, because the concepts of masculinity and femininity are pliable, which makes them vulnerable to collapse. Their transformability renders them fantasies, and as such, they are already constituted by failure. Masculinity, then, is not something D. has failed to achieve; it is something that fails by design. It does not exist outside of the cultural fantasies that animate it: in art, religion, literature, and everyday life. So what does it mean to be a "failed man," if masculinity was never there to begin with? What I am hearing is not just a complaint but a desire—a desire shaped by something called masculinity and a suffering that emerges when that fantasy is situated as cause.

Klein insisted that knowledge—especially self-knowledge—is fraught. It is not enough to know the facts of one's life or the conditions of one's marginalization. For Klein, the analyst must bracket the actual in order to attend to psychic reality—to how the mind defends against what feels unbearable, often by casting the analyst or the world into the role of persecutor. Knowledge becomes difficult not only because of repression or resistance but because *phantasy organizes reality*. The boundary between internal and external dissolves.

D.'s failed masculinity is not simply imposed upon him by culture; it is also constructed, maintained, and suffered through unconscious processes that resist thought. These are not simply internal conflicts, but Klein would call them fantasies—psychic dramas that stage the external world inside and that return through displacement, projection, and identification. From a position of unpreparedness, my listening is less concerned with locating the causes of D.'s suffering and more attuned to *how* he searches for them. In the clinic, what I have access to are my patient's constructions of the present. This is what Klein (1946) understands as projective identification—not merely a defense but a communicative process, where intolerable affect is lodged in the analyst, demanding to be thought. By listening to affect, I get a clue that something in the original experience was missed and that this "something" returns as transference.

I am listening to experiences that have not yet become thinkable, where psychic history and its affects exceed the mind's capacity to organize them. For Winnicott, history is not a fixed record but a transitional concept—something that takes shape in relation to the present. And following Freud (1936) and Klein (1952), names what is returned in such moments as a "pre-history" (p. 1): an archaic heritage—impressions without meanings—that bear on the present. To listen in this way is to enter the fray: where thinking is slow, where affects are disorganized, and where the analyst is not outside the structure but inside the scene. This is the dilemma of conceptualizing in the clinic, where the tensions between meaning and experience refuse resolution.

While many of the examples I've offered center on gender, my argument is not limited to gender alone. The difficulties of translation, the disquiet of identity, and the limits of understanding are present in all clinical situations—whether they involve sexuality, race, class, religion, or any other facet of psychic life. The question is not simply how we understand another's experience but how we remain with its unknowability—how we listen not for certitude but for the ways in which subjectivity is shaped by what is irreducible, untranslatable, and yet still deeply shared. This unknowability is not a gap to be filled but what Klein and Bion see as the condition of thinking—the place where symbolization struggles to emerge from the turbulence of affect. If we are affected before we understand, then analysis may not offer resolution so much as the capacity to stay with the contradictions of being—without retreating into the illusion that experience can be neatly assimilated, or that identity can be fully known. In this sense, situations of abandonment or rejection often become psychically fused with the material realities of discrimination, such that suffering is interpreted through the lenses of gender, race, class, or political belonging. These social inscriptions structure psychic life, without ever fully explaining it. Like the internal objects of Klein's theory, these inscriptions are not merely internalized but actively reanimated, defended against, or projected outward, marking the lived intersection of psychic and political life.

There is, of course, an attitudinal transmission at play—a reality of transphobia, racism, anti-Semitism, and other social injuries that structure psychic life. These are inconceivable experiences, felt differently by each patient, shaped by their particular translation of history. My capacity to listen—not to know who the other is but to unsettle my own theories of gender, race, and class—relies on an ability to tolerate unpreparedness: to wait, to bear the frustration of not knowing, and to revise my understanding when our imaginative engagement disrupts received certainties. Bion's suggestion that the most important part of the session lies in the unknown becomes a kind of a banister for approaching political conflict. From a position of unknowing, we can observe the unfolding of these conflicts—their movements, dispersals, intensities—without rushing to explain them away.

Bion's orientation toward the unconscious invites us to think of dreamwork as a frame for listening to the social. From this position, analysis is neither culture-bound nor culture-neutral. Subjectivity is a cultural effect, but culture itself resists direct translation. Like a dream, social and political realities are intimate, affectively charged, and beyond individual control. Psychic life, then, is not only shaped by culture, but it also expresses how we use culture to form new investments and object relations (Winnicott, 1969). The question of when the social enters the clinic is misleading: the social has never left. Winnicott's (1971) conception of culture as a borderline phenomenon—an uncanny space that is neither "me" nor "not me," an intermediate area of play—offers a way to understand that transference is already a social situation.

Randomness and the human turn

The idea that gender, race, or class can be addressed through fantasy, social experience, and desire implies that these are not fixed categories but constellations—structures of meaning that can be conceptualized in ways we do not yet, or may not wish to, imagine. Culture, in this sense, is atmospheric. It is not a backdrop but an apparatus of meaning-making. Just as Winnicott famously claimed that "there is no such thing as a baby" (as I discuss in the introduction)—only a baby and its environment—there is no gender, race, or class without the cultural surround that gives these categories symbolic life. Culture, as Clifford Geertz (2017) puts it, is a web of meanings we ourselves have spun.

Here, the line between material and emotional worlds begins to give way. And as Winnicott asks, with no easy answer: was the object created—or found? The gendered body, for example—once thought of as a given—is already mediated through narrative, fantasy, and fiction. This example allows us to ask not only how gender operates in the world but how it is lived, how it is experienced by the other. Gender, in this light, resembles Peter Pan's Never-Never Land: never fully there, never fully attainable. It promises beauty, wholeness, belonging—and then breaks those promises, often leaving behind self-hatred, anger, and the urge to escape. You must create it; you cannot simply find it. One of the things we do not know—cannot know fully—is the nature of our patient's defenses as they occur in real time. This is because our defenses constitute the ego itself, and we cannot easily step outside the ego to observe it. Klein is especially striking when she describes the most devastating defense as the *denial of denial*—a wiping out of meaning itself. This is what defenses do: they protect from the terror of having to think. And yet, in the clinic, we must go on thinking.

Bion held that it is precisely in moments of frustration that analysts are asked to think. If our task is to create the best conditions for ethical listening, then we must meet our patients with curiosity—without rushing to interpretation and with the willingness to think alongside something not yet formed. In analysis, we are attending to transference, countertransference, projective identification, and defense—all of which also pull us in. That is why we work in a space apart from everyday life: the consulting room is an intermediate area between reality and fantasy. It is a place where the world's demands are suspended, if only briefly, so that the imaginative process might unfold.

Uncanniness

As discussed earlier, the analyst's neutrality is not a fixed stance but a form of aspiration—a response to the unknowability of both the self and the other as they emerge in encounter. That aspiration—to let meaning emerge—finds one of its most unsettling forms in the experience of the uncanny. Freud's essay does not begin with definition but with disturbance: how the familiar turns strange. The uncanny, he writes, is not what we have never known but what returns from repression—too close, too known, and suddenly unrecognizable. If the womb is a first holding, then birth marks a first unhoming—an uncanniness that shadows later losses. For Freud, this anxiety gathers around helplessness, around castration, but it is also the anxiety of analysis itself: to enter a process where meaning slips, where identity is not possessed but taken apart and re-formed in transference.

To listen analytically is not to seek what is coherent. It is to enter a space where boundaries thin—where inner and outer, self and other, past and present cannot be kept apart. The uncanny, as de M'Uzan (2013) suggests, is no error of mind; it is the mind's response to the instability of sexuality, the shakiness of identity itself. Analysis begins in this space—not with knowledge but with the unmaking of certainty. Freud noted that analysts, too, cling to fantasies of mastery, of understanding that wards off disorder. The work is to resist this pull. Transference does not distort—it stages what remains unthought, what insists on being refigured. To treat emotional life as unknowable is not a retreat; it is a discipline of staying—not knowing, not yet interpreting, waiting within what has not yet taken form. As Blass (2024) writes, interpretation stirs first within the analyst's own inner life—unfinished, wavering, still without shape. To hold open this space is not passivity. It is its own labor.

If the uncanny unsettles the familiar, randomness unsettles sequence itself. Psychic life disperses, loops back, arrives where it was not summoned. Gender, race, class, sexuality—they do not present themselves as stable identities in the clinic. They return in fragments, residues, dream-traces. Identity here is no structure; it moves, frays, undoes itself. The analyst's task is not to weave these fragments into narrative but to attend to their movement—their stumbling, their returns, their dissolutions. In this space of dispersal, aesthetic experience is no adornment. It is what makes the holding possible—a way of staying with what will not yet be resolved.

Experiences of gender, sexuality, race, class, and other social identifications often emerge in analysis not as fixed narratives but as associative fragments—disjointed impressions, dream residues, moments of inexplicable affect. Just as the uncanny unsettles the seam between inner and outer life, randomness disturbs the fiction of stable identity—the fantasy that one's experience might ever be contained by category. The objects of psychic life are obscure, scattered, and in this way, the consulting room becomes something like a passport—transporting both analyst and analysand to places neither anticipated. These categories—gender, sexuality, race, religion, class—do not appear as coherent identities but as dreamlike formations: residues of the day, associative chains, impressions shaped by personal and collective history. Koichi Togashi (2022) names this unknowability a radical form of care—an abandonment of the search for immediate meaning in favor of experiencing before understanding. He proposes a "zero moment," in which the analyst must surrender to the untranslatable—to what remains between self and other, just out of reach.

To listen in this way is to encounter a deeper truth: that the other's beginnings could have been ours—not because we are the same, but because identity itself is contingent. Togashi's notion of the "zero moment" is not a call to imagine oneself as the other but to accept the randomness of psychic life—the unsettling possibility that, under different circumstances, we might have lived a different subjectivity entirely. Not identification, but contact with what cannot be seized—what stirs in the space between self and other. It is here, in this disquiet, that de M'Uzan (2013) locates what he calls the "scandal of identity"—the recognition that identity is not a coherent narrative but a psychic tension, an unstable negotiation between inside and outside, past and present, the self and what resists it. Identity, in this view, is not something we own or express but something we endure—something lived through, often without resolution.

To enter the uncanniness of social and political experience means accepting that we are affected before we understand. This is the problem of translation: the impossibility of rendering one's psychic reality into language without remainder. Every attempt to communicate leaves a gap. And yet, we persist—often mistaking that gap not as a failure of understanding but as evidence of the excess at the heart of all subjective life. As Britzman (2022) writes, all communication is a "corrupted file"—corrupted not by error but by the unconscious libidinal investments that shape it. This is the analyst's dilemma: to remain inside the uncertainty of listening, to resist the pull toward coherence, toward quick meaning. For Bion, unknowability, unpreparedness, and uncanniness are not obstacles but part of the analytic task. They demand a form of listening that, as I have written elsewhere (Gozlan, 2014), commits us to an act of differing and deferring repetition—a return to what cannot be fully re-found. When we try to resolve uncertainty too quickly—when we enter a "sword fight" with our patients as if meaning could be won—we lose what analysis seeks to cultivate: the capacity to withstand what remains unresolved.

To approach the analytic encounter as a space of unknowability is not to reject meaning but to make space for it to emerge in unexpected ways. And if we are affected before we understand, then analysis offers not resolution but the ability to stay with the contradictions of being—without retreating into the fantasy that identity can be fully known. Being affected by the other may not lead to understanding, but as Togashi suggests, it may offer the experience of not being alone. That may be enough. The analyst cannot change the world. The transformations we witness in the clinic do not always translate into public life. Still, we must enter worlds that are not our own—curious, porous, uncertain. Not to impose coherence, but to tolerate what we cannot know in time—a discipline of neutrality that is always touched by the patient's arrival. Analysis does not promise better adaptation. It offers, instead, the hope for a greater capacity: to bear frustration, to live with contradiction, to endure the ill-preparedness of being in the world.

13 Crafting of a self[1]

It is obvious to me that one of the thorniest concepts in psychoanalytic thinking today is the question of gender, particularly as it is thought about through the experience of transgender and transitioning (see, for example, recent discussions in the *International Journal of Psychology* on gender by Blass et al. (2021). An insistence of pathology under the guise of *loco parentis* (e.g., Bell, 2020; Blass, 2020; Lemma, 2015, 2018) often presents itself through preoccupation with questions about the future, worry over disruption of development, prevention of regret, and concern over the potential evasion of underlying issues which are seen as being displaced onto gender. The psychoanalytic field, however, is no longer monolithic. There is a zeitgeist of how we talk about a capacious notion of gender away from identitarian terms.

In my previous work (Gozlan, 2008, 2014), I was interested in gender and transitioning as a question of aesthetics and art, by which I mean the conceptualization of gender as an artful project, the art of creating the self. I turned to art, film, and literature to imagine transgender as psychical experience, as a question of representation, and as an enigma that belongs to gender. Today, I want to take a fragment of those experiences and move it to an understanding of different situations of transitions that are grounded in gender but that suggest a wider world of experience, with the claim that the self is a complicated matter (Klein, 1937, p. 340). Everyone knows of course how complicated the self is, but its complexity comes as a surprise because in trying to understand the self we meet its inaccessibility, like the dream's navel. What I am trying to show in this chapter are these complications and the attempt to write about them. What is interesting to me is the question of what we can learn from the study of people trying to talk about their lives via memoir.

The immediacy of the arguments over gender and gender transitioning we encounter today, I propose, might take a different turn if we look at different ways of conceptualizing transitioning. For a better grasp, I am going to be juxtaposing two memoirs of gender transitioning: one from the vantage point of a person who has transitioned and the other from a perspective of a witness to transitioning. The memoirs share something in common. They give the reader a sense of transition as a human condition, not an exception. I read them as "narrative revolts" (Kristeva, 2002). These narrative accounts are brave in the

DOI: 10.4324/9781003440758-18

sense that they resolutely face the foibles of not-knowing and the anxiety of needing to know. They open gender to the challenge of origin, the quest for an even history, and traditional notions of identity and development. Novel conceptualization of gender and transitioning also offer us original metaphors with which to consider new ways of listening to gender as a borderline concept that cannot be traced to biological or social causes; it is shaped as it is narrated.

One way of staying with the situation of gender is through thinking about the difficulties of articulating it. Part of the difficulty resides in the strange temporality of gender. Making sense of gender is a process ruled by the temporality of afterwardness (Laplanche, 1992); that is, something that can only be interpreted and made sense of from the position of the present, for which the case of reading becomes exemplary. I approach memoirs as case studies, following Forrester's (2017) insight that in reading clinical cases we can begin to conceptualize our own theory of reading. The writing of a case, Forrester suggests, is already an aftereffect of the transference, and this "combined action of anticipation and retroaction" (Gallop, 1987, p. 82) is essential to how and why we write clinical cases at all. In writing cases, we are confronted with material that does not fit together until we bring a *nachträglichkeit* temporality to bear on the case, thus revealing the meaning of disconnected bits through the deferred action of writing. This retroaction, Britzman suggests, becomes "a means to revise and construct the impact of experience felt before understanding" (Britzman, 2009, p. 52). Cases for Forrester are exemplars. Not because they can be generalized, but because they present a threshold—cases give us access to a social, political, emotional, and pedagogical situation.

Revisions and dead-ends

A 50-year-old acclaimed theater producer, P. Carl, decides to undergo gender transition. He is now a man who enjoys a free pass into misogyny, a "sudden privilege" (P. Carl, p. 3) of joining in belittling jokes about women and the "power that emanates from [his] white male skin" (p. 3). But at the same time, he experiences guilt. His is a text about the impossible attempt to put history together. In the process of transitioning, his understanding of himself transforms. Something that he knew about himself, but nonetheless could not anticipate, was announced into being, manifesting an urge to transition. Living in his pre-transition body as Polly, a dutiful daughter, and later, as a lesbian, a feminist, and an activist, P. Carl recalls existing in a constant state of discord with the categories into which he felt subsumed, swaying painfully between a longing for inclusion and the repulsion of feeling apprehended by a gaze that refracted what he felt to be a false image of himself. On the weekend of March 16, 2017, P. Carl had "crossed the line" (p. 1). He writes of taking a selfie and being overcome by a sense of agreement with his image, thinking "I am finally me" (p. 2).

P. Carl writes about a sobering change in the way he is now addressed by others. There are those who retract or attack and others who disregard or welcome. His retroactive look at his pre-transition self, who he now experiences as his twin, also invokes in him questions about his capacity to hold on to parallel realities and versions of self. He is haunted by Polly, by the persistent memory of being molested by his father, and by not being believed. As he enjoys the privilege of being accepted into the company of men, and as he muses over the thrill of momentarily identifying with the aggressor in his efforts to pass, he is also a tomboy in a fight against men. And P. Carl is a man who knows firsthand the terror of being a woman objectified by men. This doing and undoing of gender brings him to writing. Entering P. Carl's narrative, the reader is confronted with the paradox of the writer's surprise upon encountering the body he crafted and by the uncannily mixed feeling of recognition and foreignness. Unexpected welcomes and surprising dismissals are encountered in transitioning; friendly environments become hostile, and inhospitable places warm up.

I follow P. Carl from one space to another and muse over the tight link between the relative comfort with one's body and the capacity to hold on to one's mind. Here is P. Carl flaunting his masculinity in an anonymous pool, protecting a woman from another man's wrath. There, he is grappling with guilt over the masculinity that denies his wife the female partner she longs for but never had. As long as P. Carl feels he has to *prove his gender* to others, he is caught in the image of the macho man, in the elation of hormones, in the pleasure of his body, and in being seen on his own terms. There may be a terrific pleasure, a beautiful feeling of being a part of something much bigger—the world of men—but there is also something surprising that P. Carl finds. The cosmetics of gender—shaving, muscle building, climbing—are short-lived. What he faces after transitioning is the destiny of his aging body.

In gender, time also momentarily appears out of joint. P. Carl feels as if he becomes a teenager at 51. He will have his first shave, flirt with passing women in a bar, sculpt his body at the gym, conquer mountains, and discuss football with his barber. But he will also have to contend with a history: of the passionate feminist that he was, the one who envied and fought the white masculinity that hurt, humiliated, and misread him. P. Carl wonders about the man he has become. Is he now the man he used to despise? The feminist his wife had fallen in love with, he feels, is the one she misses now. The ushering of oneself into existence, we learn, also risks a devastating loss. There is a cost in transformation. Simply because he ages, gender is also subject to time. At some point, P. Carl must also face his partner's breast cancer diagnosis. Jolted by friends who doubt his capacity as a man to understand his wife's condition or to support her, P. Carl realizes the emotional situation of gender as destabilizing and conflated. He is beginning to experience the way men are seen, realizing that there is no such thing as a *man* but a *polyphony* of masculinities (Bakhtin, 1984; Fiorini, 2019) at stake, where conflicting positions are constitutive qualities of gender. "When a body faces death, a health crisis, or loss of freedom," he asks, "are there only women and men?" (p. 186).

I read *Becoming a Man* as a story of gender and of breakthrough—a push, a hatching, and a putting together. By the time P. Carl writes his memoir, *Becoming a Man* (2020), he is no longer a young man, even though transitioning allows him the psychical opportunity to be a teenager for a while and just play. It is a *nachträglichkeit* look at gender as one ages, about the childhood he wished to have had, the child and teenager he wishes to have been. P. Carl does more than narrate a unique experience of transitioning. His memoir is an attempt to represent a coming into gender by grappling with the murkiness of history and loss. There is a mourning of an image one had in mind of what one could have been, a farewell to lost time, and a beginning of an attempt to make sense of obscure family dynamics.[2] The narrative temporality of the memoir takes one into the netherworld of fantasy because

> *Nachträglichkeit* . . . not only expresses a sophisticated concept of psychical causality but also reflects how meaning in general is structured—at the same time as reflecting how its own meaning is structured on the basis of a variety of translations.
> (Civitarese, 2022, in Gozlan, 2025, p. 12)

With the construction of memoirs, one meets a history of gender through present libidinal echoes, anxieties, and wishes. We encounter gender as something that can only be understood from its deferral.

As I read *Becoming a Man*, I am also listening to gender as unconscious working-through and toward something unknown that changes as P. Carl ages. *Becoming a Man* is an explicit account of a psychic change through an encounter with something far away from gender but related to it—illness, excitement, sexuality, and relationships. Gender is never a discrete event one undergoes. Rather, gender can be thought of as an extension into life's experiences, both accidental and chosen. In P. Carl's account, beginnings are overdetermined and their narrated trajectory takes the form of a dream, encountered as it is crafted. The attempt to undo and re-do is another way of thinking of gender transitioning as repetition. What repeats, Freud (1914/1950) suggests, is memory. Everything that relies on memory is already a dilemma of repetition that is necessary, precisely because we do not have access to the origins of our conflicts. Narrating, reading, and writing structure gender's time, and we can say that its deferred temporality not only expresses sophisticated trajectories but also machinations. Meaning is in translation.

Gradually, P. Carl's narrative moves to a broader terrain than the preoccupation with questions of identity in the process of transitioning. As long as he could focus on the transitioning as something outside of other events, such as illness, age, and the shifting attitudes of friends, P. Carl could live in the ways in which his sedimentations of gender could hold. But the encounter with these events presents a crisis, not only because of the emotional difficulty they pose in the present, but also because his ways of understanding his history have been dismantled. Through P. Carl's transitioning, the reader encounters gender not as a *thing* but as an axis of innumerable relationships.

The narcissistic preoccupation with the body, in a sense of its ideal image, shifts to an understanding of gender as formed by relations with the other and with one's own otherness. Along the way, the initial question, "how do I become a man?", transitions to a more fundamental question, one concerning the pleasure of being and becoming whom he wants to be, not only as a trans man but also as a human: "what kind of a man do I want to become?"

Reparations and surrender

Where do we narrate from when we witness the other's transitioning? This is a persistent dilemma in Susan Faludi's memoir, *In the Darkroom*. Faludi, a journalist and a feminist activist, grapples with the gender transitioning of her estranged elderly father. The transitioning of her childhood father from a violent man into a delicate woman was a personal event that created a new frame of thinking for Faludi, a woman whose lifelong contributions to the feminist movement exceed her crucial coinage of the term "rape culture." The new frame meant that the old frame could not be universalized. The macho aggressive man she remembers from her childhood is now a woman who goes by the name Stepheni, who wears high heels even while hiking, and who insists on being greeted by being kissed on the hand. This transformation is shocking to the author, who wonders: is [her father's] transition "a return or a departure?" (p. 15).

At the core of Faludi's current inquiry is not physical violation, aggression, or rape but rather an entrance into something less delineated, more enigmatic and unfinished: a relationship and a loss. *In the Dark Room* bears witness to the author's own "transitioning"—a transformation of her relationship with her old self. What unfolds in her memoir is an attempt to make meaning of an intricate family story, whose traces she is compelled to examine anew, if only to discover that she is still—or again—unable to capture or undo history. Faludi movingly examines her own transformation, and she revises her relationship with her estranged father as she witnesses her transitioning in the context of a longer and larger history, bringing her to Hungary and to his Jewish family during World War II. There is a dimensionality to the father's transitioning that position's identity close to a kaleidoscopic notion of escaping: her father is an escape artist. He has escaped the Nazi regime by disguising himself as an SS officer and succeeding in outwitting the Germans into releasing his parents from captivity. He escaped from his parents, his native Hungary, his wife and his daughter, his Jewish identity, his criminal past, and finally, his masculinity. The ego, however, cannot escape itself, and so, in her attempt to discern the many faces of her father, Susan Faludi's memoir also leaves us with a question: what remains after transitioning?

Against the backdrop of Faludi's reassembling her relationship with her transitioning father, we witness a complex scene of history that is bigger than the history of the body. It includes the history of older generations, of war and anti-Semitism, of hiding and taking space. History here functions as a site of doubling, deferral, contradiction, and enigma. There is no clear "before and after," only an elusive and intermediate space of uncertainty where "the past is never past" (Faulkner, 1994, *Requiem for a Nun*). There is something in gender that resists cohesion, revealing an uncanny quality: "My father fussed with her scarf and then leaned over to deliver a strange whisper into my ear. 'I know what they are thinking,' she said, sotto voce: 'There is an overdressed shiksa'" (p. 240). What starts as a daughter's attempt to remember her childhood and make sense of her absent father's gender shift becomes a question of how one lives with uncertainty, and here the reader is doubly affected. Transitioning produces new editions of old conflicts.

In witnessing her father's transitioning, Faludi is also creating something new. The easy narrative of a violent and neglectful father is now insufficient as she confronts a larger and more complex psychic landscape, one she is not in control of and that forces her to revise the history of her own attachments and disidentifications. Eventually, Faludi shifts from a study of biographical events to a study of how people make sense of their experience. In the process of attempting to understand her father, she gradually moves to trying to simply *stand* him. The process of excavation of historical details turns to one of interpretation. She enters something much more enigmatic than the tracing of cause and effect, and she comes to see identity itself as an obstacle course where truth is elusive and ever incomplete. What the reader enters with Faludi is a surrender to obscurity. This surrendering in writing and witnessing also applies to gender transitioning. One must wait to see what unfolds.

Learning

With each story of transition, we encounter the way in which the author is pushed to reimagine their own psychic landscape, and what the memoir shows us is the ways in which transitioning are also transformations in relationality. Its not simply an individual transformation, and that transformation, as the memoirs show, is not immediate. It is a process that is overdetermined by situations that cannot be anticipated, such as the other's response. Even rationality, we come to see, much like autonomy,[3] must be assumed before it can be created. Memoirs open the dilemma of fate, the aging of all the grand markers of bodily identity, and the fact that the body is always in transition no matter what you choose and whoever you are. But this uncertainty is also a condition for desire. As we transition, we are already transforming in ways we cannot predict.

Memoirs are the work of crafting experience. As such, these memoirs enact the very temporal difficulties they attempt to apprehend, where experiences that are much anticipated but not fully comprehended have the capacity to redraw the past and the very self this past brought forward. When we aestheticize it this way, memoirs provide us ways to understand what it means to think about the self as something that is created. These memoirs are instructive, rather than indoctrinating, in the sense that they do not tell us what to do or how to think. Instead, they are depictions of how others have struggled with their situations of gender. Each memoir is the author's jacket signature that is created by others and by themselves. Their character is a place of agency, of choice. And while choices may reenact something that is already gone, such as trauma or remnants of infantile sexuality, the capacity to narrate choices already indicates that subject is not a prisoner in it. What can the analyst learn from reading memoirs of transitioning? Memoirs of gender take us outside of what we know. By reading memoirs, I am entering a world that is both mine and not mine. It is a way into an imaginative world that allows us entrance into conflicts, questions, and representations of being in the world. With the depiction of the entanglement of gender in conflicts of recognition, reparation, reconciliation, and revision, we receive a vantage through which we can appreciate the difficulty of conceptualizing gender, even though it appears to be very present. These contemporary stories of transitioning open a way to think about what happens when people try to tolerate their contradictions. If the study of character touches on the problem of self-knowledge, however, as Britzman (2010) suggests, it also elaborates the difficulties of depression and meaninglessness when they cannot bear their negative capability: "something has to fail for identity to be a preoccupation" (Peter Brooks, 2011, in Britzman, 2010, p. 14). Through the memoirs, the reader begins to see that people change their understanding of themselves because their circumstances are always in flux.

My discussion on different narratives of transitioning opens up some of the dilemmas that have been foreclosed when the phenomenology of experience is set aside. The attempt to grasp a situation by observing the terms and moves of libidinal life—its places of enjoyment, defense, performance—is also an ethical turn toward human events. If we think about gender in this intermediate way, we will be able to enter the crevices that our previous theories foreclosed and the full range of experiences and people that participate in gender transitioning. To describe gender as a situation that is both affecting and affected is also to point to a temporal difficulty that bears on the question of freedom: the situation of gender is oriented by an agency one can't possibly know because that agentic self is always already changing through the very exercise of its autonomy, which transforms any notion of autonomy related to decision-making—whether to take hormones or undergo surgery—into something one has to assume in order to make it exist. The ethical position of the analyst entails negative capability because what is put in doubt is the conceptual framing of listening: it does not matter what we know when we listen to the other. Here, ethics is not to be assumed but something that is anticipated and configured in the conditions of learning and in the therapeutic situation. This anticipatory and delayed situation gives the notion of identity its creative potential.

The capacity to tolerate enigma is also an ethical position for Freud. It is not rooted in indifference but in the capacity to tolerate difference that involves a measure of resignation, the ability to surrender to loss, to the fact that the fate of our theories or interventions cannot be known in advance (Freud, 1914, 1937a). When one listens for difference, one cannot be prepared for what one will find. Instead of locating gender, we can only find transitional space, intermediate affects, animations, dispersals, erotic pushes, anxieties, and places of pleasure. No longer a core (Stoller, 1968a), an internal stable sense of identity that Stoller associated with a hidden biological force), gender—when viewed from the vantage of *nachträglich* action—is more like a skin that surrounds emptiness. From this affective vantage, sexual difference is not a feature of gender but the "potential space that brings identity into being" (Pitt & Britzman, 2003, in Britzman & Gilbert, 2004, p. 83).

The process of transition already suggests a change, but its experience can sometimes feel like an earthquake and sometimes like a fault line that is susceptible to something unimaginable. And yet memoirs are also a way of grappling with the unimaginable: the transitioning of an aging abusive father into a delicate woman, the coming to terms with limits and death, facing disability, the question of choice that involved the dilemma of being, and not being, life or death, and of livability—in what body do I want to live? Gender is glimpsed through its vicissitudes as a performance, a space of creative self-configuration and self-expression, as a defense against and a regeneration of a lost object. And while I may understand the meaning an individual gives to their gender, gender itself remains mute.

The fact of being excluded from knowledge crumbles the sense of seeming stability of our narrative because as a retroactive action of historicity, it accrues different meanings, leaving us with many possibilities for identifications. This is all to say that memoirs of transitioning are never free of the process they attempt to describe. There is something inaccessible to knowledge, and the understanding that we cannot accomplish certitude arrives only retroactively and arbitrarily. The arbitrariness and intertwining of events leads me to think of Canguilhem's notion of error as regularity. Life, Canguilhem (1989) suggests, is already constituted by forces that cannot be predicted, traced, or prevented, and so errors are unstoppable. Through the metaphor of error, Canguilhem shows how the human is a walking advertisement of something new. Error, understood in this way, may well be another word for eros. History is indeed difficult for the psyche. But then, there is another side to this dilemma: psychical life is difficult for the telling of history because "part of the psychical life is unconscious and the unconscious is timeless, something that history cannot be" (Britzman, 2022, viii).

Our narratives are modes of self-theorizing[4]—and hence, of authorizing—and through them gender will act as a mystic pad where erasure continues to leave an impression. We cannot cut off our history because our history is also a cut, an otherness that determines our psychic susceptibility to interpretation, elaboration, and creativity, so that a new note can be made from everything that is accrued in phantasy. No matter what, no matter when, the brute reality of our body is always a problem of interpretation and theorization. Psychically speaking, anatomy has no stable meaning because, as Laplanche

(1992) insists, the human is a self-theorizing creature, which means that the self is both theoretical, subject to infantile theories, and subject to the unconscious of the other. Gender, we could say, is the fate of our givens, while givens themselves—whether they are the brute fact of anatomical differences or the enigmas of unconscious inheritance—are not laws. In this view, gender contains and frames situations of existence that render the self's truths accessible through interpretations and open to elaborations.

Notes

1 A longer version of this chapter was published in: Gozlan, O. (2025). Novel Revolts as crafting of self. *Psychoanalytic Quarterly*, *94*(1), 5–27.
2 Here I also hear an echo of Lacan's elaboration on Freud's concept of *Nachträglichkeit*: "what realizes itself in my history is not the past perfect of what was since it is no longer, not even the present perfect of what has been in what I am, but the future perfect of what I will have been for what I am in the process of becoming" (Ecrit, Seminar XI).
3 Castoriadis's (1991) notion of Autonomy as something that doesn't yet exist, that is always in relation to something else, and that therefore we must lean on the capacity to act before being ready for it, problematizes any notion of consent in recent debates about the child or adolescent's gender transitioning. This delayed notion is also the structure of learning, and the teacher as Britzman argues (2022) has to imagine the student reading before they can read. And that is close to how the learners imagining themselves accomplishing something before it is done. This brings autonomy closer to desire.
4 Self-theorizing is a Laplancian term that is used by many others, including Harris, Scarfone, and Saketopoulou. I conceptualize it as a universal theory that conveys the human's attempt to understand emotional situations with little to go on. In a way, it is the modern conception of Freud's little sex researcher.

14 What passes between[1]

We are living in an era where the body no longer obeys its previous limits. Skin, bone, and flesh have become sites of possibility—malleable, replaceable, transformable. The promise and peril of bodily transformation have never been more available, nor more contested. At the heart of these transformations lies the question of transsexuality—not simply as a medical or personal choice but as a scene where gender, ethics, and affect collide. Transsexuality today does more than multiply gender positions; it unsettles the very idea that gender is a position at all. The choice to transition—if it can even be called a choice—is often cast as a moral dilemma. Does one have the right to change one's sex? To refuse the sex assigned, to inhabit another, or to dwell between? These questions circulate not only through legal and medical discourses but also through psychic life. They echo in the classroom, the clinic, the family, and the analyst's consulting room. What passes between people—between generations, between bodies, between categories—becomes the material of transference, of phantasy, and of dread.

In recent years, a growing body of scholarship has sought to account for the clinical, cultural, and emotional lives of trans individuals. Yet what these studies reveal extends beyond trans experience alone. They offer a mirror to our shared difficulty with recognition, with autonomy, with the limits of the self. The discourse surrounding trans identity is no longer (if it ever was) just about gender. It is about the right to become, the cost of knowing, and the fragility of the categories we mistake for truth. At the same time, if we take into account the Freudian idea of the unconscious as a site of "interminable self-questioning" (Rose, p. 232 in Gozlan, 2022a), it follows that any quest for self-definition becomes inherently fraught. This impossibility is often overlooked or foreclosed, leading to what Jacqueline Rose calls a bankrupt "rhetoric of certainty." In most political discourses, the unconscious is disregarded because it cannot be fully accounted for; yet, its repression is itself traumatic. This trauma, Rose suggests, is not only about making the unspeakable into words but also about understanding trauma as an ongoing expression of one's lived experience. In her 2019 essay "The Long Scream," Rose explores the relationship between trauma and justice in South Africa, attending a 2018 conference on "Recognition and Reconciliation" in

DOI: 10.4324/9781003440758-19

Stellenbosch. She describes how trauma is often expected to be verbalized and resolved, yet she introduces the idea of trauma as something that might instead manifest in a long scream—an expression that resists easy resolution. This concept is particularly relevant to trans experience, which often exists at the intersection of visibility and silence, political demand and personal pain. Rose's insight allows us to reconsider trauma not as something to be contained but as something that reveals the vulnerability inherent in all identity formations.

This leads us to wonder: how can we think about the political in relation to the unconscious, or the unconscious as intertwined with the political? The grounds for truth and reconciliation, Rose suggests, cannot be separated from the plight of those who have been excluded, dehumanized, and oppressed. Affects that emerge from trauma can be ruthless, sometimes even generating a desire for revenge. The scream, she suggests, is both a symbolic response to the prohibition against experiencing pain and a protest against the expectation of silent endurance. Trauma, then, is not just a personal burden but can transform into a political demand. Some theorists have described trauma as a state of helplessness without a witness, leaving individuals with the internalized command: "I must be quiet." However, when this silence is broken by a long scream, it signals the return of what political structures have repressed. Rose ultimately argues that any political transformation must reconcile ideation with affect rather than rely on their dissociation. This perspective opens a crucial path for rethinking the relationship between trauma, trans experience, and political action.

To better understand these political tensions, some historical context is useful. Earlier social movements produced new ways of understanding social structures and power. For example, the women's movement's idea of choice opened a different notion of control over the body. The fight for abortion and birth control made possible the wider use of hormones and surgery, paving the way for transsexual rights. In turn, transgender demands have reconfigured what is considered feminine and masculine, de-essentializing and destabilizing gender positions. Feminist demands for political rights also wed political protest to conceptual change: transgender demands present new questions for feminism by shaping primary notions of gender. However, the language of desire that would allow for complexity in feminist and transsexual discourses is largely absent. This is because these discourses rarely move beyond the framework of rights, which often emphasizes legality and protection over deeper questions of identity and affect.

Political protest can risk collapsing politics into rigid certitude. At the same time, such a collapse is often necessary for reasons of intelligibility and political action. Certitude, however, risks wrecking the capacity for communication. If we allow for complexity, ambivalence, and potential unintelligibility, we may foster richer dialogue but at the cost of political action. On the one hand, we find absolute certainty, but on the other, we risk becoming so subtle that we become politically mute. What ethics can result from the paradoxes presented by the tension between political action and unconscious truth? Ethics, rather than being a set of fixed rules, emerges through dialogue and negotiation, much like a kind of shared fantasy. It is inherently shaped by what it seeks to contain. The tension between demand and desire also plays out in the relationship between social movements and personal preoccupations. How can we differentiate between demand and desire? Here, a series of hypothetical registers are introduced: failure, unpredictability, and difference. These registers can be read as stories of origins that link the personal to the political in novel ways, shedding new light on the complexities of identity, activism, and transformation.

Failure

Feminist demands for control of the body began with struggles for agency and choice regarding abortion, adoption, fertility, and breastfeeding. More recent demands for medical intervention in the form of infertility treatments, surrogate mothering, and artificial insemination have further shifted the notion of nature as static and given, making it a site of cultural and ideological contestation. After all, how can nature be a measurement of what is right and what is wrong when nature pays no attention to human moral codes? For instance, what kind of "natural" justice is involved when some people are able to get pregnant while others are not? These demands for medical intervention have also destabilized traditional notions of motherhood. Additionally, feminist denunciations of sexual harassment, misogyny, and violence—whose victims are generally women—have brought to the forefront Catherine MacKinnon's question of whether women were ever fully recognized as human, exposing underlying power dynamics and privilege (MacKinnon, 1999). Both feminist and gay and lesbian movements have created a path for transgender rights by interrogating and expanding fundamental structures of gender—specifically the men-versus-women binary that patriarchal laws enforce and that pervade social arrangements under the guise of natural order.

However, a cursory look at today's news headlines reveals that historic gains regarding these demands, at least in North America, are once again being contested. A re-entrenchment of patriarchal control over women's bodies is both imminent and undeniable. Simultaneously, the destabilization of traditional gender arrangements has exposed tensions within feminism's conceptions of womanhood. While feminism has long theorized gender as separate from sex, essentialist claims about genetic makeup or a shared history of female oppression have led, in some cases, to an outright dismissal of trans women's singular experiences and vulnerabilities to gendered violence. Some radical feminist perspectives view trans women as a threat, rather than allies in the fight against patriarchal oppression (Serano, 2007, in Gozlan, 2022a). The failure of feminism to address trans misogyny, some argue, allows "one of the most pervasive forms of traditional sexism to go unchecked" (Serano,

2007, 312, in Gozlan, 2022a). In turn, many trans women remain "oblivious to the impact that traditional sexism has on their lives" (Serano, 2007, 312, in Gozlan, 2022a).

Jacqueline Rose's feminist critique of feminism insists on incorporating a language of desire into feminist discourse by focusing on the tensions between rights and wants—between the concrete material demands for social transformation and the necessity of preserving subjective desire (Rose, 1993). Both rights and wants, Rose suggests, are animated by unconscious forces—and for that very reason, they remain vulnerable to retaliation and destruction. This leaves a difficult ethical question in its wake: how might feminist and trans movements grapple with the pull toward turning the tables, toward revenge, toward the satisfactions of retributive justice? To take seriously the role of personal fantasy in political life is also to confront the pull of our own omnipotent wishes—fantasies of controlling the social world, of settling its wrongs. And yet, Rose (1993, p. 235, in Gozlan, 2022a) writes that "the very moment when feminism is saying that the personal is its prerogative" is also the moment when something personal is inevitably given up, compromised. What this returns us to is not a simple political dilemma but the problem of desire—and the more unsettling condition of self-difference. Identity politics, in its effort to honor particular experiences, often strains against this self-difference. It risks closing down the unruly and unconscious dimensions of subjectivity. For Rose, this is the deeper tension: political movements are never only about the social; they are also entangled with personal fantasies—steeped in idealization and the wish for omnipotence that shadows it. Can an ethics emerge from this paradox—one that resists collapsing into an "us versus them" framework?

We might ask, here: has feminism laid claim to womanhood as its own possession? The question opens onto an impossibility. There is, on one side, the demand to make womanhood intelligible—even as this demand runs counter to the persistent reality of systemic sexual objectification, most visibly in relation to white heterosexual men. And yet, for some, the call to include and humanize women seems to hinge on the exclusion of trans women from the category of "woman." How are we to think through this refusal? The trans reading of feminist hostility and the feminist fear that trans inclusion erodes the category of gender itself both remain bound to a deeper phantasy: the wish for certainty, for a ground that will not give way. And yet it does. While feminism opened the door to the idea of self-determination over one's body, biology remains positioned as a stable ground, particularly in radical feminist movements.

Rose's recent essay, "One Long Scream" (2019, in Gozlan, 2022a), which I discussed earlier, and Sally Swartz's book, *Ruthless Winnicott* (2018), both propose new psychoanalytic perspectives on political movements that demand radical subjective change. Swartz, in particular, examines the role of ruthlessness in political protest. She provides the example of the exclusion of trans students from an exhibit organized by the "Rhodes Must Fall" (RMF) movement at a university. This exclusion led to a defiant trans protest, where activists challenged the movement's claims to inclusivity and transformation. The protest was vocal and highly visible—some protesters showed up naked, others covered in paint, and some were photographed throwing feces at a statue. As a result, the RMF movement was banned. Swartz argues that this example vividly illustrates the urgent need to think through conflicts between movements as internal conflicts—struggles of self-differentiation. These struggles, she contends, are ruthless because they concern the very integrity of the movements themselves, which are often organized around the urgent demand that a particular need be met.

Political protest often arises from rage and indignation over a lack of recognition. The less one feels recognized, the more passionate—even violent—the demand for recognition becomes. Swartz argues that the social realm must tolerate this intensity. Her theory suggests that if the political environment can withstand such demands, they may, over time, be relinquished in ways that reduce their hostility. This requires an understanding that not all demands will be met, but also that their rejection does not have to culminate in sheer destruction. However, revolt sometimes involves the destruction of meaning itself. In the process of demanding action, deeper insights are sometimes cast aside. For instance, conflicts over trans women's access to women's restrooms or all-girls schools, as well as the denial of trans misogyny in the name of women's rights, exemplify the ways in which transgender advocacy is often framed as a direct threat to the long-fought-for rights of women. In this framework, trans people's appeals for inclusion are perceived as erasing women's rights to safety and stability.

If demands for change—or transition, in any form—require a measure of ruthlessness, what kind of social framework can both "hold" these demands while setting necessary boundaries against destructive rage? Swartz finds Winnicott's concept of the "good enough mother" particularly useful in addressing this dilemma. Winnicott (1971) emphasized that it is not the perfect mother but the good-enough one who provides the child with necessary frustrations—frustrations through which resilience can grow. Swartz (2018) draws a parallel here: social movements, too, require a kind of holding—a space that can bear demands without silencing them or surrendering to them uncritically (p. 9, in Gozlan, 2022a). Change may require the destruction of old forms, but something new cannot take shape without first reckoning with the limits that mark every position, every movement. Both trans and feminist struggles must at times be ruthless, but ruthlessness alone cannot build an ethic; repair must be thought alongside rupture, not after it. Perhaps it is here that an ethic begins: in the recognition that transformation is inseparable from loss. What would it ask of trans and feminist movements, then, to listen more closely—not only to their hopes but to the ruthlessness within their demands? Or, in Rose's words, how do we build "a political movement that tells it how it uniquely is, without separating one struggle for equality and human dignity from all the rest?" (Rose, 2019, p. 10). Perhaps this task requires developing the capacity to hold both legitimate rage and legitimate fear—without allowing one to annihilate the other.

Unpredictability

The idea of self-determination over the body as a central tenet is shared by both trans and feminist discourses. Nevertheless, self-determination over the body raises a conundrum: if freedom is predicated upon self-determination, how is it possible for self-determination to have a limit? And how does one decide who has control over bodies if one believes that control over bodies is predicated on the notion of biological realism? Let us explore the tensions between trans discourse and feminism with an example. Susan Faludi's memoir, *In the Dark Room* (2016), describes her slow process of accepting her 76-year-old father's transition from male to female (Faludi, 2016). Faludi narrates the transformation in a singular manner. Hers is not a story of continuity, one of "I always was," but one of contiguity. Faludi's father is a master of disguise. He hides. He creates changes without experiencing them. Transitioning is his way of coming to life. Notably, Faludi becomes most creative when she gives up the wish to understand. She follows her father and surrenders to his questions.

In the process of witnessing her father's transition, Faludi discovers many things about him: the mystery of his femininity, his history, his relationships. Faludi learns to come to terms with the fact that, as much she tries to figure things out, her father remains opaque. She moves away from trying to understand and, in the process, her aggression becomes something else that transforms her and her father. He too must surrender. Both Faludi and her father accept experiences that have never been anticipated. At the limits of understanding, there is a coming to terms that forces Faludi to reconceptualize everything she knows. It is not only an attempt to understand the other, which would be an ethical stance, but also a study of one's own resistance to giving up something in order to understand. Those strategies are defenses and failures of imagination. Faludi's own transformation as she witnesses her father's transitioning offers a new ethical view of transitioning as discontinuous. Faludi's memoir is not just an attempt to understand but a study of her resistance to give up something in order to understand. Such a process explains how something of the self has to be surrendered or lost, like ideality or hatred, in order for truth and understanding to emerge.

As the reader follows Faludi's quest for clues, when she wonders what her father "will have been for what [he] is in the process of becoming," she sees identity as an obstacle course where truth can never be found (Faludi, 2016, in Gozlan, 2022a). Because the transitioning father is seen as a stranger, the readers, who turn into witnesses of this estrangement, have to come to terms with a similar opacity in their own selves. The opened space of intersubjectivity, that of the readers reading the text, that of Faludi and her father, is thus incommensurable. Another way of thinking about this estrangement to ourselves would be through Georg Simmel's description of the stranger as someone that comes and stays (Simmel, 1950, in Gozlan, 2022a). The unconscious, like Simmel's stranger, makes us all strangers to the others and to ourselves. Because of the agency of the unconscious, such a transformation is not a story of before and after, that is, of a strange body that is now here and then gone. Rather, the transformation affects what we might call the human condition given its power to universalize. Faludi's memoir teaches us that history, in order to be truthful, must be, as Swartz has suggested, disillusioned.

The fracture between feminist and trans movements, the split between their communities, can appear as a relational problem. Nonbinary identification, for instance, de facto challenges rigid identity labels such as "woman" or "trans" and thus excludes self-difference, which forecloses the capacity for transformation. It is at the moment when someone confronts the illegibility of nonbinary gender that essentialism emerges as a defense against anxiety. This type of anxiety is reflected, for example, in some feminist views of trans people as subjects who have appropriated and reified gender norms in their very desire for readability. It is similarly evident in the belief that trans women practice misogynist forms of femininity that preserve the patriarchal and heteronormative status quo.

The same attitude is true in radical strands of feminism that exclude trans subjects from "women only" events or facilities. These insist on the "realness" of sexual identity, whereas an F-to-M transsexual is seen as a woman who "plays" at being a man or, more threateningly, a man (with a penis) who "plays" at being a woman (Gozlan, 2016). This essentialist clinging to gender categories reflects a struggle with the enigmatic qualities of sexuality that transsexuality has exposed and thus brought a new twist to our conceptions of gender. Transsexual discourses—in their desire for stability through the insistence on the fantasized notion of righting a "wrong body"—attempt to escape from the disorienting destabilization of sexuality. As Rose argues, these defensive essentializations

> oblige the trans person, whatever the complexity of their experience, to hold fast to the rails of identity. [They] turn the demand to take control of one's own life, which is and has to be politically non-negotiable, into a vision of the mind as subordinate to the will ", the opposite of what the psychic life can ever be.
>
> (Rose, 2016, p. 12)

The meeting of feminism and trans discourses is itself affected by sexuality, hence by the murky fragility of gender, a concept that functions both as a placeholder and a prison house.

The irony is that neither feminist movements nor the transgender movement can escape the confines and fragility of gender: both are caught up in a quest for authenticity and intelligibility predicated on treacherous grounds.

The category of gender promises to render something intelligible and coherent. However, this promise of gender as offering a guarantee of meaning or stability is nothing but a fantasy, or else a defense covering over something that will always remain unintelligible. In clinging to the fantasy of "the political nature of the sexual" (1986), in which notions of self and other are supposedly known, what is left behind, Rose argues, is the sexual and hence fantasized elements of the political. Examining the ruthlessness of both feminist and trans political demands from the point of view of their unconscious underpinnings would reveal that all gender ideation is precarious and in constant tension.

Yet, if surrendering certainty can lead to transformation, as Faludi's narrative suggests, could feminist and trans movements also surrender aspects of their idealized positions in order to move beyond rigid identity categories? The demand for absolute recognition so often hardens into impasse—movements speaking past each other, unable to be altered by the encounter. If feminist struggles for authenticity have already helped make room for transgender subjectivities, the question now is less what has been gained than what must still be relinquished in order for new forms of relation to take shape. Swartz and Rose remind us: transformation asks us to confront our own exclusions—the *unthought known* (Bollas, 1987) that shadows every position we take. Recognition, in this light, becomes something more difficult—a mutual reckoning with vulnerability, not a quest for certainty. The intertwined histories of feminist and trans movements suggest this hard truth: change is not secured by demanding inclusion alone but by loosening the hold of fixed ideas, allowing something unforeseen to emerge. The deeper question insists: how much uncertainty are we willing to bear for the sake of justice that cannot yet be known?

Difference

Feminism introduced the idea that the personal is political; now feminism has to contend with the idea that the political is also personal. How do we protect the right to be non-intelligible when rights both presuppose and configure stable, legible subjects? This is not a new question. Feminism has evolved from a shared collective identity and consciousness that constantly demands self-differentiation. Present divisions between feminist and trans movements bring a new urgency to this challenge. How do we overcome binary states of mind, the logic of "us versus them," when they obscure experiential affinities and political lines of solidarity around issues such as gender violence, economic precariousness, and state and police repression? Winnicott would suggest that the only cure for immaturity is time: with time, preoccupations give up their obsessive insistence. This trajectory becomes evident in the transformation of feminist agendas from an insistence on being included in the male world to an insistence on being recognized in one's singular difference. The third and final move concerns the experience of nonbinary gender insofar as it involves a new form of subjectivity no longer oriented by an appeal to the Other.

Nonbinary identity can become a place of protest, a new ruthlessness, made of a pleasurable moment of omnipotence, a destruction of meaning, a fall of idealities. But it can also be thought of as a transitional space, a malleable in-between space to challenge the fantasy of "normal sexuality." While it is a space of play, it can turn melancholic because it is subject to disillusionment—not only because we can never have all that we want and that, when we have, we no longer want it, but also because the very thing that we value about ourselves, our identity, is in fact a defense against loss, which remains unconscious. The nonbinary subject is a reminder that gender is a conundrum and that sexuality, as Freud suggests, cannot offer any stability and does not point to any "thing" that "men and women can conquer and/ or possess" (Perelberg, 2016, p. 258, in Gozlan, 2022a). Human subjectivity concerns a relation to the void—things that we do not and cannot know. Much like dreams, our theories and ideations of gender are emblematic of the kaleidoscopic ways in which we try to make sense of ourselves at the threshold between reality and fantasy. This recalls Faludi's surrender to the unknowability of her father's transformation, where acceptance emerged not from understanding but from relinquishing the need to fully grasp the other.

Simone de Beauvoir's insistence, more than 70 years ago, that women are not "born" but become so would welcome the possibility of a new subject. We live amidst new and ever-changing reconfigurations of desire, of femininity and masculinity that appear as unstable directions and positionings. Indeed, even if we might be on the verge of freedom from the shackles of gender, difference remains a condition of human subjectivity, and thus relations are structured by a failure to find harmony; no social arrangement will ever be fully satisfactory. The idea of difference was discussed by Winnicott as a developmental achievement that he related to the concept of maiming (Winnicott, 1971). As Swartz observes, maiming is a quality of protest that Rose describes as a way of "being" that is not oriented by the quest for satisfaction or the belief that one can know, possess, and control the other.

Maiming accompanies the child's ruthlessness, which is a quality of aggression arising from the self, making a demand and an attack without collapse into compliance or retaliation. (Winnicott, 1971). Ruthlessness, Winnicott suggests, characterizes the move from relating to an object with no recognition of otherness to object usage, where the other's difference is recognized (p. 86). This process mirrors the transformation seen in Faludi's account, where coming to terms with the father's transition required a surrender of preconceived ideals, allowing for an unforeseen relational shift. In Winnicott's account, the mother cannot possibly meet every single demand of the child. She must limit the child's ruthlessness and, in doing so, let desire emerge. Containment will be based on an understanding that not all demands will be met, gradually increasing the capacity to come to terms with the other's difference.

As we have seen, Swartz and Rose imagine ruthlessness as characterizing a desperate demand that is not simply merciless but also gestures toward vulnerability. If the maiming that accompanies ruthlessness signifies a dependency on an intractable exteriority of the maternal body, which survives the baby's ruthless attacks, then maiming can also create boundaries: it generates not only a separation between the self and its outside but also a permeable boundary for the embodied self—an intermediate space between the self and itself. This recalls Faludi's father's transformation, which did not provide stable answers but instead required surrendering to ambiguity.

If we paraphrase Winnicott, we can ask: can feminist and transsexual movements allow themselves to be "used and eaten" by the protesters while "holding hatred" in a way that both contains and makes productive use of aggression? In "The Uncanny" (1919), Freud poses an intermediate, strange space of thinking. Taking inspiration from Freud's venture into aesthetics, I propose a space of in-difference, in which we discover the strangest, even the unthinkable, and at the same time familiar—a space positioned as "neuter" in opposition to the binary of loving and hating. This space of in-difference would allow one to tolerate ambivalence and to hear the other's desire as enigmatic. Just as Faludi ultimately discovered an ethical position in relinquishing mastery over her father's experience, political movements, too, must learn to surrender the need for full intelligibility. A position of in-difference should offer a way out of the ideality permeating the meeting of the political and the personal; moreover, it recognizes a limit—my worldview, whatever it may be, cannot be imposed on anyone else. The concept hinges on a shift from the "eye for an eye" (and an I for an I) that is often a feature of political activism to an ethical in-difference where people can disagree without destroying the other or themselves. We should postulate in-difference as the space for a creative engagement with something that cannot be known in advance, much like the transformative surrender that Faludi underwent in her attempt to understand her father's transition.

Note

1 A shorter version of this chapter was published in: Gozlan, O. (2022a). In-difference: Feminism and transgender in the field of fantasy. In P. Gherovici & M. Steinkoler (Eds.), *Psychoanalysis, gender, and sexualities: From feminism to trans* (pp. 212–221). Routledge. https://doi.org/10.4324/9781003284888-16

Coda

Oriented by beauty: an aesthetic turn

A coda, by nature, does not conclude. It gestures—sometimes tentatively, sometimes insistently—toward what remains unresolved. This book has traced the complex intertwining of sexuality and gender, but there is always more to say, more that resists being said. What follows is a pause—an acknowledgment of what remains unresolved. In earlier work (Gozlan, 2008, 2014), I described the uncertainties that sexuality introduces into gender—how gender, when felt as a libidinal and sensual experience, destabilizes the illusion of self-knowledge. I called this *aesthetic conflict* (Gozlan, 2015): the experience of gender not as an identity to be possessed but as something shaped through beauty, loss, pleasure, age, illness—as an emotional and psychic field in relation to something else. Drawing on Meltzer's (1990) notion of the aesthetic dimension of the drive—where libido seeks not mere satisfaction but something sublime and creative—I suggested that the meaning of gender emerges not from certainty but from the effort to translate the ungraspable into thought. This translation is never complete. It is shaped by desire, risk, and the tension between knowing and not-knowing. And in this tension, the aesthetic finds its place—not as decoration but as the very scene where identity is imagined, disoriented, and remade.

In this final gesture, I return to the question of aesthetics through two thinkers whose work unsettles the foundations of normativity and evolution. Richard Prum's theory of aesthetic evolution departs from Darwinian function and survival to place beauty and desire at the center of natural selection—not as decoration but as primary forces in the shaping of life. Georges Canguilhem, writing from a different tradition, reimagines the norm not as a standard to be enforced but as a heuristic—a response to crisis, an adaptation to instability, a gesture toward what cannot be known in advance. Taken together, these thinkers invite us to reframe sexuality and gender not as fixed identities but as expressive improvisations—situated, unstable, and inventive. Their work suggests that what is most vital in embodiment may also be what is most unruly: its capacity to surprise, to exceed its assigned form, to become beautiful in the space of its deviation. In this register, aesthetics returns—not to finalize but to open; not to conclude but to let something pass between.

DOI: 10.4324/9781003440758-20

Rethinking normativity: Canguilhem on error and adaptation

Gender has too often been pressed into the frame of biological destiny or social prescription—treated as if it were a fixed identity, grounded in stable laws. Canguilhem unsettles this picture. For him, normativity is not a system imposed from above but a fragile improvisation—an adaptive effort in the face of an uncertain world. A norm, in this view, is less a rule than a practice of orientation: a way of moving through instability, of making what is unfamiliar temporarily livable. Yet this work is shot through with affect—anxieties about what cannot be secured, the longing to stabilize what remains in flux. Without norms, the world overwhelms us; but because they are provisional, these same norms can—and do—shift. What holds us also fails to hold.

Canguilhem compels us to consider the theory of the subject as rooted in the errors of life. Even at the chromosomal level, he suggests, information must be interpreted, carrying the risk of error (1989, p. 177). He describes life as a series of errors, considering anomaly "a fundamental eventuality [that] crosses all of biology, through and through" (Foucault, p. 22). Accordingly, normalcy itself is an error insofar as "its meaning, function, and value derive from the fact that something outside itself does not meet the requirement it serves" (Canguilhem, p. 239). Normality, like consciousness, is an exception—a fragile emergence from a process full of errors, deviations, and contingencies. From this perspective, gender can be conceptualized through Canguilhem's notion of error. The instability of gender is a feature, not a flaw. Like a landscape, gender is constantly changing; it is always in flux. Thinking of the self as a system that inherently generates its own errors (as seen, for example, in the way cells are attacked by cancer) allows us to situate gender transitioning alongside questions of age, illness, and disability as fundamental aspects of human life. Gender never fully "fits," and thus, any form of gender is an "error." In other words, there is no fixed or final normative place in gender, only the provisional norms one makes and remakes in the living of it.

Canguilhem's move highlights an aesthetic aspect to the norm when he argues that it is bound up with affect (anxiety) and desire (for stability). Like gender, norms are constituted in opposition to what they exclude, sanction, or repulse. Yet, as with narratives, social norms are easily inverted because the "reference and regulation the norm offers also leave room for possibilities that are other to it" (Canguilhem, 1989). Much like age, gender changes us in ways we cannot predict. The aporia of gender might also create the conditions for an aesthetic conflict that is hard to bear. I bring together errors, aesthetics, and wayfinding as metaphors with which to think about gender as stories of becoming that are also myths, both created and received. What is foreclosed in the conceptualization of gender as monolithic and ontological or in the fear that gender transitioning is ruinous is the idea that we have experiences in the world that can affect the accident of birth—transitioning, immigration, adoption—and that we can do something else other than what we have been doing.

In turning to Canguilhem, I am moving outside of psychoanalysis as a way to enliven the field by thinking deeply about the world and bringing new metaphors and new situations to bear on the questions we are asking. I find Canguilhem's discussion on the subject of norms as something that is both socially and scientifically relevant to the inquiry into gender from the vantage point of aesthetics. His notion of normalcy as fantastic and functional, as bound by social and organizational interests, and as always relative is also an assertion that error, or experiences that fall outside of the norm, are not exceptions but rather potential for variability. Both in nature and in culture, Canguilhem suggests, sexuality is not a straight line but a tangle—diverse, multiple, always threatening to unravel and re-thread itself elsewhere. Gender, we can say, owes its mutability to the slip, the breaks, the exquisite accident of error. Error is not a deviation but a generative force, a crack that allows something unexpected to breathe through.

The norm, for Canguilhem, is a fable dressed up as law: an artifice we stitch to steady ourselves against the unruliness of existence, a human strategy for organizing the chaotic textures of life into something legible, bearable. But here's the twist—every time the norm draws its line, it simultaneously condemns and calls forth its inversion. It is as if the norm, in its eagerness to stabilize, leaves the door ajar for everything it wishes to exclude. "A norm," Canguilhem writes, "offers itself as a possible mode of unifying diversity, resolving a difference, settling a disagreement"—though what it unifies is a provisional peace, always haunted by its exclusions (1979, p. 240). The norm, Canguilhem proposes, is a story we create as a way of imposing regularity on an existential condition in which we have no control. Normativity, then, is less a structure than a mythology—a story that obscures the arbitrariness of biology, the errancy of identity, and the randomness of life. We are not propelled forward by moral or natural teleology; we are assembled, piece by errant piece, through socialization, desire, and the Oedipal scrim. Experience cannot be separated from this randomness, from the accidents of biology and identity that are later enculturated, socialized, or Oedipalized. No moral or natural design of development carries us to safety (Gozlan, 2022c).

Canguilhem's thinking of development as constituted by an avalanche of errors allows us to press on familiar narratives of gender as tied to biology, whose destiny is bound to notions of anatomy, naturality, and utility. But it also allows us to consider narratives of gender as very personal stories of destruction, rebuilding, and to the question of fate. And here is where we might press against the familiar narratives that bind gender to anatomy, utility, and naturality. We might, instead, read gender as a ruin and a reconstruction, a fate as fragile and strange as any myth. The psychoanalytic concept of gender, when placed beside Canguilhem's notion of error, unfurls not as fixed taxonomy but as a question posed to fate itself. It is through error, beauty, myth, and the delicate art of wayfinding that I wish to approach gender—not as a medical object to be fixed or diagnosed but as a poetic situation. A lived experience negotiated through language, seduction, and the improvisational creativity of the psyche.

By turning to questions of error, beauty, mythology, and wayfinding as metaphors that describe the emotional situation of gender and our methods of handling it, I attempt through this manuscript to move the psychoanalytic understanding of gender away from the medicalization of the body and towards the creativity of language and, hence, of agency. In listening to theories as creative and seductive narratives, we can consider their function as containers or placeholders for the anxiety of the unpredictability inherent in desire, but also as a claustrum that encircles and forecloses the dimensions of our thinking. We can treat theories as fictions that seduce us, tools designed to contain the unpredictable nature of desire. Yet, like any container, they also risk trapping us—becoming, in their rigidity, a claustrum that limits the open, evolving nature of becoming.

Prum and aesthetic evolution: beyond utility

The idea that we are subject to something that has nothing to do with us—errors, coincidental occurrences, and forces of drives that are polymorphous, blind, and impersonal, contingent and unpredictable—is difficult for the human. In this sense, we are also able to consider the ways in which theories of gender function as aesthetic "wayfinding" devices in the new terrain of gender, offering orientations rather than fixed destinies. Here, Prum's understanding of aesthetic evolution becomes relevant: just as birds develop extravagant plumage and elaborate courtship rituals not for survival but for the sheer pleasure of attraction, gender too can be seen as a process of aesthetic flourishing—one that is neither strictly functional nor reducible to biological determinism but rather an unfolding of desire, creativity, and embodied improvisation.

Prum's theory of aesthetic evolution challenges functionalist accounts of biological development. He argues that evolution is not solely driven by natural selection but also by arbitrary, aesthetic choices made through desire and attraction. This perspective destabilizes traditional Darwinian models that frame adaptation as purely utilitarian, instead foregrounding pleasure, affect, and contingency in shaping life. Prum widens the understanding of variability by introducing something akin to a drive for beauty. In *The Evolution of Beauty* (2017), he proposes that evolution is propelled not by utility but by aesthetics. His theory suggests that desire shapes evolutionary trajectories, shedding light on the enduring mystery of variation in human sexual attraction. From Prum's vantage point, beauty is constituted through pleasure, fashion, and appearance—elements often dismissed in evolutionary accounts that prioritize reproductive function. He critiques the reductive tendency in evolutionary biology to link all sexual behaviors to reproductive success, using the example of oral sex to illustrate how such activities defy reproductive logic yet persist across species. For Prum, this suggests that sexual behaviors cannot be fully explained by their utility. Instead, he calls for an inquiry into the evolutionary origins and maintenance of variation in the *subjective* experience of sexual desire—pleasure for its own sake.

Psychoanalysis offers us an aesthetic vision of what it means to be human in the idea that we are structurally susceptible and affected by that which we do not know. The desire to know creates pressure for interpretation. If we stay in the realm of aesthetics, we might recall Prum's conceptualization of a drive for beauty, and here we might pause to consider Freud's drive as an aesthetic mythology—a force of sexuality that, while tied to social effects and structures, does not have a reason as a final end (1905), and that cannot be reducible to a biological instinct, but is mediated through phantasy and representation (1921). In this sense, psychoanalysis shares with Prum and Canguilhem an insistence on the instability of identity: error is also the very foundation of the psyche.

Robert Macfarlane (2020), too, gestures toward this fundamental instability when he turns to *wayfinding*—a concept that, although drawn from geography, resonates deeply with questions of gender, identity, and narrative. In *The Landscapes Within Us* (2021), Macfarlane describes how new technologies, particularly GPS, have transformed human orientation to time and place, disrupting the instinctive ability to navigate. He asks, have we become disabled by our dependence on external systems of mapping? What does it mean to be lost in an era where the very possibility of losing oneself has been foreclosed? If gender is an aesthetic process of orientation, we might say, following Macfarlane, that we have lost the coordinates that once tethered us to a singular, intuitive map of the self.

Although Macfarlane does not frame his inquiry in relation to gender, his reflections on deep time—on the randomness, contingency, and errancy of landscape—can be brought to bear on the changing landscape of gender itself. His notion of *deep time* resists a chronological, linear unfolding, instead emphasizing coincidence, disruption, and an open-ended relation to the past. This temporal dislocation finds an echo in Freud's concept of *nachträglichkeit*, the way meaning is belatedly assigned to past experiences, and in the view of gender (Gozlan, 2018, 2022, 2025) as a process of belated narration. To experience gender, then, is to experience a state of aesthetic wayfinding—negotiating the excesses of the psyche, the forces of beauty and error, and the impossibility of a singular origin. If Macfarlane suggests that we are losing our ability to situate ourselves in time and space, then perhaps gender has never been about a stable location to begin with but about an unfolding story—one that must be continually rewritten in relation to what is not yet known.

With Macfarlane, I imagine wayfinding as the necessary transition in our very capacity to situate ourselves in time and space in a way that permits us to have a place in the world. It involves turning internally. Quoting Agnes Varda, he writes: "If we opened people up, we would find landscapes" (Varda, 2008, in MacFarlane, 2021, p. 2). Storytelling, McFarlane suggests, is the navigation capacity of the human. This turn requires a step into the unconscious of psychic time; that is, to "tell stories about ourselves that unfold both backwards and forwards in time" (p. 2). Telling a new story involves the tremendous pain and anxiety of separation, because the stories that we tell are not so far from our phantasies and, hence, we can add, are also affected by and are an effect of our transference to our infantile theories or gender.

Macfarlane's idea of wayfinding as storytelling speaks to the predicament of gender today, especially to the ways mental health clinicians, analysts among them, try to orient themselves amid new formations while still holding on to old banisters of thought. In the analytic situation, the question might be put this way: when orientation collapses because knowledge is tethered to an inherited story, can the analyst risk turning ruthlessly on their own theories of gender? This question points to the analyst's capacity to bear helplessness and unknowability, since history is arbitrary, contingent, and already over-written—every narrative of gender a palimpsest (Gozlan, 2022). Helplessness becomes a condition of encounter, an experience of being moved by what exceeds one's grasp. Transference attaches to bodies, clothes, and language, and with it comes the inevitability of failure in every effort to stabilize or convey gender.

The experience of gender can never equal the thing itself, and this implies that in listening to gender, we are hearing its web of intricacies; the urges and draws, pushes and pulls of emotional logic. Our narratives will bear the tension of the drives and the paradox, where any attempt to symbolize will also present a challenge to symbolization as our theories of gender inevitably bump up against something other to it. This experience is hard to put into words. In a way, storytelling provides a way of conceptualizing gender as an art project because the stories we tell also implicate questions of aesthetics.

Framed in this way, gender is central to psychoanalytic thinking not only because it is a central linchpin in the capacity to imagine something like psychical life, but also because what we hear in the clinic are the derivatives of gender: "I hate my body," "I want to be beautiful." These experiences are tied to desire and belong to the self, and as long as pleasure vacillates across the categories of gender, it is very difficult to separate gender from sexuality. Even so, femininity and masculinity are social experiences that play out in the field of gender as the ongoing project of being recognized on our own terms. And while identifying gender's derivative will not lead us to an origin, gender contains and frames situations of existence that render the self's truths accessible through interpretations and open to elaborations. In listening to stories of gender, I therefore enter a *dynamic*. Within the intersubjective situation of learning and therapy, questions of gender are not only a site of passion and conflict but also are emotional situations, and in psychoanalysis, emotional situations are also matters of the body: what I put on every day, what gives my body pleasure or pain, and how I am seen in the world.

This tangle between ideas and affects and gender and sexuality bring the impossibility of separating experience from fiction to the fore and brings us closer to Bion's understanding of the analyst's position. The focal point of any analytic session, he suggests, is being oriented by the unknown. "Progress," Bion writes, "will be measured by the increased variety of moods, ideas, and attitudes seen in any given session" (pp. 136–37). The attempt to understand the other's situation and their place in the world leans on this capacity for tolerating the unknown. The capacity to listen to gender through negative capabilities—the unexpected, the indispensable, the surprise—brings us closer to imagining its experience as something atmospheric and dynamic, where multiple forces occur at once. At the same time, there is an involuntary experience with categories of gender that are not contained but are saturated. Our narrative of coming to gender, the story we tell ourselves about who we are, is not unlike Canguilhem's function of a norm as a conforming narrative, in a sense that it too is grounded in mythology and is invested with meaning. We know this in the clinic and in our psychoanalytic education—the places that call upon our eros.

Because normativity binds itself to social structures and institutions, any attempt to step outside discourse is already caught in an unconscious attitude that gives shape to every concept we hold. Stepping outside the discourse of heteronormativity may indeed feel for some as difficult as trying to step outside of one's ego. The added complication is our unavoidable desire to participate in the identity structures (Foucault, 2004; Foucault & Sennett, 1981), even though there is nothing voluntary about the formation of identity as such. We are born into a discourse of gender, and we believe it to be ours. Here we are in the realm of phantasy and desire. Narratives are fragile attempts to make the unknown intelligible. In our stories of gender, this fragility shows itself in the desire to symbolize archaic identifications and the elements entangled with gender. Yet, as with the floppiness of our narratives of gender, social norms can easily be inverted, because norms, as Canguilhem suggests, are not laws of nature, only conditions of "reference and regulation" that make space for possibilities that are other to it (Canguilhem, 1979). Canguilhem shows that norms are not immutable laws but shifting points of reference, provisional measures of order that, in their very attempt to regulate, open the door to what exceeds them.

Oedipus—an uncanny story

While this chapter does not undertake a full study of the history of the concept of gender, it is important to recognize how such inquiry opens conditions for change. Tracing the conceptual history of gender unsettles the naturalization of heteronormativity and exposes the powerful equation between the everyday and heterosexuality. This involves the study of errors, because the history of gender entails a way to trace its trajectory along defensive functions and paradoxical situations. These are also the places where the very attempt to repress the ambiguous qualities of sexuality brings to the creation of demitarian categories, producing a sexuality that is banned. The prohibition is so deeply unconscious and implanted that it is difficult to unlearn. The unconscious history of gender poses a fundamental challenge to the development of a new psychoanalytic theory of gender. This difficulty lies not just in what gender is, but in how it has been received, internalized, and resisted over time. André Green approaches this dilemma through what he calls the work of the negative—the "difficulty of psychical life" (2000, p. 2). Any effort to historicize our gender will inevitably be marked by error: denials, delusions, and acts of negation.

Gender can be understood as a kind of wayfinding—a fugitive tracing of forms, a negotiation between the given and the yet-to-be imagined. Sophocles' story of Oedipus carries the same structure: a map drawn in the ink of disorientation, its coordinates scrambled by time.

Oedipus does not move only through prophecy; he moves through the structure of knowledge itself, where recognition arrives belatedly and action follows as the echo of what was already set in motion. His tragedy can be read not simply as the failure to outrun fate but as a crisis of orientation—the vertigo of realizing that the chosen path was charted in the very effort to avoid it. Freud's fascination with this myth was less the sketch of a psychic law than the staging of the psyche's continual reckoning with what it cannot fully grasp.

I have always been struck by the way Oedipus doesn't just arrive at the truth—he collides with it. The moment of recognition isn't a triumph of knowledge; it's a fall, a rupture, a haunting. And isn't this what Freud meant when he spoke of the uncanny—that eerie sensation when something long-buried resurfaces, not as something new but as something we somehow always knew? Oedipus's tragedy is not only a crisis of knowledge but a crisis of recognition—a confrontation with what was always already there, obscured until it is too late. Freud's theory of the uncanny captures this paradox, tracing the moment when the familiar becomes estranged, and the known reveals itself as ungovernable. In this sense, the Oedipal story is itself uncanny: it stages the return of the repressed, the eruption of a hidden logic that, once exposed, unmoors the subject from their world.

Gender, too, belongs to this haunted terrain, where psychic life becomes entangled with historical movements we did not choose but nevertheless inhabit. It functions as a banister concept—something we hold onto to steady ourselves in the face of internal difference, even as it fails to contain the excess it seeks to manage. Oedipus does not simply stumble upon a truth—he is swallowed by it, consumed by the slow, belated recognition that what he has sought all along was always circling back to him. His tragedy is that of the uncanny, the moment when the world folds in on itself, revealing not a new reality but the terrifying return of what was always there, waiting. Freud saw in this myth not just a developmental drama but a deeper disturbance: the psyche's encounter with what it cannot fully know yet cannot escape. What if gender, too, is structured by this ghostly return—by the impossible task of recognizing something we never quite forgot?

But perhaps this ghostly return points not only to the failure of recognition but also to the impossibility of symbolic completion. The traditional symbolic order—the so-called name-of-the-father—has too often been treated as a shorthand for intelligibility itself. Yet the symbolic is less a finalizing structure than an aesthetic scene: a place where meaning blurs, repeats, and is taken up otherwise. Not to close contradiction, but to make room for the improvisation of thought. For Lacan, the status of the father is symbolic, but can there be an imaginary father as well—an imaginary implicit in the law as such? Or is there a smudge of the Real across the imaginary and the symbolic too? To turn toward aesthetics is not to abandon the symbolic but to tarry with its textures—to dwell in a symbolic that does not foreclose gender or subjectivity but instead sustains a space for transference, uncertainty, and psychic labor.

My aim here is not to negate the developmental or transitional frames that have long scaffolded psychoanalytic thought but to turn them slightly—toward their aesthetic underside. I am drawn to approach gender not as the product of a developmental arc—not a movement from pre-Oedipal to Oedipal, nor from confusion to clarity—but as a scene of aesthetic negotiation: a space where libidinal attachments take on form, only to be lived, revised, and encountered again. From this angle, the symbolic does not descend as imposed order. It takes shape through the labor of psychic learning—where the subject must come to bear the weight of meaning through conflict, ambivalence, and failure. In this light, transition—across its many iterations—emerges as a transformative aesthetic: a practice of form always in negotiation with what cannot be fully contained.

The symbolic, then, is less a law that fixes subjectivity than a scene that stages it—repetition, rupture, and the glimmer of something unforeseen. What matters here is not the search for a new law—maternal, fraternal, or a reversal of the paternal—but the suspension that comes with listening. In this suspension, symbolization slips and returns in altered form, exposing its unfinished work. To think gender aesthetically is to linger with this lag in meaning, to accompany its uneven rhythms, and to resist the temptation of coherence. Psychoanalysis, when it listens most acutely, does not aim to settle gender but to read it—and to read again, each time otherwise. Freud's 1919 essay *The Uncanny* turns to E.T.A. Hoffmann's *The Sandman* (1816), where Nathaniel is haunted by a figure who threatens to steal children's eyes and entranced by Olimpia, the automaton he mistakes for a woman. Olimpia unsettles not because she is strange, but because she fulfills too completely the fantasy of a femininity without opacity or desire. Her blank compliance and her affective vacancy enact a fantasy of difference abolished. What horrifies Nathaniel is not her mimicry itself but the exposure of his dependence on an object that cannot return his desire. The uncanny here is double. It reveals how fantasy secures coherence and at the same time undoes it. Olimpia condenses projection, anxiety, and castration dread, while also exposing the persistence of attachment to what is not there. Freud shows that the uncanny is not only the return of the repressed but also the tenacity of ties that cannot be relinquished. The experience of gender we remain bound to it, compelled to repeat and to rework its impossible promise. What comes into view is a surface worn thin, where invention shows through. The uncanniness lies not in strangeness but in overexposure—when form becomes too exact, too legible, too complete. In that saturation, attachments reveal their fragility: provisional, patched, rehearsed, unable to settle into coherence yet impossible to abandon. This is the wound of belatedness: entering a story already inscribed, desire shaped as much by absence as by insistence. To narrate gender is to work within this condition, to return again to the point where certainty has already collapsed.

The hero, Freud suggests, is the one who can wrest themselves from group psychology, and Freud praises the imagination of the writer (Sophocles): "He relates to the group his hero's deeds which he has invented. At bottom this hero is no one but himself" (*Group Psychology*, 1921, pp. 136–137). Freud's assertion gets at the heart of the value of narrating one's experience, which of course writers do. And, as Felman argues, as a story of misrecognition a project of narrating, analysis itself is as an act of "historical integration of the spoken, but misrecognized parts of the subject" (1987, p. 130). Psychoanalysis was constituted by Freud's capacity to transform his narratives about himself and others into theory. Freud, Shoshana Felman observes, was able to tell stories "that made history" (1987, p. 100).

From the question of misrecognition, we can only ponder how the history of our reading shapes our current narratives of gender. Darian Leader's archive of "Freud's footnotes" presents evidence for Freud's struggle with the three essays through continuous revisions. The additions of footnotes (see Darian Leader's "Freud's footnotes, 2000) reflect his arguments with the social climate and with the tensions within the psychoanalytic movement itself. His narrative is bound to historical events and culture and includes its unfolding in the aftermath of the Holocaust, whose effects were devastating and ground shifting both on a personal and theoretical levels (as I elaborated in Chapter 2). In reviewing psychoanalytic theory in the context of history, we are therefore also responsible in articulating how it is, and from which place, we are reading.

The dilemma of reading brings us back to the question of aesthetics. Here I am pressing on us to retain in our reading the impenetrable edge that is so central to analytic thinking. Deborah Britzman frames this insistence as a queer question: "can we stop reading straight?" (Britzman, 1995). This question states a feeling of alienation at the incapacity for pedagogy to "read otherwise" (p. 16). It applies to psychoanalysis as well. It is the question of how we can talk about gender in ways that do not produce questions of exclusion and disavowal. It is also a question that relates to history because it engages our capacity to account for how we arrived at our understanding of gender. To interrogate the relationship between masculinity and femininity we must move, in other words, to a queer position; a new, non-defended pedagogy that is asking what makes something like gender intelligible. It is a question that challenges our relation to the experience of gender and is decentering because it has not been deeply thought of before but is also liberating because new ideas can come into being.

Can we bear the aesthetics of unintelligibility? Can we read gender from the "queer" place of aesthetics and sexuality, in all its forms—straight, gay, trans, nonbinary? These questions move us towards the analyst's capacity to use a kaleidoscopic lens for looking at something that may have been totally foreclosed; to be oriented by interest in sexuality and movement beyond the binary. In psychoanalytic training and in the therapeutic clinic, the queerest pedagogy would be interpretation of the transference that leans upon free association where new ideas come to the analyst and the patient's mind. Reading theory from an inexplicable, queer, and alienating place requires us to bear the uneven logic of affects, fantasies, gaps, unlikely proximities to confront our infantile theories. There will be a delay in meaning, and we will be swept away by experience, before we understand and therefore we will be subject to miscommunications, misreading, and fantasies. Our understand-ing—our necessarily provisional positing of a norm—will be a fragile edifice made from an avalanche of errors.

The topology of gender cannot be mapped. It shares with geography a queer temporality—an accumulation of traces, unsituated, unstable, resistant to prediction. Witnessing narratives of gender is never a neutral act; it is to become entangled in them, to find oneself already spinning a thread of inter-pretation. In this, I find myself within the pull of *nachträglichkeit*:

> In attempting to understand, we also step back in time. We lean on familiar coordinates at the same time that something new is recon-stituted through the weaving of a historical narrative. This process is always already marked by the present.
>
> (Gozlan, 2025, p. 27)

Here lies the analyst's difficulty: what we receive is always incomplete, and our effort to make more of it is shaped—and constrained—by what we can bear to associate. Resistance emerges where this associative movement is defended against, through the fantasy of knowability.

This tension surfaces through the very act of reading. Reading is never neutral, Felman suggests, because the unconscious of the reader is caught within the text of the other (1987, p. 23). What is read is never just the words before us but also what they stir, what they revive, what they dis-place. Reading becomes a site of recognition—and of misrecognition. So it is with gender. In the analytic space, we read gender as we hear it: through projection, interpretation, and the distortions of transference. The terrain is uncanny: haunted by both the strange and the over-familiar, where experi-ence precedes meaning. Gender is not a stable essence but a scene endlessly re-narrated. Something lived before it can be spoken and spoken always incompletely.

The experience of being gendered hinges upon recognition but also upon the slippages of recognition, the places where identity is neither fully affirmed nor wholly denied. Coming into gender is never the simple assumption of a role. It is a passage through projections, desires, misreadings, and the pleasures of losing one's way. Gender may be *written on the body* (Winterson, 1992, p. 190), but this inscription is errant, palimpsestic—subject to endless rewriting. Its idioms move through art, fashion, gesture—where gender's affective life and imaginary excess take fleeting form. One senses this uncanniness in gender memoirs, which do not capture an identity so much as perform the uncertain labor of becoming. Here, gender appears in retroactive sparks, what comes to be known only through *nachträglichkeit*, through belated intelligibility. To narrate gender is to stage this doubled temporality: a force that acts upon the writer and reader alike, even as it is shaped by the history of its own telling. In this sense, gender remains an aesthetic object—always exceeding its own frame, always in the process of being read anew.

Aesthetic as condition for change

For the analyst, approaching the formations and representations of gender—those patterns we are drawn to and yet unsettled by—requires an aesthetic openness to what cannot be known in advance. It asks of us the work of the negative (Green, 1999): a refusal to foreclose meaning too soon, a capacity to dwell in contradiction. To frame the conditions for a changing mind as an aesthetic question is to approach the analytic act itself as a kind of artwork: not a mirror of reality but an encounter with obscurity, with gaps that invite the imagination. Here, time slackens; narrative opens toward emptiness, timelessness, and, when crossed by sexuality, enters the unsteady currents of drive. This movement begins in helplessness—in the analyst's encounter with what cannot yet be symbolized and the effort to remain within that space. It asks us to attend to questions of beauty, knowledge, and truth not as problems to be solved but as aesthetic conflicts to be sustained. The work of the negative exposes what earlier theories closed off; it shows the points where thought breaks down and experience slips. Approached aesthetically, gender narratives appear less as stable accounts of identity than as openings—sites where the self's fragile, affectively charged formation can be sensed. In this register, gender is an aesthetic object (Gozlan, 2015), whose expression always exceeds symbolic articulation. As an unfinished project, gender neither stabilizes the subject nor offers closure. It calls instead for interpretation and for bearing what remains unresolved.

In listening to narratives of gender as aesthetic procedures of handling life events, we also consider experience from a *nachträglich* temporality, and hence not far away from phantasy. From the temporal vantage of deferral, the carving of gender identity is not as a process of forming in relation to presence and absence but in the moments of contradictory states where absence and presence, femininity and masculinity, unite. The analyst's own capacity to sustain the inscrutability of sexuality and tolerate the aesthetic conflict—the sensorial and affective apprehension of the object, the registration of its otherness, the desire to know and the limits of knowledge—as an essential aspect of the analytic experience of transformation (Gozlan, 2008) and, hence, of gender. The analyst must become a protean of thought, attuned to the play of meanings, lingering in the liminal space between conviction and improvisation. To take gender apart is to expose its fictions; to put it back together is to face the fragility of the effort—an assemblage in flux, unfinished, never secure in its form.

The capacity to reside between the wholesomeness of identity and the perversity of fantasy—without reducing one to pathology or the other to privilege—relies not on separating social identity from sexual desire but on understanding their entanglement: the way gender, too, is a site of eros, a space of psychic and bodily possibility, of "what could be, what might be, what will be" (Green, 2000, pp. 2–3). Psychoanalysis suggests that freedom is not the negation of limits but their imaginative reworking, and gender becomes one of the most profound expressions of this freedom—an ongoing act of aesthetic and existential creation. The idea that gender identity is carved in the "moments of contradictory states" finds a striking parallel in Horn's visual and conceptual language.

Roni Horn's work returns us to the tension between identity, desire, and transformation. Her art dwells in fluidity—in the play of doubling, reversal, and shifts that refuse to hold. In *You Are the Weather* (1997) and *Things That Happen Again* (1986–88), the gaze does not settle. What repeats begins to slip; what differs returns. The scene does not resolve into knowing. Gender, too, resists this settling. It is not a possession to be named but a relation that shifts with its surroundings—gathered here, scattered there, caught in the folds of encounter. Horn brings this sensibility to *Island Zombie*: "There is no distinction between the path and the place itself . . . it takes the shape of each place, intimately" (2020, p. 27). Gender's path too isimpossible to trace from the outside; it takes shape in movement, improvised as it goes. The gendered subject inherits no map. It navigates by stitching fragments—past and imagined—into a scene that might hold. In this labor, novel revolts (Gozlan, 2025) speak: not a return to a forgotten self but the invention of a form not yet known.

To listen from within this movement is to resist capture. Gender unsettles the scene—not as survival but as allure, as the pull of what exceeds use. Prum demonstrates that beauty shapes life beyond function, while Canguilhem insists that refusal marks the living. So too with gender: it insists on its pleasures, its contradictions, its errant forms. The drive here does not resolve but unsettles—pressing against form, scattering its edges, refusing its frame. What draws us is not the promise of coherence but the spaces where meaning slips, where it undoes itself, only to return in altered guise. The analyst, like the artist, lingers here: a space where presence strains toward absence, where fantasy recomposes the real, and where no final reading can be made. To remain with aesthetic conflict is not to master gender's meaning but to stay within its folds, to listen in the subjunctive mood of its becoming.

References

Amir, D. (2018). *Bearing witness to the witness*. Routledge.

Amir, D. (2022). On revenge, pardon, and forgiveness. *Journal of the American Psychoanalytic Association, 70*(6), 1037–1051. https://doi.org/10.1177/00030651221141694

Amir, D. (2024a). *Psychoanalysis as radical hospitality: Six perspectives on turning-to versus turning-away* (1st ed.). Routledge. https://doi.org/10.4324/9781032715766

Amir, D. (2024b). From mind-deadness to mindedness, from collaboration to cooperation. *The International Journal of Applied Psychoanalytic Studies*. https://doi.org/10.1002/aps.1888

Arendt, H. (1976). *The origins of totalitarianism* (New ed.). Harcourt Brace Jovanovich.

Arendt, H. (1998). *The human condition* (2nd ed.). University of Chicago Press.

Aulagnier, P. (2001). *The violence of interpretation: From pictogram to statement* (A. Sheridan, Trans.). Brunner-Routledge.

Bakhtin, M. M. (1984). *Problems of Dostoevsky's poetics* (C. Emerson, Ed. & Trans.). University of Minnesota Press.

Baudrillard, J. (2004). *The spirit of terrorism* (C. Turner, Trans.). Verso. (Original work published 2002)

Bazzi, D. (2022). Approaches to a contemporary psychoanalytic field theory: From Kurt Lewin, Georges Politzer and José Bleger, to Antonino Ferro and Giuseppe Civitarese. *International Journal of Psychoanalysis, 103*(1), 46–70.

Bell, D. (2020). First do no harm: Psychoanalysis, ethics, and the cultural politics of identity. *International Journal of Psychoanalysis, 101*(5), 1031–1038. https://doi.org/10.1080/00207578.2020.1810885

Benjamin, J. (1990). *The bonds of love: Psychoanalysis, feminism, and the problem of domination*. Pantheon Books.

Benjamin, W. (1940). *Theses on the philosophy of history*. In H. Arendt (Ed.), *Illuminations* (pp. 253–264). Schocken Books.

Benvenuto, S. (2024, February 23). Gendrification: "Pas de sexe, rien que des Genders". In *La néosexualité: norme et pathologie* (pp. 124–135). Parrhesia. https://www.parrhesia-sergiobenvenuto.it/fr/gendrification/

Bion, W. R. (1962). *Learning from experience*. Heinemann.

Bion, W. R. (1965). *Transformations: Change from learning to growth*. Butterworth-Heinemann.

Bion, W. R. (1975). "Forward." In L. Grinberg, S. Dario, & E. Tabak de Bianchedi (Eds.), *Introduction to the work of Bion* (A. Hahn, Trans.). Roland Harris Educational Trust.

Bion, W. R. (2000). *Seven servants: Four works by Wilfred R. Bion* (p. 321). Karnac. (Original work published 1962)

Bion, W. R. (2005). *Elements of psychoanalysis*. Routledge. (Original work published 1967)

Bion, W. R., Aguayo, J., & Malin, B. (2013). *Los Angeles seminars and supervision*. Routledge.

Blass, R. (2024). Remembering, repeating and working-through as a step in Freud's ongoing struggle with the 'What', 'Why', and 'How' of analytic knowing in the curative process. In U. Hock & D. Scarfone (Eds.), *On Freud's 'remembering, repeating and working-through'* (pp. 88–105). Taylor & Francis.

Blass, R. B. (2020). Introduction to "Can we think psychoanalytically about transgenderism?" *International Journal of Psychoanalysis, 101,* 1014–1018.

Blass, R. B., Bell, D., & Saketopoulou, A. (2021). Can we think psychoanalytically about transgenderism? An expanded live Zoom debate with David Bell and Avgi Saketopoulou, moderated by Rachel Blass. *International Journal of Psychoanalysis, 102,* 968–1000.

Blechner, M. J. (2005). The gay Harry Stack Sullivan. *Contemporary Psychoanalysis, 41*(1), 1–20.

Bollas, C. (1987). *The shadow of the object: Psychoanalysis of the unthought known.* Columbia University Press.

Britzman, D. P. (1995). Is there a queer pedagogy? Or, stop reading straight. *Educational Theory, 45*(2), 151–165.

Britzman, D. P. (2000). Teacher education in the confusion of our times. *Journal of Teacher Education, 51*(3), 200–205. https://doi.org/10.1177/0022487100051003007

Britzman, D. P. (2006). *Novel education: Psychoanalytic studies of learning and not learning.* Peter Lang.

Britzman, D. P. (2009). *The very thought of education: Psychoanalysis and the impossible professions.* State University of New York Press.

Britzman, D. P. (2015). *A psychoanalyst in the classroom: On the human condition in education.* State University of New York Press.

Britzman, D. P. (2020). Freudian theory: History, theory, and culture in adolescence theories of adolescent development. In S. Hupp and J. Jewel (Eds.), *The encyclopedia of child and adolescent development.* John Wiley & Sons, Inc. https://onlinelibrary.wiley.com/doi/abs/10.1002/9781119171492.wecad306

Britzman, D. P. (2021). *Anticipating education: Concepts for imaginary work.* State University of New York Press.

Britzman, D. P. (2022b). *Novel education: Psychoanalytic studies of learning and not learning* (2nd ed.). Peter Lang.

Britzman, D. P. (2024). *When history returns: Psychoanalysis and the future of education.* State University of New York Press.

Britzman, P. D. (1998). *Lost subjects, contested objects: Toward a psychoanalytic inquiry of learning.* SUNY Press.

Britzman, P. D. (2004). What will have been said about gayness in teacher education. *Teaching Education, 15,* 81–96.

Britzman, P. D. (2010). *Freud and education.* Routledge.

Britzman, P. D., & Gilbert, J. (2004). What will have been said about gayness in teacher education. *Teaching Education, 15,* 81–96.

Butler, J. (1990). *Gender trouble: Feminism and the subversion of identity.* Routledge.

Canguilhem, G. (1989). *The normal and the pathological* (C. R. Fawcett & R. S. Cohen, Trans.). Zone Books. (Original work published 1966)

Caper, R. (1999). *A mind of one's own: A Kleinian view of self and object.* Routledge.

Carl, P. (2020). *Becoming a man.* Simon & Schuster.

Castoriadis, C. (1991). Power, politics, autonomy. In D. A. Curtis (Ed.), *Philosophy, politics, autonomy: Essays in political philosophy* (pp. 143–174). Oxford University Press.

Castoriadis, C. (1994). *Speculations after Freud: Psychoanalysis, philosophy, and culture* (S. Shamdasani & M. Munchow, Eds.). Routledge.

Chervet, B. (2024). The advent of the superego: An après-coup of *Beyond the pleasure principle.* In F. Busch & N. Delgado (Eds.), *The ego and the id: 100 years later* (pp. 76–88). Routledge.

Civitarese, G. (2022). Not a literal translation … In fact, rather performative: A review of *Translation/Transformation: 100 Years of the International Journal of Psychoanalysis* (D. Birksted-Breen, Ed.). *International Journal of Psychoanalysis, 103*(4), 692–702.

Civitarese, G. (2024). *On arrogance: A psychoanalytic essay* (1st ed.). Routledge. https://doi.org/10.4324/9781032669427

Cooper, S. H. (2022). The activity of neutrality. *The Psychoanalytic Quarterly, 91*(2), 355–369. https://doi.org/10.1080/00332828.2022.2078156

Dalal, F. (2001). The social unconscious: A post-Foulksian perspective. *Group Analysis, 34*(4), 539–555.

D'Angelo, R. (2025). Do we want to know? *The International Journal of Psychoanalysis, 106*(1), 82–108. https://doi.org/10.1080/00207578.2024.2391419

de Certeau, M. (1993). *Heterologies: Discourse on the other* (B. Massumi, Trans.). University of Minnesota Press.

de M'Uzan, M. (2013). *Death and identity: Being and the psycho-sexual drama* (A. Weller, Trans.). Karnac Books.

Derrida, J. (1978). *Writing and difference* (A. Bass, Trans.). University of Chicago Press. (Original work published 1967)

Dorenbaum, D. (2021, November 24). *Ecocide times.*

Drescher, J. (2023). Is it really about freedom of thought? *BJPsych Bulletin* (2022), pp. 1–3.

Dufourmantelle, A. (2019). *In praise of risk* (Steven Miller, Trans.). Fordham, University Press.

Evzonas, N. (2021). Countertransference madness: Supervision, trans*, and the sexual. *Psychoanalytic Review, 108*, 475–509.

Faludi, S. (2016). *In the dark room*. Metropolitan Books.

Farley, L. (2018). *Childhood beyond education*. State University of New York Press.

Faulkner, W. (Ed.). (1994). *Requiem for a nun*. Vintage Books. (Original work published 1950)

Felman, S. (1987). Jacques Lacan and the adventure of insight. In *The literary speech of psychoanalysis* (pp. 107–130). The Johns Hopkins University Press.

Ferenczi, S. (1955). Confusion of tongues between the adults and the child. In M. Balint (Ed.), *Final contributions to the problems and methods of psychoanalysis* (pp. 156–167). Karnac Books.

Ferro, A., & Civitarese, G. (2015). *The analytic field and its transformations*. Karnac.

Fiorini, L. G. (2019). Polyphonies of sexuality: Debates about theories/debates about paradigms. *International Journal of Psychoanalysis, 100*, 1256–1269.

Forrester, J. (2017). *Thinking in cases*. Polity Press.

Foucault, M. (1982). Truth, power, self. Interview by R. Martin recorded on October 25th, 1982. In L. H. Martin, H. Gutman, and P. H. Hutton (Eds.), *Technologies of the self: A seminar with Michel Foucault* (pp. 9–15). University of Massachusetts Press.

Foucault, M. (2004). *The birth of biopolitics: Michel Foucault's lecture at the Collège de France on neo-liberalism* (A. I. Davidson, Trans.). Palgrave Macmillan. (Original lectures published 2004)

Foucault, M., & Sennett, R. (1981, May 7). The mask of solitude. *The London Review of Books, 3*(10), 3–8.

Freud, A. (1958). Child observation and prediction of development—a memorial lecture in Honor of Ernst Kris. *Psychoanalytic Study of the Child, 13*, 92–116.

Freud, A. (1974). Psychoanalysis and education. In *The writings of Anna Freud: Volume I. Introduction to psychoanalysis: Lectures for child analysts and teachers, 1922–1935* (pp. 123–145). International Universities Press.

Freud, S. (1899). Screen memories. In J. Strachey (Ed. & Trans.), *The standard edition of the complete psychological works of Sigmund Freud* (Vol. 3, pp. 299–322). London: Hogarth Press and the Institute of Psycho-Analysis.

Freud, S. (1900). The interpretation of dreams. In J. Strachey (Ed. & Trans.), *The standard edition of the complete psychological works of Sigmund Freud* (Vols. 4–5). Hogarth Press.

Freud, S. (1901). Letter from Freud to Fliess, August 7, 1901. *The Complete Letters of Sigmund Freud to Wilhelm Fliess, 1887–1904, 42,* 446–448.

Freud, S. (1905). Three essays on the theory of sexuality. In J. Strachey (Ed. & Trans.), *The standard edition of the complete psychological works of Sigmund Freud* (Vol. 7, pp. 123–246). Hogarth Press.

Freud, S. (1908). On the sexual theories of children. In J. Strachey (Ed. & Trans.), *The standard edition of the complete psychological works of Sigmund Freud* (Vol. 9, pp. 205–226). Hogarth Press.

Freud, S. (1911). The interpretation of dreams: Supplement. In J. Strachey (Ed. & Trans.), *The standard edition of the complete psychological works of Sigmund Freud* (Vol. 5, pp. 563–621). Hogarth Press.

Freud, S. (1913). Totem and taboo. In J. Strachey (Ed. & Trans.), *The standard edition of the complete psychological works of Sigmund Freud* (Vol. 13, pp. 1–161). Hogarth Press.

Freud, S. (1915a). The unconscious. In J. Strachey (Ed. & Trans.), *The standard edition of the complete psychological works of Sigmund Freud* (Vol. 14, pp. 159–190). Hogarth Press.

Freud, S. (1915b). Instincts and their vicissitudes. In J. Strachey (Ed. & Trans.), *The standard edition of the complete psychological works of Sigmund Freud* (Vol. 14, pp. 117–140). Hogarth Press.

Freud, S. (1917). Mourning and melancholia (J. Strachey, Trans.). *The Standard Edition, 14,* 243–258.

Freud, S. (1918). From the history of an infantile neurosis (The "Wolf-Man"). *The Standard Edition, 17.*

Freud, S. (1919). The uncanny. *The Standard Edition, 17,* 217–256.

Freud, S. (1920). Beyond the pleasure principle. In J. Strachey (Ed. & Trans.), *The standard edition of the complete psychological works of Sigmund Freud* (Vol. 18, pp. 1–64). Hogarth Press.

Freud, S. (1921). *Group psychology and the analysis of the ego* (J. Strachey, Trans.). The International Psychoanalytical Press.

Freud, S. (1924). The economic problem of masochism. *The Standard Edition, 19.*

Freud, S. (1930). Civilization and its discontents. *The Standard Edition, 21,* 57–145.

Freud, S. (1933). *New introductory lectures on psychoanalysis.* Hogarth Press.

Freud, S. (1936). A disturbance of memory on the Acropolis. In J. Strachey (Ed. & Trans.), *The standard edition of the complete psychological works of Sigmund Freud* (Vol. 22, pp. 239–248). Hogarth Press.

Freud, S. (1937a). Analysis terminable and interminable. In J. Strachey (Ed. & Trans.), *The standard edition of the complete psychological works of Sigmund Freud* (Vol. 23, pp. 209–253). Hogarth Press.

Freud, S. (1937b). Constructions in analysis. *The Standard Edition, 23.*

Freud, S. (1950a). Remembering, repeating and working-through (Further recommendations on the technique of psycho-analysis II). In J. Strachey (Ed. & Trans.), *The standard edition of the complete psychological works of Sigmund Freud* (Vol. 12, pp. 145–156). Hogarth Press and the Institute of Psychoanalysis. (Original work published 1914)

Freud, S. (1950b). *Project for a scientific psychology.* In J. Strachey (Ed. & Trans.), *The standard edition of the complete psychological works of Sigmund Freud* (Vol. 1, pp. 281–391). Hogarth Press and the Institute of Psychoanalysis. (Original work published 1895)

Freud, S. (1955). The sexual theories of children. In J. Strachey (Ed.), *The standard edition of the complete psychological works of Sigmund Freud* (Vol. 9, pp. 209–226). Hogarth Press.

Fromm, E. (1941). *Escape from freedom*. Farrar and Rinehart.

Gabbard, G. O. (1994). Sexual excitement and countertransference love in the analyst. *Journal of the American Psychoanalytic Association, 42*(4), 1083–1106. https://doi.org/10.1177/000306519404200402

Gallop, J. (1987). *Reading Lacan*. Cornell University Press.

Garfinkel, H. (1980). *Studies in ethnomethodology*. Prentice-Hall. (Original work published 1967)

Geertz, C. (2017). *The interpretation of cultures*. Basic Books.

Gherovici, P. (2010). *Please select your gender: From the invention of hysteria to the democratizing of transgenderism*. Routledge.

Gherovici, P., & Steinkoler, M. (Eds.). (2022). *Psychoanalysis, gender, and sexualities: From feminism to trans*. Routledge.

Glocer Fiorini, L. (2017). *Sexual difference in debate bodies, desires, and fiction*. Routledge.

Gloria, A. (2022). *Borderlands/La Frontera: The New Mestiza* (5th ed.). Aunt Lute Books.

Gozlan, O. (2008). The accident of gender. *The Psychoanalytic Review, 95*, 541–70.

Gozlan, O. (2014). *Transsexuality and the art of transitioning: A Lacanian approach*. Routledge.

Gozlan, O. (2016). The transsexual's turn: Uncanniness at Wellesley College. *Studies in Gender and Sexuality, 17*(4), 297–305. https://doi.org/10.1080/15240657.2016.1236552

Gozlan, O. (2018). From continuity to contiguity: On the fraught temporality of gender. *The Psychoanalytic Review, 105*, 1–29.

Gozlan, O. (2022a). In-difference: Feminism and transgender in the field of fantasy. In P. Gherovici & M. Steinkoler (Eds.), *Psychoanalysis, gender, and sexualities: From feminism to trans* (pp. 212–221). Routledge. https://doi.org/10.4324/9781003284888-16

Gozlan, O. (2022b). Adolescent ruthlessness and the transitioning of the analyst's mind. *Journal of the American Psychoanalytic Association, 70*(3), 459–484.

Gozlan, O. (2022c). Has psychoanalysis reached its limits in the question of the trans child and adolescent? *The Psychoanalytic Review, 109*, 309–332.

Gozlan, O. (2023). Transsexuality bibliography. In S. Thurer (Ed.), *Beyond the binary: Essays on gender* (pp. 87–99). Karnac Books.

Gozlan, O. (2025). Novel Revolts as Crafting of a Self. *The Psychoanalytic Quarterly, 94*(1), 5–27, DOI: 10.1080/00332828.2024.2442119

Gozlan, O. (2025a). Revolts as crafting of self. *Psychoanalytic Quarterly, 94*(1), 5–27.

Gozlan, O. (2025b). Unmasking the moral fantasy of the "underlying conflict": A critique of Roberto D'Angelo's "Do we want to know?". *The International Journal of Psychoanalysis, 106*(4), 849–850.

Green, A. (2000). *The work of the negative* (A. Weller, Trans.). Free Association Books.

Grossman, D. (2014). *Falling out of time* (J. Cohen, Trans.). Knopf.

Gullestad, S. (2024). Transgender—a challenge for psychoanalysis? *The Scandinavian Psychoanalytic Review, 47*, 129–136.

Gullette, M. M. (1997). *Declining to decline: Cultural combat and the politics of the midlife*. University of Virginia Press.

Halperin, D. (2004). *How to do the history of homosexuality*. University of Chicago Press.

Hansbury, G. (2017). The masculine vaginal: Working with queer men's embodiment at the transgender edge. *Journal of the American Psychoanalytic Association, 65*, 1009–1031.

Harris, A. (2009). *Gender as soft assembly*. Routledge. (Original work published 2005)

Hoffer, A. (1985). Toward a definition of psychoanalytic neutrality. *Journal of the American Psychoanalytic Association, 33*(4), 771–795. https://doi.org/10.1177/000306518503300402

Hoffmann, E. T. A. (1816). The sandman. In W. A. O'Neil (Trans.), *The golden pot and other tales* (pp. 193–234). Dodo Press. (Original work published 1816)

Hopper, E. (2002). *The social unconscious. Selected papers*. Hachette Publishing.

Horn, R. (1986–1988). *Things that happen again* [Pair object VII; sculptural installation]. Chinati Foundation; Dia Art Foundation archives.

Horn, R. (1997). *You are the weather* [Artist's book]. Scalo.

Horn, R. (2020). *Island Zombie: Iceland writings*. Princeton University Press

Joynt, C. (Director), & Schilt, K. (Writer). (2019). *Framing Agnes* [Short documentary film]. University of Southern California.

Kahn, L. (2022). *What Nazism did to psychoanalysis*. Routledge.

Keats, J. (1817). Letter to George and Tom Keats, December 21, 1817. In H. E. Rollins (Ed.), *The letters of John Keats* (Vol. 1, pp. 193–194). Cambridge University Press.

Kernberg, O. F. (2016). *Psychoanalytic education at the crossroads*. New Haven, CT: Yale University Press.

Klein, M. (1921). The development of a child. *International Journal of Psycho-Analysis, 2*(3–4), 167–185.

Klein, M. (1940). Mourning and its relation to manic–depressive states. *The International Journal of Psycho–Analysis, 21*, 125–153.

Klein, M. (1946). Notes on some schizoid mechanisms. *International Journal of Psycho-Analysis, 27*, 99–110.

Klein, M. (1952). The origins of transference. *International Journal of Psycho-Analysis, 33*, 433–438.

Kristeva, J. (1989). *Black sun: Depression and melancholia* (L. S. Roudiez, Trans.). Columbia University Press.

Kristeva, J. (1997). *New maladies of the soul* (R. M. Guberman, Trans.). Columbia University Press.

Kristeva, J. (2002). *Intimate revolt: The powers and the limits of psychoanalysis* (J. Herman, Trans.). Columbia University Press.

Kristeva, J. (2009). *This incredible need to believe*. Columbia University Press.

Kristeva, J. (2012). *Hatred and forgiveness* (J. Herman, Trans.). Columbia University Press.

Kuhn, T. (1962). *The structure of scientific revolution*. The University of Chicago Press.

Lacan, J. (1977). *Écrits: A selection* (A. Sheridan, Trans.). Tavistock Publications.

Laplanche, J. (1992). Interpretation between determinism and hermeneutics: A restatement of the problem. *The International Journal of Psycho-Analysis, 73*, 429–445.

Laplanche, J. (1995). Seduction, persecution, revelation. *International Journal of Psychoanalysis, 76*, 663–682.

Laplanche, J. (2016). *New foundations for psychoanalysis* (J. House, Trans.). Unconscious in Translation. (Original work published 1987)

Layton, L. (2020). *Towards a social psychoanalysis: Culture, character, and normative unconscious*. Routledge.

Leader, D. (2000). *Freud's footnotes: On the history of psychoanalysis*. The Tapestry Press.

Leiber, E. (2023). The politics of the navel: Psychoanalysis and affiliation. *American Imago, 80*(3), 527–552.

Lemma, A. (2015). *Minding the body: The body in psychoanalysis and beyond*. Routledge.

Lemma, A. (2018). Transitory identities: Some psychoanalytic reflections on transgender identities. *The International Journal of Psychoanalysis, 99*, 1089–1106.

Levine, H. B. (Ed.). (2023). *The Freudian matrix of André Green: Towards a psychoanalysis for the twenty-first century*. Routledge.

Macfarlane, R. (2020). *Underland: A journey in deep time*. Penguin Press.

Macfarlane, R. (2021, July 1). The landscapes inside us. *The New York Review of Books*. https://www.nybooks.com/articles/2021/07/01/wayfinding-landscapes-inside-us/

MacKinnon, C. (1999). "Are women human?": Reflection on the universal declaration of human rights. In B. van der Heijden & B. Tahzib-Lie (Eds.), *Universal declaration of human rights: 50 years and beyond* (pp. 171–191). Martinus Nijhoff Publishers.

McDougall, J. (1989). *Theatres of the mind: Illusion and truth on the psychoanalytic stage*. Brunner-Routledge.

McDougall, J. (1993). *Plea for a measure of abnormality* (1st ed.). Brunner/Mazel.

McDougall, J. (1995). *The many faces of Eros: A psychoanalytic exploration of human sexuality*. W.W. Norton & Company.

McDougall, J. (2001). Gender identity and creativity. *Journal of Gay & Lesbian Psychotherapy*, 5(1), 56–78. https://doi.org/10.1300/J236v05n01_04

Meltzer, D. (1990). *The claustrum: An investigation of claustrophobic phenomena*. Clunie Press.

Milner, M. (1950). *On not being able to paint*. Heinemann.

Mitchell, J. (1999). *Psychoanalysis and feminism. A radical reassessment of Freudian psychoanalysis*. Basic Books.

Moss, D. (2021). On having whiteness. *Journal of the American Psychoanalytic Association*, 69(2), 355–371. https://doi.org/10.1177/00030651211008507

Musil, R. (1995). *The man without qualities* (S. Wilkins & B. Pike, Trans.). Knopf. (Original work published 1930–1943)

Perelberg, R. J. (2018). *Psychic bisexuality: A British-French dialogue*. Routledge.

Pitt, A., & Britzman, D. P. (2003). Speculations on qualities of difficult knowledge in teaching and learning: An experiment in psychoanalytic research. *International Journal of Qualitative Studies in Education*, 16(6), 745–758. https://doi.org/10.1080/0951839030001632135

Polgreen, L. (2024, September 1). The cass report: Biased or balanced? *The New York Times*. https://www.nytimes.com/2024/09/01/opinion/transgender-cass-report.html

Prum, R. O. (2017). *The evolution of beauty: How Darwin's forgotten theory of mate choice shapes the animal world—and us*. Doubleday.

Quinodoz, D. (2002). The case of the transsexual patient Simone: Psychoanalytic treatment and the question of gender identity. *International Journal of Psychoanalysis*, 83(6), 1357–1376.

Rancière, J. (1991). *The ignorant schoolmaster: Five lessons in intellectual emancipation* (K. Ross, Trans.). Stanford University Press. (Original work published 1987)

Rose, J. (1986). *Sexuality in the field of vision*. Verso.

Rose, J. (1993). *Why war? Psychoanalysis, politics and the return to Melanie Klein*. Blackwell Publishing.

Rose, J. (2000). Preface. In M. Safouan, *Jacques Lacan and the question of psychoanalytic training* (pp. vii–xiii). (J. Rose, Trans. & Ed.). St. Martin's Press.

Rose, J. (2016). Who do you think you are? *London Review of Books*, 38(9).

Rose, J. (2019). One long scream: Jacqueline Rose on trauma and justice in South Africa. *London Review of Books*, 41(10), 10–14.

Roudinesco, É. (2016). *Freud: In his time and ours* (C. Porter, Trans.). Harvard University Press.

Safouan, M. (2000). *Jacques Lacan and the question of psychoanalytic training* (J. Rose, Trans. & Intro.). St. Martin's Press.

Safouan, M. (2004). *Four lessons to psychoanalysis*. Penguin.

Saito, T. (2013). *Hikikomori: Adolescence without end*. Routledge.

Saito, T. J. (2011). *Beautiful fighting girl*. University of Minnesota Press.

Saketopoulou, A., & Pelegrini, A. (2023). *Gender without identity*. The Unconscious in Translation.

Scarfone, D. (2015). *The Unpast*. The Unconscious in Translation.

Sedgwick, E. K. (1990). *Epistemology of the closet*. University of California Press.

Sedgwick, E. K. (1991). How to bring your kids up gay: The war on effeminate boys. In M. Warner (Ed.), *Fear of a queer planet: Queer politics and social theory* (pp. 69–81). University of Minnesota Press.

Sedgwick, E. K. (1999). *A dialogue on love*. Beacon Press.

Sedgwick, E. K. (2003). Paranoid reading and reparative reading. In *Touching feeling: Affect, pedagogy, performativity* (pp. 123–151). Duke University Press.

Sedgwick, E. K. (2011). *The weather in Proust* (J. Goldberg, Ed.). Duke University Press.

Serano, J. (2007). *Whipping girl: A transsexual woman on sexism and the scapegoating of femininity*. Seal Press.

Simmel, G. (1950). *The sociology of Georg Simmel* (K. Wolff, Trans.). The Free Press.

Simon, W., & Stoller, R. J. (2020). Documents: "How much closer to Freud's very nervous, sexual world i feel than to that of my students": Correspondence between sexology and psychoanalysis, 1988–1989. *Psychoanalysis and History, 22*, 53–73.

Simpson, R. B. (2022). Analytic work: The essential and the accidental in psychoanalysis. *Psychoanalytic Quarterly, 91*, 119–144.

Soreanu, R. (2018). *Working-through collective wounds: Trauma, denial, recognition in the Brazilian uprising*. Palgrave Macmillan.

Stengers, I. (2005). The cosmopolitical proposal (L. Carey-Libbrecht, Trans.). In B. Latour & P. Weibel (Eds.), *Making things public: Atmospheres of democracy* (pp. 994–1003). MIT Press.

Stengers, I. (2017). *In catastrophic times: Resisting the coming barbarism*. Semiotext(e).

Stengers, I. (2018). *Another science is possible: A manifesto for slow science* (S. Muecke, Trans.). Polity Press. (Original work published 2013)

Stoller, R. J. (1964). A contribution to the study of gender identity. *International Journal of Psychoanalysis, 45*, 220–226.

Stoller, R. J. (1968a). *Sex and gender: On the development of masculinity and femininity*. Science House.

Stoller, R. J. (1968b) A further contribution to the study of gender identity. *International Journal of Psychoanalysis, 49*, 364–368.

Stoller, R. J. (1973). *Sex and gender: The development of masculinity and femininity*. Science House.

Stoller, R. J. (1979). *Sexual excitement: Dynamics of erotic life*. Pantheon Books.

Stoller, R. J. (1985). *Presentations of gender*. Yale University Press.

Stoller, R. J., Auerbach, A., & Marmor, J. (1960). The hermaphroditic identity. *Journal of Nervous and Mental Disease, 131*(1), 43–54. https://doi.org/10.1097/00005053-196007000-00001

Swartz, S. (2018). *Ruthless Winnicott: The role of ruthlessness in psychoanalysis and political protest*. Routledge.

Togashi, K. (2019). *The psychoanalytic zero: A decolonizing study of therapeutic dialogues*. Routledge Press.

Togashi, K. (2022, May 14). *Naming, traumatizing and being a player-witness, presentation*. Toronto Psychoanalytic Society & Institute.

Varda, A. (Director). (2008). *The beaches of Agnès* [Film]. Ciné-Tamaris.

Waddell, M. (2018). *On adolescence: Inside stories*. Routledge.

Wake, N. (2011). *Private practices: Harry Stack Sullivan, the science of homosexuality, and American liberalism*. Rutgers University Press.

Walsh, J. (2020). Robert Stoller and the gender binary. *International Journal of Psychoanalysis, 101*(3), 429–446.

Watson, E. (2022). Gender transitioning and variance in children and adolescents: Some temporal and ethical considerations. *The Psychoanalytic Study of the Child, 75*, 184–190.

Weber, S. (2000). *The legend of Freud* (Expanded ed.). Stanford University Press.

Weber, S. (2024). Reconsidering Freud's uncanny: The Coppola perspective. *Humanities, 13*(1), 4. https://doi.org/10.3390/h13010004f

Winnicott, D. W. (1969). The use of an object and relating through identifications. *International Journal of Psycho-Analysis, 50*, 711–716.

Winnicott, D. W. (1971). *Playing in reality*. Routledge.

Winterson, J. (1992). *Written on the body*. Vintage.

Young-Bruehl, E. (1996). *The anatomy of prejudices*. Harvard Press.

Young-Bruehl, E. (2000). Beyond "the female homosexual". *Studies in Gender and Sexuality*, *1*(1), 97–124.

Young-Bruehl, E. (2010). Sexual diversity in cosmopolitan perspective. *Studies in Gender and Sexuality*, *11*(1), 1–9.

Žižek, S. (2001). The subject of tragedy: Lacan, Hegel, and the end of history. *Journal of European Psychoanalysis*, *13*, 5–18.

Index

For Product Safety Concerns and Information please contact our EU
representative GPSR@taylorandfrancis.com
Taylor & Francis Verlag GmbH, Kaufingerstraße 24, 80331 München, Germany

www.ingramcontent.com/pod-product-compliance
Lightning Source LLC
Chambersburg PA
CBHW052001270326
41929CB00015B/2747

9 7 8 1 0 3 2 5 7 7 3 6 4